Eleanor's Story

Eleanor's Story

An American Girl in Hitler's Germany

ELEANOR RAMRATH GARNER

PEACHTREE
ATLANTA

To my grandchildren,
Tommaso, Giacomo, and Samuel
Kathryn and Ingrid,
and to the generations to come.

Published by
PEACHTREE PUBLISHERS
1700 Chattahoochee Avenue
Atlanta, Georgia 30318-2112

www.peachtree-online.com

Text © 1999 by Eleanor Ramrath Garner

First trade paperback edition published in 2003

Cover photos courtesy of Eleanor Ramrath Garner
Author photo © 1999 by Dick Snyder

Book and cover design by Loraine M. Joyner
Composition by Melanie M. McMahon
Manufactured in November 2012 in the United States of America by R.R. Donnelley and Sons in Harrisonburg, Virginia
10 9 8 7 6 5 (hardcover)
10 9 8 7 6 5 4 (trade paperback)

Library of Congress Cataloging-in-Publication Data

Garner, Eleanor Ramrath
    Eleanor's story : an American girl in Hitler's Germany / Eleanor Ramrath Garner. — 1st ed.
      p. cm.
   ISBN 13: 978-1-56145-193-7 / ISBN 10: 1-56145-193-2 (hardcover)
   ISBN 13: 978-1-56145-296-5 / ISBN 10: 1-56145-296-3 (trade paperback)
    1. Garner, Eleanor Ramrath. 2. World War, 1939–1945—Germany Juvenile literature. 3. World War, 1939–1945—Personal narratives, American Juvenile literature. 4. World War, 1939–1945—Children–Germany Biography Juvenile literature. 5. World War, 1939–1945—Children–United States Biography Juvenile literature.   I. Title.
D811.5.G26   1999
940.54'8173'092—dc21
  [B]   99-22964
                                                   CIP

CONTENTS

ACKNOWLEDGMENTS

MY BOOK was not created in a vacuum. Many individuals contributed to this work either directly or indirectly, and it is to them that I wish to express my deepest, most heartfelt thanks.

First and foremost to my editor, Sarah Helyar Smith, without whose vision and loving encouragement my story would never have been written. She guided me with patience and kindness through the manuscript's many revisions, always sensitive to the painful material I was working with. And finally it was her sensitivity and remarkable editorial skills that made my story come together as a whole. Also special thanks to the caring, skilled staff at Peachtree who contributed their expertise to my book: Amy Sproull and Vicky Holifield, editors; Loraine Joyner, art director; and Melanie McMahon, production manager.

Thank you to my beloved Mother, who was the anchor in my life, and in loving memory of Father, who I know would have been proud of me. My heartfelt thanks also to my brother Frank, who helped me out when memory failed me, and who contributed facts and anecdotes throughout the book. To my brother Thomas, whose unfailing enthusiasm for the project buoyed me when my spirits flagged. To my dear little sister, Elizabeth, who is always there when I need her.

Special thanks also to my wonderful sons, Jim and Tom, and their families who supported this project wholeheartedly with words of encouragement and expressions of pride in their mother.

To Annemarie, my beloved friend, who helped me to remember. To Rosemarie Dion for her invaluable help in computer logistics in the first draft, and to all my wonderful friends, you know who you are, who were the enthusiastic midwives in giving birth to this book.

Finally, but always first, my deepest love and gratitude to my husband, Lou, a World War II veteran who, in the U.S. Army's 78th Infantry Division, was among the first American troops into Berlin. He, more than anyone else, understood how difficult it was to write a memoir of those tragic times. He made many insightful suggestions to the book, in addition to taking over numerous household tasks to free up writing time for me. I couldn't have done it without him.

Events, places, and most of the names in this narrative are true to the best of my recollection and perception. In some cases, I have changed names to protect the privacy of individuals and families still living.

PROLOGUE

AT THE END of the Great War (later known as World War I) in 1918, the victorious Allies forced Germany to pay immense reparations and rearranged Europe, limiting Germany's borders and taking away large amounts of land, people, and natural resources. This put an enormous financial burden on Germany, which led to inflation, unemployment, and finally economic collapse. Thousands of Germans had to emigrate to find jobs elsewhere.

Adolf Hitler, leader of the National Socialist German Workers' (or Nazi) Party, promised economic solutions and the restoration of patriotic values. German President Paul von Hindenburg appointed Hitler chancellor in 1933. Germans wanted to rebuild their lives, and, indeed, a remarkable economic recovery took place. But when Hitler was declared dictator of Germany a few months later, the shadowy racism of his Nazi Party became apparent. Joseph Goebbels, the efficient propaganda minister, controlled the news media to assure that Hitler and Nazi Germany were viewed in the best possible light the world over.

Hitler and his operatives in the Third Reich felt that Germany was overpopulated and needed what he called Lebensraum, living space. In 1936 they began a crusade to take back territories that had been denied Germany after World War I, such as the Rhineland, then annexed Austria in 1938, followed by the Sudetenland and soon the rest of Czechoslovakia in 1938–39. The other European powers did not respond.

In addition to expanding Germany's borders, Hitler and the Nazis wanted to "purify" the German populace. They targeted Jews, Gypsies, and other groups and systematically began to separate them from the rest of the population.

Greed for even more land and resources pushed Hitler to invade Poland on September 1, 1939. Britain and France declared war on Germany two days later. Hitler directed a series of blitzkriegs, lightning campaigns, in 1940 and 1941 against other European countries, including Holland, Belgium, and France, and ordered the bombing of Britain to the west and the invasion of Russia to the east. After Japan, Germany's ally, bombed Pearl Harbor on December 7, 1941, Hitler also declared war on the United States. England, France, the United States, and the Soviet Union were now allied against the Axis powers of Germany, Italy, and Japan.

With the Soviet defeat of the German army to the east at Stalingrad in January 1943, and confrontation of the overwhelming Allies to the west, combined with the relentless Allied bombing of German military and civilian targets, Germany began to collapse. The Germans surrendered on May 7, 1945. The Third Reich had ended in a horrendous bloodbath. The atomic bombings of Hiroshima and Nagasaki by the Americans in August 1945 finally ended World War II.

The aftermath of this terrible war revealed unbelievable horrors that seared the soul. It wasn't until the Allies discovered the extermination camps in 1945 that the world, including most Germans, were shocked beyond belief to learn to what extremes Hitler's hatred and racial obsessions had driven him. More than 6 million Jews, along with other so-called undesirables, like homosexuals, Gypsies, Communists, Poles, resistance fighters or anybody who opposed the regime, were executed in these death camps.

Staggering statistics emerged out of this horrendous war. An estimated three-fourths of the world's population participated in or suffered from the effects of the war. Of those, 25 million military personnel died and almost 40 million civilians were killed, including those in the Nazi death camps. Countless millions more were maimed or wounded.

Statistics are numbers, but numbers represent individual lives, people who lived and breathed, who laughed and cried, who loved and suffered. Each one of the millions who died and every person who miraculously survived has a story. Mine is only one of them. This war lives on in infamy. It should never be forgotten, lest we forget our humanity.

It is a terrible thing
To be so open; it is as if my
      heart
Put on a face and walked into
      the world....

—Sylvia Plath, from "Three Women," stanza 43

Berlin, 1938

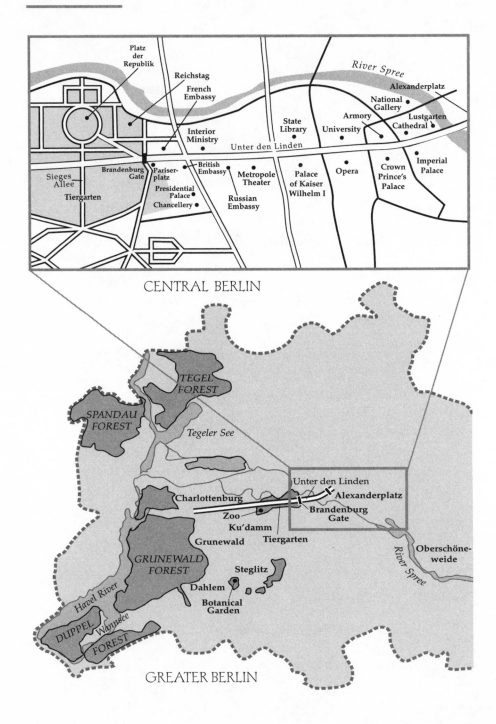

CENTRAL BERLIN

Platz der Republik · Reichstag · French Embassy · Interior Ministry · Unter den Linden · State Library · Armory · University · National Gallery · Lustgarten · Alexanderplatz · Cathedral · River Spree · Sieges Allee · Brandenburg Gate · Pariser-platz · British Embassy · Metropole Theater · Palace of Kaiser Wilhelm I · Opera · Crown Prince's Palace · Imperial Palace · Tiergarten · Presidential Palace · Chancellery · Russian Embassy

TEGEL FOREST · SPANDAU FOREST · Tegeler See · Charlottenburg · Zoo · Ku'damm · Grunewald · Tiergarten · Unter den Linden · Alexanderplatz · Brandenburg Gate · Oberschöneweide · GRUNEWALD FOREST · Steglitz · Dahlem · Botanical Garden · Havel River · Wannsee · DUPPEL FOREST · River Spree

GREATER BERLIN

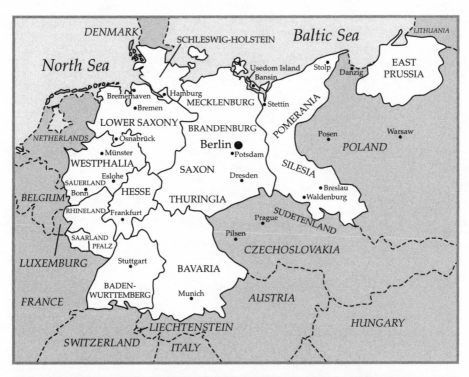

Allied
Occupation
Zones of
Germany,
1945–1949

*Berlin itself also
was divided into
the four sectors.*

Hope is the thing with
feathers
That perches in the soul,
And sings the tune without
the words,
And never stops at all.

—Emily Dickinson

CHAPTER ONE

STRATFORD

SEPTEMBER 1938—AUGUST 1939

IN THE FALL of 1938, when I was eight years old, Adolf Hitler came to my neighborhood.

He didn't come in person, of course, but the thought of him came into people's minds in Stratford, New Jersey. At the beginning of October, news reports on the radio declared, "Adolf Hitler, Germany's leader, has taken over the Sudetenland province of Czechoslovakia." Our neighbors across the street had immigrated from Czechoslovakia a year earlier. Their kids suddenly turned angry and started being mean to us.

I usually walked alone to school, since my brother, Frank, preferred to go on ahead with his friends. One morning soon after that report, the Czech kids came up behind me and chanted, "Hitler in his casket, brown and yellow basket…." Then they ran off, laughing.

I was bewildered. *Why are they saying that to me? Who is this guy Hitler anyway? And what does he have to do with me?* Then I got angry. *I'm not German. I'm American.* After that episode, I walked with Frank and his buddies to school. Frank was better able to cope with the teasing. He and his pals stood up to the kids across the street.

∾

One warm Sunday afternoon that fall, my parents' friends gathered at our house, as they often did. These old friends, who had immigrated in the 1920s from Germany, as my parents had, were like our extended family. Frank and I called them Tante and Onkel, aunt and uncle.

Mother set the table under the apple tree and served homemade plum cake and streusel kuchen with whipped cream. Along with coffee, she set out some of the wine Father made from the grapes in our yard.

Mother, Father, and their friends all joked and laughed. Then their discussion turned to the economy and how hard it was to get and keep a good job in these tough times. But as it did many Sundays that fall, the conversation led to the subject of Hitler.

Frank and I weren't allowed to interrupt our elders and ask questions, so we just listened as the grown-ups talked noisily. We sat together on the hammock, quietly swinging back and forth, and stuffed ourselves with cake. We didn't understand everything they said, but we heard about Germany and the changes going on there. We heard about Hitler, who promised a stronger, better Germany and who was inviting the immigrants back with offers of employment.

"Adolf Hitler promises a better economy and new jobs…."

"Hitler is power hungry. He had himself declared dictator!"

"But he's restructured the army and stabilized the economy."

"The things his Nazi party is doing scare me. And that swastika flag is pompous! The old one was much nicer."

I liked it better when the grown-ups told jokes and laughed.

Their talk about the German flag reminded me of the time I had seen it myself. A year earlier, in the spring, we had just finished dinner and turned on the radio when we heard the announcer crying.

"Oh, the humanity and all the passengers," he wept. "The wreckage is flaming up again!… I can't talk, ladies and gentlemen."

The *Hindenburg*, the giant dirigible, was flying passengers here from Germany when it exploded during a thunderstorm as it was trying to moor in Lakehurst, about fifty miles from my home. We went there the next day. I still get goosebumps thinking about what we saw.

We stood at the edge of the field and stared at the collapsed skeleton of the airship, what had been Germany's pride and joy. Wisps of smoke still rose from the remains. The red and black symbol on the fins of the airship—"the Nazi swastika!" Frank whispered to me—lay twisted and charred among the wreckage. The heavy, bitter smell of smoke and ashes hung in the air. As we stood behind the rope barrier, I clutched my arms as shivers ran down my spine. I thought of the people aboard the airship who had died. I shuddered.

~

My attention was drawn back to the grown-ups' conversation. They had stopped discussing politics and were talking about their families in Germany. I tried to remember what Germany had been like. When I was two and Frank four, when my family still lived in Philadelphia, Mother took us to Germany on the ocean liner *S.S. Bremen.* She left me with Omi Ramrath, Father's mother. I had never seen her before. Omi lived in Eslohe, a small farming village surrounded by mountains, in the Sauerland region of Germany. Frank stayed with Mother's parents, Grossmutter and Grossvater Rump, who lived in Münster, in Germany's Westphalia province.

At first, I was terrified that my mother had abandoned me. I was separated from my brother, in a strange country, in a strange house, and with people I didn't know. All around me I heard the language I had heard before only in our home.

But gradually, over weeks and months, I forgot about my parents in America and began to enjoy being spoiled by Omi and my two aunts, Tante Maria and Tante Adele. I became the center of attention in the village too. Everyone called me Mäti, the pet name my parents had given me. I often toddled down the street by myself to the butcher shop, where I begged for a piece of sausage, then on to the bakery for a cookie.

Grossmutter and Grossvater Rump sometimes brought Frank to Eslohe for the day. He and I played in the sandbox, climbed the fruit trees, burrowed through hay in the barn, and fed the pig, cow, and chickens. The grown-ups sat in the gazebo, drinking coffee and eating cake. I always cried when Frank had to leave again in the evening.

After Frank and I were in Germany for two years—I was four and he was six—our grandparents put us on a ship in Bremerhaven. With only a steward to watch over us, we traveled the nine days across the ocean back to the United States. When we arrived, I barely remembered Mother, and Father had become a complete stranger. I called him uncle.

I didn't understand until later that Mother and Father had a good reason to send us away. Mother explained how Father used to be an electrical engineer but lost his job because of the Great Depression. He and Mother didn't have any money to support us, so they sent us to live with our grandparents.

While we were gone, Mother's brother, Onkel Franz, and some immigrant friends moved into an apartment in Philadelphia together to help pay the rent. Mother and Father both pumped gas and mended tires at a service station until Father finally got another job and made enough money to send for us. Onkel Franz, my godfather, moved back to Germany when we returned.

I wasn't happy to be back in America and resented the strangers who called themselves my parents. Mother and Father made us follow lots of rules. I couldn't wander around as I had in Eslohe, and my parents always scolded me.

"You're so spoiled!" Mother often scolded, her dark eyes fixed on me.

It took us all a long time to adjust to living together again.

Then when I was six, we moved from Philadelphia to this house on Union Avenue in Stratford. Mother said housing in big cities was expensive, so after looking for a long time, Father finally found this old house to rent. He liked the house because it was near his job at RCA in Camden.

I liked the house because it was roomy and comfortable, all covered with brown shingles. On cold or rainy days we played on the glassed-in front porch or watched Father in his workshop in the big basement. But most of all I loved the big garden out back. We had fruit trees, Concord grapevines, and thick hedges of sweet-smelling honeysuckle. The only thing I didn't like was the cesspool that regularly overflowed.

Mother dug her vegetable garden near the cesspool. "Plants grow much better there," she explained. "Rich soil."

Next to our house stood a tall, twisted old apple tree that grew nothing but wormy, puckered apples. But Mother made them into delicious applesauce that she stored in jars in the cellar for winter. Father built a wooden table and attached it to the tree trunk, so when it was hot we could eat in the tree's cool shade. On warm weekend mornings we ate breakfast there too.

I loved the tree. Sometimes when I felt sad or rejected, the tree helped me feel better. When I pressed my ear against its rough bark, I was sure I could hear its heart beat.

High up in the tree's thick branches, Frank built himself a tree house. "Girls," he declared, "are *not* invited."

My job was to provide cookies and stuff for him and his friends up there. Whatever I could snitch I put into a basket, and then Frank hauled it up into the tree house by rope. I was definitely not happy about this job, so we often argued about it.

Once we moved to the house, Father started to give us lots of chores. Before he left for work in the morning, he gave Frank and me instructions. "Help Mother with household chores," he told us. "Sweep the driveway" or "Clean out the garage." During the summer, we had to fill a basketful of weeds every day from the vegetable garden. If we didn't finish our chores by the time Father got home, then he whipped us or grounded us.

I was afraid of Father, and I tried hard to please him. But sometimes I forgot to do a chore after school because I got so caught up in playing hopscotch or jumping rope with my friends. Before I knew it, Father was home and all heck would break loose. He never bothered to listen to why I hadn't finished my chores anyway. When I tried to explain he hit me across the mouth to shut me up.

If Frank or I complained about being punished, Mother just scowled. "Do as your father says!" she said. She never interfered when he disciplined us, or comforted us afterward. When she caught us doing something wrong, she would threaten to tell Father. But sometimes she wouldn't actually tell him. Then I hoped that she was on our side after all.

Frank and I noticed that many of our friends in the neighborhood had dogs. We begged Father for one.

"No dog!" snapped Father each time we asked.

So Frank and I made up a dog. We called him Pudel and created adventures for him, just like Rin-Tin-Tin. Pudel always got himself into dangerous situations, and we took turns rescuing him.

Frank arranged our midnight Pudel meetings. They were secret. If Mother or Father found out, we knew they would quickly put an end to these nighttime sessions. At midnight Frank tiptoed into my room and woke me up. I could never figure out how he managed to wake up exactly at twelve without an alarm clock, but he always did it.

We took turns beginning and ending a story, always in whispers. Sometimes we finished the story by sharing a stolen cookie or piece of chocolate.

I loved the secret world we shared, and I loved Frank, knobby knees and all. He was tall and strong and handsome, with his light brown hair cropped short. I hoped to marry him when I grew up. But when I told Mother about my plans, she said, "That's nonsense! Sisters can't marry brothers."

"Why not?" I cried. At six years old, I just couldn't understand.

~

As Frank and I rocked in the hammock, listening to the conversations going on around us, I noticed dirty smudges on his knees and across the front of his sailor suit. Then I spotted some grass stains on my own white organdy dress and tried to brush them off. *Uh-oh,* I thought, *Mother isn't going to be pleased about how we've messed up our Sunday-best clothes.* She always had us dress up for these occasions.

Mother looked elegant in her flowery dress, her brown curls neatly brushed. Her eyes sparkled as she smiled and talked with Tante Lina and Onkel Carl. She got up and refilled the grown-ups' coffee cups, then motioned to me to carry a plate of sweets around.

When the plate was almost empty, I took it inside and put more plum cake and cookies on it. As I passed the mirror in the front hall, I caught my reflection, my suntanned face covered with freckles—"fly dirt," Frank called them—and my straight blond hair pulled tightly into short, thin braids. With my free hand I fingered the ribbon on a braid. *I wish my hair was as curly and beautiful as Shirley Temple's,* I thought for the hundredth time.

I placed the full tray on the table outside and settled back into the hammock with Frank. I noticed that Father, in his polo shirt and white trousers, was smiling and relaxed. I turned to Frank and whispered, "Don't you think Father looks like an Indian chief, with his hawk nose and reddish skin?" Frank nodded and smiled, punching my arm.

Father enjoyed company and entertaining, and he liked being the center of attention, especially with women. He also loved to drink alcohol. Frank and I liked it when Father drank. He never got drunk, but he relaxed and wasn't so mean. He actually became fun to be with. Sometimes he told stories of when he was a young boy in Germany—tales he shared over and over again.

I loved stories. Fairy tales, adventures, the stories of Huckleberry Finn, stories about Indians and about Abraham Lincoln and the Civil War.

When Father read to us, he preferred to read the more grown-up books. "Fairy tales bore me," he said.

So from him we learned about Hawkeye of the Mohicans and the Count of Monte Cristo. Often I didn't know the meanings of many words, but I understood enough to be fascinated by the characters and their adventures. Frank and I became the characters we heard or read about.

My favorite story was about the wolf boy, Mowgli, from *The Jungle Book.* Mowgli, who was abandoned by his real parents, was raised by wolves and became master of the jungle. I envied Mowgli for having a wolf mother. Shortly after hearing the story when I was around six years old, I created a wolf history for myself.

On our dining room wall was a picture of a lonely hut that I always liked to look at. I told a friend, "This is the house I was born in. My mother didn't want me when I was a baby. She left me there, and then a wolf found me and raised me as her own." I could see my friend was impressed, her eyes big as quarters, so I continued. "My wolf mama carried me around in her mouth. And I had wolf brothers and sisters to play with."

Mother overheard me and stormed in, furious. "Stop telling lies!" she yelled. "You know what happens to liars?"

I nodded. Yes, I knew all right. "If you lie," she often warned Frank and me, "you'll grow horns like the devil!"

I had seen pictures of this horned, goatlike devil in *Grimm's Fairy Tales.* As Mother was sending my friend home, I carefully stole looks at myself in the mirror and studied my forehead. I thought I saw little knobby things that could indeed be the beginning of horns.

When she came back into the room, Mother glared at me with her dark, piercing eyes and said, "Don't lie ever again!" But it hadn't seemed like a lie to me. It had seemed true. After that, though, I kept my stories in a safe place inside me and didn't share them with anyone, except sometimes with my brother, who was also my best friend.

Frank was the leader of our neighborhood pack in Stratford. As his sister I was allowed to be the only girl private in an all-boys' army. Frank could order me around all he wanted to—well, most of the time—but he got angry if the others tried to do it too. He always came to my defense, and he even took time out to retie a ribbon to the end of my braid.

The boys finally accepted me as part of the gang last summer when I managed to steal a watermelon from one of the nearby farms. Stolen watermelons always tasted best.

We re-enacted the Civil War, fought Indians, and warred with neighborhood bullies. We looked for and found arrowheads in the nearby fields, where the Delaware and Sankhikan tribes had lived a long time ago.

The empty lot next to our house was a perfect hiding place from our parents—the weeds there grew over six feet tall. We dug an underground fort in this jungle. When it was finished, since I was the smallest—and the girl—I was given the honor of sitting inside while the boys jumped on the roof to test its strength. With creaks and then a snap, the roof collapsed, burying me under piles of dirt and old rotten wood. I was scared and angry. The boys hauled me out.

"I'm telling!" I screamed, rubbing dirt from my eyes and hair.

Frank quickly offered a deal. "Eleanor, if you don't tell Mother and Father, I'll let you go in my tree house."

A visit to the boys-only tree house was an offer I couldn't resist. "Okay," I sniffed. "I won't tell."

∼

"It's a school night," Mother said after our immigrant friends had left and we had cleaned up. "Make sure to finish your homework, and then off to bed."

At our old, red brick schoolhouse on Princeton Avenue, two grades shared a classroom, so Frank and I were always in the same room. I learned a lot just by listening to the lessons of the next higher level.

After school, we played, did chores and our homework, then sat down to dinner. But dinner, too, was often a chore. Father ordered us to speak in German at the dinner table. "That way," he said, pointing at us, "you won't forget the language you learned in Germany." For every English word we spoke at the table, we lost a penny of our nickel allowance for the month. A penny bought a whole bag of candy that'd last all afternoon. So I definitely had to think twice before opening my mouth. I silently rehearsed in German, "Please pass me the sugar" or "May I have the saltshaker, please?" Often I just went without rather than risk making a mistake.

When we were trying to eat, Father gave us arithmetic problems to solve. Since arithmetic wasn't my best subject—actually, it was my worst—I often struggled to come up with the right answer. If I hesitated or made a mistake, Father shook his head and angrily called me "dumb cow," "stupid old owl," or "dumb chicken."

I knew that the animal insults were part of German culture, but they still made me feel bad. I hated it when he called me those animal names. They made me feel even dumber than I already thought I was. Sometimes to make myself feel better, I tried to think about happy things.

One of my favorite thoughts was of the special Christmas package from Grossmutter Rump; it arrived every year at the end of November. We marveled at the July postmark on the box. It had taken the box five months to reach us. Because it took so long to send a package by freighter from Europe, every year Grossmutter had to make the Christmas cookies in July. "To get myself into the spirit," she wrote us, "I sing Christmas carols while baking." Frank and I lifted the great box to see how heavy it was. We shook it and sniffed it. But we had no clue about what was inside, other than the cookies.

My family started celebrating Christmas on St. Nikolaus Day, the sixth of December. That night, as Mother and Father told us, St. Nikolaus comes by on his donkey. Frank and I put on the windowsill a plate filled with old bread for the donkey. If we had been good that year, St. Nikolaus would leave a gift or some candy in the dish. But if we had been bad, he would leave a switch instead.

Last year he left us a switch. We tried hard to determine which of our naughty deeds deserved such a horrible punishment. But we never figured it out.

This year Frank and I tried to stay awake and catch a glimpse of St. Nikolaus, but we fell asleep well before morning. When we awoke, we were thrilled—and relieved—to see that he had left candy.

A couple of weeks later, on Christmas Eve, we waited for the Christkind to bring the Christmas tree with shiny silver tinsel and real waxed candles. And there, tucked under the tree with other gifts, was Grossmutter's special box. At last we were allowed to open it. When we lifted the cover, we smelled the pine branches from the German forest mixed with the aromas of spekulatius, stollen, and pfeffernüsse, all traditional Christmas goodies. The wonderful box held gifts for everyone.

Opening Grossmutter's package was always the best part of Christmas. It made me feel loved and connected to my family across the sea.

∼

In March 1939, Hitler invaded the rest of Czechoslovakia. This time, our neighbors across the street avoided us and ignored Mother's greetings. Their kids called us names and continued to taunt us.

I was angry and embarrassed. *How can they blame us for something we didn't do?* I wondered. *We're Americans with immigrant parents, just like they are. We didn't invade their country. Hitler did.* I felt strange, as if they were telling me that I didn't belong.

Soon after, the hostilities escalated and erupted into violence. I watched from inside the gate on our front lawn as Frank and his friends fought the kids across the street. This wasn't a make-believe battle, though, like those we had waged in years past. Rocks now flew back and forth. Then a stone hit my forehead, barely missing my eye. My head stung, and blood gushed down my face. I panicked and started scream-ing. Mother ran out of the house waving Father's BB gun, scaring the kids away. She hauled Frank and me into the house.

"Don't get pulled into fights with those kids!" she lectured us. She began bandaging my cut.

"But Mother, they blame us for what Hitler's doing—" I started.

"Just ignore them!" Mother sighed. "If you tried reasoning with them and it didn't work, just ignore them."

The trouble didn't stop there. The Czechoslovakian immigrants reported Mother to the police for possession of a weapon and for threat-ening kids with a gun, even though it had been unloaded. The police came to our house, took the BB gun, and gave Mother a stern warning.

After that, our neighborhood didn't feel as safe and friendly anymore. I worried that things could turn violent again.

But by the end of May, the sunny days and the scent of the white blos-soms on the apple tree greatly picked up my spirits. As I walked to school on May 25, my birthday, I noticed the tiny green leaves unfolding on the trees and listened to the birds singing in the bushes nearby. *Today I'm nine years old,* I rejoiced with them. *Third grade will be over soon, and then comes summer vacation!*

All day long I thought about my birthday party after school. Mother had already sent out invitations, but I felt sorry for those girls who hadn't been invited. So on the way home from school, I told them, "Why don't you come over anyway?" They were delighted and raced home to change into their Sunday dresses.

Mother set a beautiful table under the apple tree, with a hand-embroidered tablecloth, cups and plates for the invited guests, and colorful favors. I didn't dare tell her about the other children I had invited—deep down I realized I had made a big mistake. When they arrived, Mother made it very clear that she was angry with me. Her dark eyes glared as she sliced the cake into smaller and smaller pieces, trying to make it stretch to feed everybody.

When the party was over, she turned to me, furious. "This," she hissed, "was your last birthday party." I knew she meant it. She always kept her word.

Shortly after my birthday, Father called Frank and me into the living room. "Sit down," he said. "I have something to tell you."

Frank and I looked at each other, and I knew we were both thinking the same thing: *Now what have we done?* I mentally ran down a list of things that might have gotten us into trouble with Father. But his face didn't show anger, so we knew it had to be something even more serious.

"We're going to Germany in the fall," he announced.

"For a vacation?" I ventured.

"No, not exactly, Eleanor. I was offered a challenging job as an engineer in Berlin at the AEG, the Allgemeine Elektrizitäts-Gesellschaft," he said proudly. "The offer was made by a famous professor named Dr. Biermans." Father's eyes sparkled as he continued. "It's in my field of electrical engineering. It's a great opportunity. And the AEG has offered us housing and a very generous exchange rate of four German marks to the dollar."

I was stunned. Questions swirled in my head. *We're leaving Stratford? Our friends? Will we have to go to German schools? What about our house? Our furniture? Will we come back?*

Sensing my rising panic, he quickly tried to reassure me. "Don't worry. I accepted the position with the understanding that I will return to the United States in two years." I knew that Father now had only a drafting position at RCA, even though he was trained as an engineer. His excitement showed us that he felt this offer from Berlin was too good to pass up.

Frank and I remained silent. Father added, "Anyway, it will give us all a chance to visit your grandparents."

Because of the many letters and photographs sent to and from Germany, I had long been aware that Mother and Father often missed their families. Travel to Europe was expensive and took nine days by ocean liner. Many immigrants never saw their families again. This was an opportunity my parents might not have had otherwise.

After the initial shock wore off, Frank and I began thinking of the move across the ocean as another adventure. We looked forward to the voyage. *Anyway,* I reminded myself, *in two years we'll be coming back, hopefully even to the same house.* And I was excited about seeing my beloved Omi, Grossmutter, and Grossvater.

After Germany invaded Austria and then Czechoslovakia, our immigrant friends had talked often about the possibility of war in Germany. When Father told them about accepting the new job in Germany, all of them tried to convince him to stay in America.

"Don't go, Josef," one said. "Hitler isn't going to be content with just annexing Austria and Czechoslovakia."

"Oh, I don't believe it," Father replied. "That's just the newspaper reporters trying to sound dramatic. Germany can't afford to get involved in another war."

"Mark my words," warned another friend. "He'll go after Poland next."

Father shrugged. "Why would Hitler want to jeopardize Germany's strong economy now by starting a war? It wouldn't make sense."

～

Frank and I eagerly looked forward to the big community picnic in Laurel Springs on the Fourth of July. Knowing that it would be the last time we would participate in the festivities for a couple of years made it even more special. For days before the event, Frank and I went with the gang to watch booths going up in the park, musicians practicing on the bandstand, flags being unfurled and hung, and preparations being made for the fireworks. We galloped for hours through all the busy confusion.

On the big day, our whole family went to the picnic. Frank and I lost no time disappearing into the crowd with our friends, as far away as possible from the critical eyes of our parents. We sang the "Star Spangled Banner" and "America the Beautiful" and marched to "Stars and Stripes

Forever," proudly waving paper flags. We were Americans! We stuffed ourselves with hot dogs and hamburgers.

This was one evening we didn't have to be home at dusk, and Father was in a more lenient mood. So as night settled in, we lay back on the cool grass, our heads cradled in crossed arms, and watched the magnificent fireworks display.

"Much better than last year," Frank said. We all agreed.

Through the long, warm days of July and early August, Frank and I played with our neighborhood buddies, exploring and creating more adventures for ourselves.

We were Robinson Crusoe, marooned for years on the tiny island of the tree house.

We were Huck Finn, making a raft of logs and tying it together with ropes. We crammed ten kids on board and floated the raft on Kirkwood Lake. None of us could swim.

We played chicken with the daily train that rumbled through town on its way to Laurel Springs. We ran onto the tracks and then jumped off at the last minute. The first of us to jump away was chicken.

My family drove up to Kuhn's Farm in the Poconos for a week, as we had each summer. I loved the Poconos. The simple farm was on the edge of a great, dark forest, which was full of all kinds of dangerous wild animals—snakes, bears, mountain lions—the perfect place for adventurers like Frank and me.

The last few years, we had gone up there in our old Model-A Ford with the rumble seat in the back. Frank and I sat securely strapped in our special seat, surrounded by pillows and luggage, with the rush of wind in our faces and a wide open view of passing scenery. We felt as if we were flying. This time, though, we drove up in Father's Ford V-8, which he had bought last fall. We cranked down all the windows, but the trip just wasn't as much fun as before.

On a couple of weekends my family went with our Danish neighbors, the Holms, to their summer cottage in Stone Harbor. Frank and I buried each other in the sand, jumped the waves, and pedaled the Holms's paddleboat in the harbor. But one Sunday, as Frank and I were digging a moat around a huge sand castle, trying to stop the waves from collapsing the walls, a big horsefly stung Frank right on his eyelid. His lid puffed way up and turned red and purple. He had to keep an ice pack on it for hours.

"I'm not going back there anymore," Frank declared. We didn't.

I had one last visit to see my favorite immigrant relatives, Tante Lina and Onkel Carl in Routledge. I loved going there because Tante Lina hugged me often and made me feel special. But I was happy to go there for another reason too. I couldn't wait to run over to Bobbsy Kurash's house, down the street from Tante Lina's. Bobbsy, his sister Eleanore, and his brother Hans—whose parents also had immigrated from Germany—and I roamed the neighborhood and played cowboys and Indians until darkness forced us back home.

Just before I had to leave Tante Lina's, Bobbsy came over and offered me a small ring from the five-and-dime store. "Eleanor," he said, "I'm going to marry you someday." I was flattered and proudly wore the ring home to Stratford.

Toward the end of August, Mother and Father put our furniture in storage and packed our clothes and books and stuff into large steamer trunks, which they shipped to New York Harbor. We said good-bye to our immigrant family and Stratford friends.

A few days before we left, I buried a tin cigar box filled with treasures at the base of the apple tree. Of the many small treasures I had collected through the years, I selected for this special box a smooth round pebble from the Pocono Mountains, a pink seashell from the ocean, and a scrap of black glittery material that I thought was especially pretty. As I buried the box, I looked up at the tree. "I'll be back," I said. "I promise."

Then one day all the hurrying was over, the house emptied of the familiar things that had made it our home. I walked through the garden one last time, hugging my magic apple tree, breathing in the sweet fragrance of honeysuckle, and waving good-bye to the towering jungle weeds of the empty lot next door, where Frank and I had spent so many happy hours at play. And then I bid one last farewell to the old house. As I listened to my footsteps echoing through the empty rooms, I was suddenly gripped by an odd feeling of foreboding, a vague sense that something bad was going to happen. I pushed the feeling to the back of my mind and ran outside to the car.

The day before we were to board ship, we visited the New York World's Fair. We walked down the Avenue of Nations, with its spraying fountains, then past the British and Russian pavilions to the magnificent Perisphere and Trylon, which symbolized progress through peace. On the inside of this immense building, we stood with other visitors on a slow-moving circular platform and looked down below at the pristine World of Tomorrow, which included jet airplanes, streamlined cars, beautiful houses, lush gardens, and green forests. As I peered over the rail I was struck by how peaceful and safe it looked down there, everything clean and bright. *That's where I want to live,* I told myself.

On August 29, 1939, we boarded the *S.S. Hamburg,* a huge German luxury ocean liner. As the ship pulled away from the wharf and through New York Harbor, Mother, Father, Frank, and I stood by the rail. We watched the Statue of Liberty vanish into the mist. As the city disappeared, Father turned to Mother.

"You know," he said, an uneasy edge to his voice, "when we were walking up the gangplank earlier, I heard a voice behind me say 'Don't go!'" Father rubbed his forehead. "It was so loud and clear, I turned around to see who was talking to me."

"Well?" Mother asked. "Who was it?"

Softly he replied, "Nobody was there!"

Father was always so sure of himself and wasn't given to what he considered flights of imagination. Hearing him talk like that made me anxious. *What did it mean?*

CHAPTER TWO

CHANGES
AUGUST 1939–SEPTEMBER 1939

AFTER MY FAMILY SETTLED into our cabin, we strolled around the decks. We met the Basedows, another German-American family. Frank and I were delighted to find that they had eleven children, several of them close to our own age. Together we kids began exploring the ship from stem to stern, and before long we were racing up and down the gangways. After we had tired of running around the ship, we settled into the enormous playroom with its toys, jungle gyms, and games. We stayed busy from morning till night, and we rarely saw our parents. In the evening, the stewards who oversaw all our activities put us to bed.

On our fourth day at sea, September 1, 1939, the captain addressed all the passengers over the loudspeaker. "Attention, please, ladies and gentlemen!" his voice boomed, reaching into every corner of the ship. "Germany has just declared war on Poland!"

Frank and I, who were out on deck with the Basedow kids, just stared at each other. Then we glanced at the grown-ups around us. All of them looked as if somebody had just punched them in their stomachs.

"I don't believe it!" somebody exclaimed.

"Is Hitler nuts? What does he think he's doing?"

The grown-ups began to gather in small groups. Germany's declaration of war became the only topic of conversation on deck, in the lounges, and at the dinner table. Even Frank and I were subdued by the news, sensing that something was very wrong.

Two days later, when Frank and I were spending a rare moment with our parents on deck, the captain made a second, more devastating announcement over the speaker. "Britain and France have declared war on Germany," he reported solemnly.

Everyone murmured their disbelief, and a woman near us started to sob.

"My God, Germany is actually at war!" Father exclaimed. "I didn't believe this would happen."

Mother just looked at Father, her brow furrowed.

I turned to Frank, alarmed. "What does it mean?"

"It means that we're probably going to be torpedoed by the Brits."

"Torpedoed!" I cried.

"Yup, that's what war is. Shooting."

The captain immediately addressed the torpedo threat. Shortly after his announcement, the ship halted in the middle of the ocean. We watched in amazement as sailors scrambled over the smokestacks with buckets of paint. Soon the red, white, and black colors of Germany gave way to the blue, white, and red colors of France. The German trim on each side of the ship vanished and reappeared as French. In a few hours, with some deft brushstrokes, the crew had magically transformed the German ship into a French one.

That evening we third-class passengers were served a fancy dinner, which had been intended for the many first-class passengers who had decided not to sail at the last minute. For a little while the somber feeling on the ship gave way to a tense gaiety. A band played, and the grownups danced and laughed. And all of us children, at our own tables, were treated to a party, with paper umbrellas, party favors, and cake. Our steward watchdogs were too busy entertaining and tending to the adults to keep an eye on us, so we did as we pleased and didn't go to bed until very late, dropping with fatigue, fully dressed, on our berths.

The next day, the purser told my parents that the captain was not taking his normal ocean route. To avoid enemy encounters, the captain ordered his crew to turn the ship north toward the Norwegian coast once we passed Iceland. Soon after that the ship stopped again, and for the second time the crew transformed the smokestacks, this time into Norwegian colors.

Up to this point, our parents had received a daily ship newspaper that kept them abreast of news around the world. But all news now stopped. Neither Father nor Mother said much to Frank and me about what was going on. Frank and I continued running around the ship with the other children and hiding from our stewards, but our games were less lively after the announcements of war.

A couple of days later the weather turned much colder, and Mother had to dig through our steamer trunks for warmer clothing. The captain explained that we were entering the Norwegian fjords, a route he hadn't taken before. We watched with increasing worry as the crew lowered lifeboats into the water and trailed them behind our ship. The purser later told us that the captain had been making preparations under order of the German High Command. If the British attacked the ship, the captain was to scuttle the *S.S. Hamburg* on the rocky coast of Norway.

Fortunately, we were not detected and did not have to wreck the ship. We were able to continue down the coast of Schleswig-Holstein and Helgoland to Cuxhaven, Germany. But on our arrival in Cuxhaven we learned that the port had been taken over by the German Navy, and we couldn't dock there. Tugboats pulled the ship into Hamburg harbor at noon on September 9, after eleven days at sea.

Onkel Franz, Mother's brother who now worked in Hamburg, was waiting for us at the pier. Frank and I were delighted to see him as we walked down the gangplank. I was eager to show him how much I had grown since he had last seen us. When we met him on the pier, however, his dark eyes, so like Mother's, were serious, and his face showed no hint of a smile.

"You've got to turn around and go back to the United States right away," he told us. "It's going to get bad here."

Frightened now by the turn of events, Father immediately tried to arrange for a return passage to America. But ships that were still sailing to the United States from neutral countries accepted only U.S. dollars. Unfortunately, Father had exchanged his U.S. money for German marks just before we left New York, and the Reichsbank refused to re-exchange the marks for dollars.

We were stuck in Germany just days after war had broken out with England and France, America's allies.

~

I sensed the nervousness and fear in the adults around me. A feeling of dread began to nag at me almost all the time.

Because we couldn't go back, Mother and Father decided to make the best of our situation and go forward with the plans they had already made. Before going to our new home in Berlin, we visited our Eslohe and Münster grandparents.

I had not seen my Eslohe Omi since I was four, and I was now a grown-up nine. As soon as I saw the old house with the red geranium boxes in the windows, memories came rushing back. Omi wrapped Frank and me in a hug and then greeted my parents. Father's two younger sisters, Tante Adele and Tante Maria, no longer lived with Omi. They were now married and had families of their own.

While the adults talked, Frank and I set off exploring. The bubbling brook still meandered across the street from her house and through the village, inviting us to play in it as we had done so many years before. The garden climbed up the hill behind the house, still covered with the fruit trees, vegetables, wild raspberries, and blackberry vines.

With my beloved Omi, in the small village of Eslohe, tucked between dark forested mountains and green meadows, I felt safe. The warm, early fall days were filled with bright autumn colors. Omi and I spent a lot of time in the garden, picking yellow mums, bright red dahlias, and multicolored zinnias and arranging them into bouquets. I climbed the apple and plum trees, pulling down the last of the ripe fruit.

Early one Sunday morning, Omi and I walked through the forest behind the house to the Hexenplatz, the place of the witches, as we had done so many years before. According to local legend, witches danced there at full moon. In my imagination I could see them as they danced wildly to music only they could hear, black hair flying in the wind, naked bodies writhing in the silvery moonlight.

We sat on the bench where we had always liked to rest. "It was here at the witches' place," Omi reminded me, "that your father proposed to your mother, and here that she agreed to return with him to the United States to become his wife. Your father was so excited and happy," she said, smiling, "that he immediately ran down into the village and bought an engagement ring to seal the promise before your mother had a chance to change her mind."

I knew the story well. This engagement had been no easy feat for Father, as he had had barely three weeks to convince Mother of his love for her. They had met on board the *S.S. Bremen* on a trip from the United States to Germany. Mother was returning home from a year spent as a governess in Toledo, Ohio, while Father was on vacation from his job in Philadelphia. He had fallen madly in love with the beautiful young lady seated next to him at the ship's dinner table and had decided at that moment to marry her.

Mother, however, was less than enchanted with the idea of putting her life into the hands of someone she had known such a short time. Their shipboard romance had been brief. But Father persevered and eventually Mother surrendered to his charm.

On our walk home, Omi and I took a path along the edge of a meadow. We could see people in the middle of the field grouped around what looked like an altar. Behind the altar hung a large blood-red flag with a twisted cross, the National Socialist, or Nazi, swastika. Images of the burned and twisted swastika on the *Hindenburg* flashed through my mind, and I shivered.

Uniformed young men—some men dressed in black, a few soldiers in gray—gathered near someone who looked like a priest in a white robe. I wondered if it was some kind of church service. Omi and I looked on in astonishment as they performed a ritual, which included repeatedly raising their right hands, arms outstretched.

"What is this, Omi?" I asked.

Omi shook her head. "I don't know," she replied. "I wonder why they aren't worshipping in church like everybody else." After that, Omi seemed preoccupied. We walked home in silence.

～

After my family's visit to Eslohe, we went to Münster to see Grossmutter and Grossvater Rump, Mother's parents, and Tante Elsbeth, her sister.

Mother had told us that when she was young, the family lived in a big house and had servants. Grossmutter was always a stickler for appearances and also for good manners, especially at the dinner table. Food at her house was always served formally on white linen tablecloths with fine china and silver flatware.

Frank and I ate in the American style, with fork in our right hands and our left hands resting on our laps. Grossmutter was aghast at what she saw as our horribly bad manners.

"In Germany," she informed us, eyebrows raised, "we hold our fork in the left hand and our knife in the right hand. Like this." She demonstrated. "Then when you're finished eating, you place knife and fork neatly side by side on your dinner plate."

Frank and I looked at each other, then tried to juggle our food on the upside-down forks, as she had shown us. It took some awkward juggling to attempt this new way of eating.

With a disapproving glance at Mother, Grossmutter said, "Don't they teach children manners in your country?" Mother didn't respond.

But our lessons from Grossmutter didn't stop at the dinner table. Shortly after we arrived in Münster, Grossmutter found out that Frank and I no longer believed in the Christkind.

"The Christkind is nothing but stories made up by adults," we informed her.

Grossmutter was horrified. She promptly dropped on the table the cut flowers she had been arranging and sat us down. She told us in no uncertain terms how she knew firsthand that there was indeed a Christkind.

"Every year around Christmas," she declared, "I take a zeppelin to heaven and help the angels and the Christkind with their Christmas baking." When she saw our raised eyebrows and smirks she sternly shook a finger at us. "Take my word for it, there is a Christkind."

Seeing our doubting expressions, she continued. "Now don't tell me you haven't seen the pink sky around that time of year."

Yes, we nodded, we had to admit that we had.

"Well," she explained, "the sky turns pink from the warm glow of the baking. Don't you see?"

When I glanced quickly at Frank, I saw that he wasn't buying Grossmutter's story.

But she had managed to sow a little seed of uncertainty in my mind. *Maybe I do believe in the Christkind,* I thought. *After all, I do believe in angels.*

After that we kept any doubts about Grossmutter's influence with heaven to ourselves, not wanting to jeopardize our Christmas presents.

～

Doors inside our grandparents' home, as in all the homes we visited in Germany, were kept shut tight. But as Frank and I played and entertained ourselves in Grossmutter and Grossvater's house, we soon discovered that we could peer through the keyholes to find out what was happening behind each door.

We rarely saw anything of interest, but one morning our persistent spying paid off. What we saw in our grandparents' room sent us into fits of stifled laughter. Grossvater stood in his long johns, bracing one foot against the bed frame, grasping the laces to Grossmutter's full-bodied, boned corset in both hands and leaning back. He was pulling as hard as he could to cinch in her stout body. Grossmutter repeatedly took deep breaths and then demanded, "Harder, Augustus, harder!"

When she emerged later, fully dressed and dignified, Frank and I still hadn't stopped giggling. We tried to disguise our peals of laughter as coughs.

One night, after we had been in Münster for about a week, I was awakened by the wail of a siren that shot chills through my body. "What's that?" I cried, jumping out of bed and running into the hallway.

"Air raid!" Grossvater shouted. "Air-raid alarm! Everybody to the bunker."

We all dressed quickly and rushed into the cold night air. Neighbors were already heading for the bunker at the end of the block. I was bewildered. "What's happening?" I cried.

Grossvater took my hand in his. "Don't worry," he said. "It's only a drill. No enemy airplanes are around. We're going to the bunker to practice for the planes that might come later."

I cried hysterically, begging Mother, "Please, please, let's go back to Stratford! I don't like it here!"

The next day we watched as a group of draftees marched down the street past my grandparents' home. Grossvater shook his head sadly as he looked at the young men barely out of their teens. "Now it's happening all over again!" he muttered.

"What does he mean 'all over again'?" I whispered to Frank.

Frank whispered back, "He's talking about the Great War that Germany fought years ago against England, France, and the United States."

I nodded. I remembered hearing Grossvater talk about how many of his friends had lost their lives in that war.

Soon after that, our parents left for Berlin. Frank and I stayed a few more days in Münster and joined them in late September 1939.

CHAPTER THREE

EARLY DAYS IN BERLIN

FALL 1939—SPRING 1940

OUR APARTMENT BUILDING, which we shared with five other families, was located at Breitenbachplatz 15 in Steglitz, a suburb in the southwestern part of Berlin. The first-floor apartment provided to us by the AEG, Father's employer, was comfortable, but small compared to our house in Stratford. It had a living room, dining room, kitchen, three bedrooms—one about the size of a large closet—and a small balcony to the back that overlooked a rose garden.

From the front windows I could see everything that went on in the little park across the street. Elderly people often sat on the benches under the tall chestnut trees while little children ran about in the playground. Streams of Berliners went in and out of the entrance to the U-Bahn, the subway system that took them to the city or to outlying areas. On the far side of the park were apartment buildings like ours, with shops on the first floors.

Mother and I had to shop for groceries every day, as we had only a pantry with thick walls to keep food cool. We crossed the little park in the morning to fetch freshly baked rolls for breakfast. Milk was delivered to each apartment house by horse-drawn buggy every morning. Housewives waited on the front steps with big, blue milk cans. Once a week the open-air market was held in downtown Steglitz, and we could find bargains on anything from clothing to fresh fruit and vegetables to pots and pans.

The first time I went on an errand to a store in Germany, I was astonished to see a sign in the window that read "Entering anywhere, your greeting must be 'Heil Hitler,'" Hail Hitler. That sounded conceited to me. I tried to imagine telling my friends in America that they must greet everyone with Hail Eleanor instead of Hi or Good morning or How are you? I knew they would laugh and make fun of me.

But no one I saw laughed as they entered stores around me. They gave raised-arm salutes—like Omi Ramrath and I had seen the uniformed men give beneath the giant swastika flag. As I stepped in the shop and raised my right arm, I felt peculiar and more than a little uncomfortable. After all, I didn't even know this guy Hitler. But after a while it was easier. I just flopped my arm in a fast upward motion and followed it by the friendly Guten Morgen, Good morning, or Guten Tag, Good day. I noticed most others did the same.

Everyone in Berlin seemed to be going to work, to school, to shops, and to shows as though there weren't a war going on. Ration cards for food, blacked-out lights at night, and occasional air-raid drills reminded us that Germany was at war, but most everyone seemed cheerful. People talked as if peace were just around the corner.

Berlin was an exciting, cosmopolitan city. Because the opera, concerts, and plays were affordable in Berlin, my family began attending these events. One Saturday night we went to a performance of *Hansel and Gretel,* and I was fascinated by a lovely song Gretel sang as an evening prayer before she went to sleep. She sang of being surrounded by fourteen angels: eight surrounding her, two to cover her, two to wake her, and two to take her to heavenly paradise. I had no trouble imagining invisible angels floating around me, watching over me. I was comforted. I could almost feel their wings fluttering against my skin.

On Sundays, weather permitting, my family took long walks in one of Berlin's many forest and lake areas. Pfaueninsel, Peacock Island, was an island in the Havel River, which laces the boundaries of Berlin. We took the ferry there, and upon landing we were greeted by peacocks almost as tall as I was, squawking and strutting around in their shimmering finery. The island was covered with green meadows and thick oak trees, and

Frank and I explored the fairy tale–like castles and ruins that were scattered here and there. I had no trouble transporting myself back to the eighteenth century when the royal families had played on those grounds. I pretended that one of the castles belonged to me.

The Grunewald, a wooded park practically within walking distance from our house, quickly became one of my family's favorite places. It contained more than fifteen square miles of pines and birch trees and was crisscrossed by footpaths. An old royal hunting lodge, which had been used by princes for boar hunts, still stood there. We were told that the forest still contained a number of wild boars, although we never saw any on our walks.

I spent many happy afternoons playing in that forest. It was a fascinating place of discovery, reminding me of the dark, sometimes creepy Grimm's fairy tales I loved. The forest's rotting tree trunks became little trolls with bulging eyes, ready to chase me through the damp forest undergrowth. Fallen logs became dragons I was forced to face and fight to the bitter death. Dried, twisted twigs grew into otherworldly creatures.

One day when we became tired on a walk in the forest, my family stopped at a café overlooking a lake, the Grunewaldsee, for cake and coffee while a band played lively folk music and couples danced. Frank and I sprinted across the dance floor, pretending to dance but exaggerating the dance steps and making silly faces. Our behavior embarrassed Mother, and we infuriated Father to the point that he ordered us out of the café and canceled our cake order.

Frank and I were tutored daily that fall in preparation for attending school. I could speak German pretty well, but I couldn't write or read the language. The Gothic letters were so different from English letters, and very difficult to master. Our tutor warned us that in school, if a student's letters stubbornly refused to touch the paper's lines or wiggled backward and forward, the student's grade immediately went down, no matter how good the content of the paper might be. Writing took me hours of practice, and I began to worry about going to school.

But I didn't let my anxieties spoil our Sunday explorations of the city. Some days my family caught the subway at the station across the street and rode to Unter den Linden, a boulevard lined with giant linden trees. The broad street ran through the heart of the city from the Brandenburg Gate all the way to the square called Alexanderplatz.

"Unter den Linden," Father told us on our first trip there, "is the centerpiece of classical Berlin. For hundreds of years it has been the main political artery, where ceremonies, processions, and parades take place."

Father walked us through the Brandenburg Gate, with the goddess of victory on top, standing proudly in her chariot drawn by four prancing horses. Then he led us down the avenue, pointing out stately old buildings, embassies, palaces, and the royal opera house built for Frederick the Great in the 1740s. He took us to see the imposing medieval churches that dotted the area, including the Dom, the Berlin Cathedral and the thirteenth-century Marienkirche, Saint Mary's Church. Their spires towered over us.

I loved visiting the Tiergarten, which had once been a royal game and hunting preserve. It contained bridle paths, a small lake with ducks, and a meandering stream. Siegesallee, Victory Avenue, cut through the middle of the park and led to a towering pillar crowned by a gold statue of Winged Victory that glistened in the sun. All along this avenue posed statues of the conquering heroes of the past—kings, emperors, and generals with plumed helmets and coats of mail.

For Sunday walks in the park, Berliners dressed in their finery. "It is a way of honoring the beautiful surroundings," Mother explained to us. She insisted that we polish our shoes and dress neatly when we went on Sunday excursions.

Walking among the civilians were men wearing the many uniforms of Nazi organizations. Frank had already memorized them all. "Those are the Schutzstaffel, or the SS, troops in black," he explained to me. "The Sturmabteilung, Hitler's bodyguards, are wearing brown. The men in gray are field soldiers, and those are Hitler Youth in black shorts and brown shirts. And the Gestapo, secret police, are everywhere."

To me the men's stiff faces and formal strides always seemed out of place on these peaceful Sunday strolls. When the soldiers strutted by in their shiny black boots, an uneasiness crept over me as if I had done something wrong and was about to get caught. *If I don't look at them,* I reassured myself, *they won't notice me.*

We began a tradition of finishing a Sunday in town with coffee and cake at Café Kempinski on the Kurfürstendamm, or Ku'damm, as everyone called the stylish shopping avenue. Sunny afternoons through the middle of autumn, we sat in the outdoor café with the last rays of sun warming our faces, watching the busy street awakening to evening life. Here on this avenue were the big department stores, the Kadewe and Wertheim, where Mother and I had already been shopping for school clothes. Just down the street near the beginning of the Ku'damm, in the middle of a busy intersection, stood the old gothic Kaiser Wilhelm Memorial Church with its giant spire.

One of Frank's and my very favorite places to visit was Sanssouci Palace in Potsdam, southwest of Berlin. "Often referred to as the Prussian Versailles," the tour guides told us, "the fabulously beautiful palace was built in rococo style around 1745 by Frederick the Second, King of Prussia." Through its windows I could see terraced vineyards and sculptured gardens. But it wasn't the beauty of the palace that interested Frank and me so much as putting on the big felt slippers. All visitors were required to wear the slippers over their shoes to prevent scratching the delicately inlaid wooden floors. It was much more fun for Frank and me to slide at breakneck speed across the highly polished floors than to look at boring artwork and fancy furniture. Stern reprimands from our parents didn't stop us. We just slid quickly out of their sight.

When our Münster grandparents came to visit us that fall, we all went into the city for Sunday dinner. Father knew of some restaurants serving a type of meat that did not require ration cards. Everyone called the meat Berliner Schnitzel, or Berlin steak. Frank and I knew the disgusting truth about where the meat came from, but we were sworn to secrecy. "Under no circumstances do you tell your grandmother what it is," Mother warned us, her dark eyes glaring.

The waiter brought the food to our table and placed the dishes in front of us. The pale white Berlin steak was covered with a heavy sauce and decorated with parsley. Actually, it was tender and I liked how it tasted.

Grossmutter seemed to enjoy it as well. Frank and I giggled as she ate everything on her plate. When we stepped out onto the sidewalk after dinner, she praised the meal. Then she became curious. "I wonder what kind of meat they could serve without requiring ration cards," Grossmutter said.

Mother and Father didn't respond, but Frank grinned. "You know what you just ate, Grossmutter?" he blurted out, ignoring Mother and Father's dagger looks. "Cow udder!" he exclaimed with glee.

Upon hearing that, our proper Grossmutter gave a big heave, and her dinner landed in the gutter. After Father finished punishing Frank, he couldn't sit down comfortably for several days.

Sometimes my family went to Berlin's Botanical Gardens. There we saw a display of a plant with a skull and crossbones sign in front of it. "Careful!" it read. "Do Not Touch! Extremely poisonous. Grows in North America." And indeed everybody kept a respectful distance. We all laughed as we recalled the many itchy run-ins we had had with this plant in the Poconos and on picnics around New Jersey. It was just poison ivy.

Our months of play and exploration came to an end. In late November, the dreaded day arrived: my first day of German elementary school. While I could now speak the language, despite my tutoring I still could not read or write it easily.

What scared me most, though, was that for the first time I would be in school without Frank. He had to go to the boys' school, while I was to attend the girls' school. In Stratford we had always shared a classroom. I didn't know what I was going to do now without being able to look over and see Frank.

Mother went with me that first morning to the old, dark, brick building that looked like a prison. I felt as if I were going to jail, with Mother's full consent. *Don't leave me! Please, please don't leave me!* I screamed deep inside as I watched Mother disappearing down the corridor without a backward glance.

When I entered the classroom, all eyes focused on me. In that instant I became intensely aware that I was not a German girl as they were. I was a foreigner. *Soon all of them will know that I can't even read or write German.* I became so nervous, I could hardly walk to my seat.

"This is Annemarie Tesch," the teacher said, motioning me to a seat next to a pretty brown-haired girl. "Eleanor, you will share the desk with her." The girl glanced at me with her blue eyes and smiled warmly. The smile seemed to say, Don't worry. Everything is going to be okay. Somehow I knew that this girl would become an important part of my life.

Because my German parents were strict, I had assumed that school would be strict too. I was right. I was constantly worried about misunderstanding school rules or doing something to offend a teacher and being hit for it. Then one day I was caught talking to Annemarie in Lehrer—Teacher—Lautsch's class. Talking in class was strictly forbidden.

Lehrer Lautsch was a big man with a red face. "Come here, Amerikaner," he growled, pointing a finger at me like a pistol.

The room became so quiet that I heard every squeak my shoes made as I walked weak-kneed to the front of the room. His desk was up on a platform, so he always seemed to be looking down on us like a prosecutor.

"You know why you need to be punished?" he barked. I nodded, terrified at what was about to happen. "Hold out your hand," he said, and when I did, his ruler hit my fingertips with a *crack* that echoed through the room. My fingers burned. "This will teach you not to talk in my class." I tried hard not to cry as I went back to my desk. I knew crying would be considered giving Lehrer Lautsch satisfaction, and I knew my classmates wouldn't like me if I showed weakness now. As I sat down, Annemarie squeezed my arm under the desk, trying to comfort me.

I was still battling tears when Lehrer Lautsch suddenly shouted, "Hey, Amerikaner! Come back here!"

My heart skipped a beat. *What did I do wrong now?* I tried to be brave as I walked back to his desk.

"Here, shake my hand," he demanded with a snarl, "and thank me for disciplining you."

I did as I was told and shook his moist, fleshy hand, murmuring, "Thank you for disciplining me."

"Louder!" he shouted. "I can't hear you!"

"*Thank you!*" I yelled at the top of my lungs, suddenly furious. My need to cry had disappeared. Head held high, I marched back to my seat. My classmates gave me reassuring looks. They now accepted me as one of them.

Frank had his own difficulties adjusting to the German school. He said that the boys teased and taunted him because he was a newcomer and an American. One day, after being harassed by the other boys because of the knickers he wore that weren't popular in Germany, he lunged at his main tormentor, to the cheers of the boys gathered around, and gave him a beating. After that, his classmates were more friendly to him.

"I think they wanted me to prove I could fight," Frank said to me that afternoon, shaking his head.

I knew what he meant.

It wasn't long before I had another run-in with a teacher. During music hour, the elderly music teacher, who always had a sour expression, often liked to play the violin for us, his captive audience. He demanded absolute silence and attention. We had to sit with our hands folded in front of us on our desks and could not interrupt him, even to ask a question. Even a request to go to the bathroom was denied.

He directed us to listen to the music and think of images that expressed what the music might be saying. I loved classical music and enjoyed this part of the music lessons. This particular day, the teacher was playing a piece by Mozart from *The Magic Flute,* and I was conjuring up magnificent scenes in my head. I was totally absorbed in the music, unaware that my hands were no longer folded in front of me, but were pulling absentmindedly on the puffed sleeves of my dress. All of a sudden I felt my elbows being repeatedly slammed down on the desktop.

The music teacher's face, flushed red with anger, loomed above me. He kept yelling, "Puff, puff, puff sleeves! This will teach you to pay attention in my class instead of fiddling with your sleeves."

I was shocked. Bitter tears streamed down my cheeks, because I had been doing exactly what he had instructed us to do. I had lost myself in the music. But I bit my tongue. I knew that, like my father, the teacher wouldn't accept any explanation.

I continued to have trouble writing in German. When my class was given a dictation by Herr Kolander, the director of the school, I struggled hard to write quickly, keep the letters in line, and still listen to the words that he dictated. But soon I was hopelessly lost. I panicked. *I'll fail if I don't do something,* I thought. *I'm just going to write everything in English.*

The next day Herr Kolander returned the corrected papers to the class. I cringed, awaiting his reprimand. "Overall, the dictations were very good," he said. "But there was one exception. I couldn't correct that one since it was written in a foreign language."

My heart pounded so hard I feared he might hear it. All eyes turned to me. Anxiously I looked at the teacher for signs of disapproval. Instead, a smile spread across his face. I sighed with relief and dared a small smile in return.

Besides reading and writing, I also had trouble with mathematics, particularly in learning the multiplication table. Father dealt with the problem by demanding that I learn one set every day. I was to recite all ten, backward and forward, and each time I missed one, he slapped me. I worked hard each day to memorize the tables. By evening I could recite them easily, both ways, to Mother or Frank. But as soon as I heard Father's key in the front door, my mind went blank. Even though Mother and Frank witnessed for me, Father did not believe I had practiced. He accused me of deliberately disobeying orders and punished me. After weeks of frustration and frequent slaps, he finally gave up. I knew his opinion of me had dropped to an all-time low.

My reading slowly improved. One of the first stories I was able to struggle through on my own was a German childrens' classic, *Der Struwwelpeter,* Shaggy-Haired Peter. On the front cover was a boy with a thick mop of shaggy blond hair and long fingernails like spikes. In the story, the boy became an outcast in society because he refused to have his hair and nails cut.

In the same book, I read other stories of children who disobeyed their parents. Paulinchen was told not to play with matches, but when her parents went out she disobeyed them and accidentally burned herself to death. Only her red shoes remained.

Another story was about Konrad, who sucked his thumbs. "Don't suck your thumbs," his mother warned, "or the tailor will come with his big scissors and cut them off." When Konrad sucked his thumb, the tailor did cut them off, leaving only bloody stumps.

I also read about naughty white children who made fun of a black boy. As punishment, Santa Claus dipped them into an inkwell so they were even blacker than the black boy they had teased. I was both fascinated and repelled by the stories in the book. The verses were fun and easy to learn because the words rhymed. But I was frightened by the stories. The children who disobeyed their elders suffered serious consequences, worse even than beatings.

I wondered if the children in the stories felt as I did. Even when my ideas and actions made perfect sense to me, they often displeased my parents and resulted in punishment.

Mother went shopping one rainy afternoon, and in her absence I painstakingly braided the silk tassels of the lace tablecloth on our dining room table into tight little braids. I envisioned her returning home and exclaiming happily about the interesting new look I had created.

But to my surprise, when Mother came home, she was enraged. "You stupid girl! You ruined my tablecloth!" she screamed, chasing me around the table with a bamboo rug beater.

I sat the rest of the day undoing each tight little braid, which left the long silk tassels wavy. With a certain satisfaction I thought the tablecloth looked like it had a perm. It did have a new look, after all.

On nights when Father wasn't home for dinner, Frank and I played a game of rolling our wooden napkin rings back and forth across the table to each other. Our giggles and the noisy collision of the napkin rings drove Mother mad.

"Stop that right now!" she yelled, exasperated.

But we were too wound up and persisted with the irresistible game. Finally she hauled out a wooden spoon and slapped our rear ends with it. She hit Frank so hard that the wooden spoon broke in two. Frank burst out laughing and I did too, even though being hit with the spoon had hurt. Finally Mother laughed with us. I couldn't remember many times when she had laughed with Frank and me.

Despite our troubles with our parents and our teachers, Frank and I adjusted to our new lives and began to make friends. Frank had begun to be interested in aquariums and soon discovered that one of his new friends, Georg Geutler, had the same hobby. Together, they set up an aquarium in our apartment. They read up on everything to do with aquariums: how to arrange them, how to feed the fish, and which plants to place in the tank. They began to trade fish regularly with each other.

And Frank and I were delighted to discover that the Basedow family we'd met on the *Hamburg* had settled in Berlin. They lived in a tall, old apartment house that was built as solidly as a fortress. The Basedows were a noisy, fun family, with not nearly as many rules as ours, so Frank and I preferred to play at their home. We practiced our English together and talked about our lives in America—where we had lived, what we had done there, and what we were going to do when we returned. Often when their mother had had enough of our screaming and shooed all of us out of the apartment, we rode the elevator in their building, up and down, punching all the buttons and delighting in watching the scowls of the adults who tried to squeeze into the elevator with us.

But visits with the Basedows weren't as frequent as I wanted, and I would have become lonely if I hadn't started to become close to Annemarie. Her family's villa was located on the Fichteberg, a wealthy section of Steglitz, with many large villas along broad, tree-lined streets. Her house was nestled in the middle of a formal garden near the Botanical Gardens. From her home I could see the giant glass domes that housed palms and rare tropical plants.

The Teschs were a wealthy old Berlin family, and three generations of the family still lived in the house: Frau Tesch's mother, a spry eighty-seven year old who in her youth had been a celebrated opera singer at the courts of Europe; Annemarie's other grandmother, Herr Tesch's mother; and the young family Tesch, including Annemarie's brother Christoph, who was the same age as Frank.

Although she hadn't been an opera singer for many, many years, Frau Tesch's mother, Ömi, expected the family to wait on her hand and foot. And Herr Tesch's mother had lived in wealth all her life, so she couldn't understand why things had suddenly become rationed. She complained constantly.

However, Annemarie's sunny and kind disposition soothed the family's ruffled feathers. She was adored by everyone in the household, especially Papa Petke, the head servant who had worked for the Tesch family for many years. He was truly a loved and trusted member of the Tesch family. He was devoted to Annemarie and watched over her.

I saw the affection and intimacy that spun so naturally between Frau Tesch and Annemarie and wanted some of it for myself. Annemarie and her mother were trusted friends. I never felt I could confide my deepest feelings to my own mother, who always seemed critical and distant.

Annemarie's father was an architect, but he had been drafted into the army as an officer. Herr Tesch, unlike my father, had a warm, loving relationship with his children. He called Annemarie "Entchen," little duck, never "dumb cow."

The rooms in their house had high, ornate ceilings and were filled with furniture lavishly carved and inlaid with gold. The bright, glassed-in veranda held a winter garden with tropical plants and wicker furniture. Annemarie received and practiced her piano lessons in a separate music room on a grand piano. But my favorite part of the house was a large library with deep, soft leather chairs and floor-to-ceiling bookcases stacked with books. Plush oriental carpets covered the shiny wooden floors, and on the walls hung magnificent, gilt-framed paintings—one pictured golden-haired Valkyries carrying dead heroes on winged horses to Valhalla, the realm of the warrior god Wotan, chief of the Germanic gods, a terrifying figure. When I looked at him, Wagner's powerful music of *The Ring of the Nibelungen*, which I had seen on stage at the Berlin State Opera, played in my head.

Occasionally Annemarie invited me to spend the night, and we were allowed to choose any of the empty bedrooms for our sleepovers. One night, after telling each other chilling ghost stories in one of the canopied beds, Annemarie left the room. As I waited for her, a storm outside unleashed pouring rain, lightning, and great rumbling thunder. In the flashes of lightning, the tree branches that swept and scratched against the window looked like witches' broomsticks. Shivering, I pulled the goose-down comforter all the way up to my chin and wished Annemarie would hurry back.

Suddenly I heard the floorboards creaking. Somebody was moving about in the room. "Is that you, Annemarie?" I whispered. No one answered. A cold breeze passed over my face, even though the windows were closed. *What is it? A ghost?* My heart pounded wildly. Too scared to scream, I remained motionless, hoping that whoever or whatever it was would leave. I willed the Invisibles, my guardian angels, to protect me. Some time later, Annemarie came back to the room. When the first rays of sun streamed into the room my fear vanished. I never told anyone about my encounter with the ghost. I was afraid they would make fun of me.

It was always more fun to play at Annemarie's house than at my family's apartment. One reason was her attic. Nothing was more exciting on a rainy afternoon than exploring the chests that belonged to Annemarie's opera Ömi. They were filled with elegant velvet and satin gowns, flow-ered hats, soft feathery wraps, delicate ivory-handled fans, and beaded purses. And over everything lingered a faint scent of roses. We tried on the gowns and hats and admired ourselves in an oval, full-length mirror.

Ever since I had seen my first opera, I had secretly wanted to be an opera singer. I couldn't hold a tune, but when I dressed in one of those elegant gowns and played a record of famous arias on the Victrola, I mouthed the words in front of the mirror and became a diva. At the end of the aria, I curtsied low before my adoring audience and regally received the thundering applause and a showering of red roses, as befit-ted a great star.

The old attic also held a secret room. About the size of a closet, it was a perfect hiding place, because the entrance blended smoothly into a wooden wall. From another area in the attic, stairs led up to a flat rooftop that once had held a garden. On warm days we climbed up there and sunned ourselves in the nude.

In the garden behind some tall shrubs, we dug a hole and covered it with logs and branches. Inside we fixed up a cozy little hideaway with an old rug and candles. We kept special treasures there, and hid inside to share stories and secrets. I told Annemarie about the underground club-house in Stratford, and she told me about the wonderful times she had on her family's island.

At the back of the garden, a high stone wall surrounded the Tesch property and bordered a narrow lane that ran along the back of the homes. It was called Zigeuner, or Gypsy, Promenade, but was also known as Lover's Lane, since couples often sat on benches tucked away in bushy alcoves. Annemarie and I liked to sit on top of the wall and spy on the lovers as they walked by holding hands or kissed on the park benches.

One day a man stopped next to our wall and looked up at us. "Would you like to see something?" he asked, winking at us.

"Sure!" we giggled, feeling safe on our high perch and curious about what surprise he might have.

With both fascination and revulsion, we watched as he opened his zipper and revealed his extended private part. After a moment of shocked silence, we jumped off the wall and ran screaming into the house. From then on we were forbidden to go near the Gypsy Promenade.

One evening, however, around dusk, I had to tell Annemarie some-thing important that I had forgotten to tell her earlier. Since we lived no more than a twenty-minute walk from each other, I figured I could eas-ily make it to her house and home before dark. Even though I wasn't supposed to, I decided to take the shortcut along the Gypsy Promenade. *I'll walk fast,* I thought.

As I came around a bend, I saw a man standing motionless by a bench. Since the shadows were long, I couldn't tell what he was doing. My instincts warned me to turn around and take the long way. But that would take time and would probably mean punishment at home if I returned after dark. I decided to go on anyway. Every muscle in my body tensed. I was ready to break into a run if I had to.

As I approached, I realized that the man seemed to be floating in midair. When I came near him, I saw with horror that he was a young soldier who had hanged himself from a tree. His limbs were completely still, his face a frozen blue-gray mask. The rope around his neck had forced his tongue out. *I never knew a tongue was that long,* I couldn't help but think.

I raced the rest of the way to Annemarie's house, where I breathlessly spilled my story. While Frau Tesch called the police, Annemarie and I wondered why the man had taken his life.

"Maybe his girlfriend jilted him," Annemarie suggested.

"Or maybe he had received orders to go to war," I replied.

The next time we looked over the wall, the body was gone. But the end of the rope hung there for a long time, a grisly warning and a reminder of the first dead person I had ever seen. I thought of him every time I considered taking the forbidden shortcut.

In spite of how busy I was with all my new adventures, school problems, and adjustments to life in Germany, I was seized at the oddest moments by a terrible longing to be back in my beloved Stratford. At those moments I felt as if a cloud passed over the sun, leaving me in the dark and cold. *Two years, Father had said, and we will be back in America.* But why couldn't I believe it?

CHAPTER FOUR

HITLER YOUTH AND A VISIT TO STOLP

SPRING 1940–SUMMER 1941

FATHER INSISTED ON complete quiet from Frank and me when he listened to the evening news on the German National Radio. He wouldn't tolerate any interruptions. So although I was bored by it, in the spring and summer of 1940 I heard many reports about the victories of the German army in western Europe.

"Germany invades Denmark and Norway," the radio announcer proudly proclaimed on April 9.

Father shook his head in disbelief. "It's going to get serious now," he declared. "Hitler's trying to take over all of Europe." My parents looked at each other, the worry lines in their foreheads carving deeper with each broadcast.

The reports all began to sound like a lot of bragging to me. The announcers never talked about how the people felt when their countries were invaded. I imagined strangers coming in our apartment, into my room, and seizing all of it as their property. I recalled the angry reaction of the Czech family in Stratford when the news came of Hitler's invasion of their country. *Now here we are again,* I thought.

~

At age ten, all German boys and girls were automatically inducted into the Hitler Youth, which to me appeared to be like the Girl or Boy Scouts in America. I had eagerly looked forward to joining the Scouts before we moved from America, so I was intrigued by the Jungmädchen, a junior branch of the BDM, the Bund Deutscher Mädchen. Girls belonged to the Jungmädchen until age fourteen, when they graduated to the senior BDM. Boys started out in the Jungvolk and moved up at age fourteen to the Hitler Jungen.

Since Frank and I were Americans—foreigners—we were exempted from the Hitler Youth. But all my new friends were in the Jungmädchen and told me how much fun they had together. I wanted to join too.

At first when I asked Mother about it, she said "Hitler Youth? Absolutely not!" I told her how much fun the Youth was, how it taught discipline and would also help me grow closer to my new friends. Frank wanted to join as well.

"You can go to the social events," Mother finally told us. "But I forbid you to attend the political indoctrination sessions." That suited me fine. I had no interest in politics anyway.

Each week the Hitler Youth attended a political evening which stressed Nazi ideology. To be excused from this evening, a Hitler Youth had to provide a written note from a parent explaining why he or she was absent. This rule annoyed Mother greatly. "Why should I have to explain anything to some dumb little goose?" she said, referring to my troop leader, who was just sixteen years old. Mother simply wrote one sentence for me to take to the girl, "Eleanor couldn't come," and signed the note with an almost unreadable flourish. For some reason, my leader never challenged those notes.

At the Hitler Youth swearing-in ceremony, we had to raise three fingers of our right hand and say all together, "I promise in the Hitler Youth to do my duty at all times in love and faithfulness to help the Führer— so help me God!" I felt strangely guilty—disloyal—saying the oath, but I'd been in Germany long enough to know it was best not to criticize the Nazis or to voice my opinion. I didn't want to be singled out and punished or kicked out of the Hitler Youth if I didn't take the pledge.

Then we sang the Hitler Youth anthem, "Forward, forward, sound the bright fanfares. We march for Hitler through night and suffering with the flag of freedom and bread. Our flag means more to us than death. Youth knows no dangers." As I looked at the scary black, twisted cross on the blood-red Nazi flag, I thought about the beautiful red, white, and blue, star-studded flag of my country.

Most of my group—with the exception of the fanatics, whose parents were members of the Nazi party—were in the Hitler Youth not to serve the Fatherland, but because it was fun and popular. Like me, they seemed to enjoy the excitement and the feeling of belonging to a group, to something bigger than ourselves.

We kept busy with marches, parades, hiking, campfires, and song festivals. We learned many old hiking songs, folk songs, and Hitler Youth songs. We were encouraged to learn a musical instrument. I tried the recorder, without much success. Bodybuilding was taught through calisthenics, push-ups, running, and broad jumping. The Hitler Youth motto was to be hard as Krupp steel, tough as leather, and fast as greyhounds. But cleanliness and neatness were stressed above all. Scuffed shoes, a dirty blouse, or stains on a skirt were not acceptable. If a girl failed the inspection held before every meeting, she was sent home and forbidden to participate in upcoming events.

Now on Sundays instead of taking walks with my family through the the Grunewald, I sometimes went to the Grunewald for Hitler Youth Pfadspiele, path-finding games. One troop left a trail through the woods, marked by signs on the ground or ribbons attached to tree trunks, and other troops had to find that trail and follow it. The first troop to reach the goal was the winner.

The Hitler Youth placed a heavy emphasis on competitions, especially in sports. But I was forever dropping the ball or stumbling or getting winded in my eagerness to win. The kids on my team groaned and rolled their eyes in exasperation. Even the leaders often sighed, "Eleanor is hopeless!" Unfortunately, the harder I tried, the more destined I seemed to fail.

For months we trained for one big event in particular: the day of the Reichswettbewerb, the Hitler Youth Olympics, held at the immense stadium in Berlin. The day of the event, the arena was filled to bursting with Nazi officials in uniform and thousands of parents and other spectators. Hitler himself sat prominently in the center of the dignitaries' section.

Like all of the other kids, I was excited to see the thousands of people watching us and nervous about showing off all we had practiced. We stood in formation at attention for what seemed like hours on the stadium field in our black shorts and white T-shirts with the swastika emblem. Giant red swastika flags flapped in the breeze above the grandstands. Torches flared and waved in the wind. The military band played the German national anthem with pomp and solemnity, "Germany above everything in the world…." The band played the Horst Wessel song, the Nazi anthem, "The flag held high, the rows unbroken, storm troopers march in quiet, firm steps,…" to which everybody raised their right arms in rousing salute.

Speeches followed. Baldur von Schirach was the director for the Hitler Youth. It was hard to hear everything he said because his voice echoed around the stadium. When I heard him say, "The future of Germany rests on the shoulders of our youth," I glanced at the skinny little shoulders of the girls in front of me and wondered how the whole future of a country could rest on them.

My mind kept wandering during the endless speeches. Finally I heard somebody yell, "One Nation! One State! One Leader!" and everybody in the grandstands rose to their feet, right arms raised, shouting in a frenzy, "Sieg Heil! Sieg Heil!"—the Hitler salute.

After that we marched off the field and waited until it was our turn to compete. We were all scared and quiet. I was feeling quite sick to my stomach, and only the fear of throwing up in front of the immense crowd at the stadium prevented me from heaving. I swallowed hard and ordered my stomach to calm down. I kept telling myself, *I have been practicing for months and toughening my body for this event, and now the big moment has arrived. Surely I can do it.* Then I prayed, *Oh please, God—if you exist—don't let me mess up.* I figured that my teammates must have been thinking the same thing—about me—as we marched out onto the field.

Another team lined up opposite my team for the relay race. Bodies tensed. "Ready! Set! Go!" shrieked the official, and amidst a deafening roar from the spectators, we were off and running. After just the first lap, it was clear to me that my worst nightmare was coming true. I was falling behind, and no matter how hard I tried, my legs felt like lead weights pulling me into the earth. The distance between the last row of girls and me grew longer and longer until it seemed as though the entire distance of the stadium lay between us. I was breathing so hard I thought my lungs would burst.

What will those Nazi men in uniform do to a loser? I worried as I finally crossed the finish line. Obviously I was a disappointment to the Führer and Director Schirach. I didn't need the berating of my troop leader nor the ridicule of my teammates afterward to point this out to me. The American had proven herself to be unworthy of being a good Hitler Youth.

~

April 20 was Hitler's birthday, and Germany celebrated with a national holiday, which meant no school for us kids. Mother and I went to run errands and saw that every window in Berlin was decked out in festive flags, as required. We turned onto our street, and Mother suddenly stopped, frozen in terror. But I was thrilled. There, between all the bright red swastika flags draped from the windows of our apartment, fluttered the Stars and Stripes. I had never felt so proud of Father.

Mother tore into the house, yanked the flag from the windowsill, and destroyed it. "How could you do this?" she yelled at Father. "You endangered the whole family! Somebody might report us to the Gestapo. Don't you know people are arrested for a lot less than this?"

I had never seen Mother so angry. We had heard rumors of people being taken away by the Gestapo for having said something negative about Hitler or the war. Even Frank and I as Hitler Youth were supposed to report negative comments that were made against the Third Reich— even if those comments were spoken by our own parents.

To me this rule was absurd. It was unthinkable for me to report my parents for anything. They were my parents and had a right to say whatever they wanted to without judgment from anyone else. For a few tense days we worried about who might have seen the flag and reported us.

When nothing happened, we considered ourselves lucky. But secretly I was pleased, and relieved, to see whose side Father was on.

Father had been right about the situation getting much more serious. "Germany invades Holland, Belgium, and Luxembourg," the radio announcer reported on May 10. Two days later, on May 12, he announced, "Germany invades France."

"France is one of America's allies," Frank whispered to me.

I was horrified. "Does this mean we can't go back to America soon?" I asked Father, fearing the answer.

Father shook his head grimly. "No, I don't think we can."

Why did Father bring us here? He's put us all in such danger. I bit my tongue. *Stratford is moving a little bit farther away from me every day.*

∼

Once summer finally arrived and school was out, Frank and I spent our days with our new friends. On sunny days, Annemarie and I took the subway to the Grunewaldsee, lazed around in the warm sand by the lake, swam, or hiked in the woods, looking for mushrooms. Sometimes we rented a paddleboat and pedaled along the shore of the lake. On rainy days, Annemarie came to my house and we knitted or sewed, or I went to hers and we played in her attic. Other times we went into town and wandered through the Kadewe department store, pretending we could buy anything we wanted to.

Frank liked to spend entire days exploring the subway system with friends or just by himself, riding around the various lines for hours, trying to see where and how far he could travel on one fare. Many nights he told me about all of the people he'd seen and the places he'd visited that day.

∼

On June 14, another war update blared over the radio and splashed across newspaper headlines: "Paris has fallen to the glorious sons of the Third Reich!" Shortly after that announcement, a big victory parade was organized along Unter den Linden, through the Brandenburg Gate. My troop was chosen to attend the military parade. We went by subway, proudly wearing our crisp uniforms of black skirts, white blouses, black bandannas knotted around our necks, and white knee socks.

I wasn't prepared for the masses of people gathered in front of the elegant old Adlon Hotel at the Pariser Platz, where we assembled. Thousands of people lined the long Linden promenade. It looked and felt as if all of Berlin were present. Swastika flags waved from every window, and flowers were strewn the length of the parade route. People were screaming "Sieg Heil! Sieg Heil!" Soldiers and polizei, city police, were trying to control the enthusiastic crowds. It felt like a carnival. Since we were so small, our troop was ordered to stand just inside the cordoned-off area near the Brandenburg Gate.

It was a dreadfully hot, sticky day. We had been standing at attention in one spot for hours in the sun, waiting for the parade to begin. I began to feel as if all the oxygen had been sucked out of the air. My head began to spin round and round. "I can't breathe! I'm suffocating!" I shouted desperately to anyone who might hear me in the crowds that pressed around us. But my voice was drowned in a sudden deafening roar that spread out all around me, like a giant tidal wave, as a black limousine glided by carrying a smiling Hitler in the back. He was standing, saluting the crowds.

The roar grew fainter and fainter as the limousine and the cheering crowds merged into one tiny dot that receded into nothingness. Sometime later I found myself lying on a cot while a woman held smelling salts under my nose. I had no idea how I got there. I had missed the parade. When I felt stronger, I was given permission to go home. I was never so happy to be back in the cool quiet of our apartment as on that day.

In August, we began to hear radio reports daily about the German air force, the Luftwaffe, bombing London and other parts of England. One night soon after those reports, the air-raid siren sounded, and we all scrambled for the basement.

Berlin was being bombed by the British Royal Air Force.

We could hear the faint, low-droning buzz of airplanes high above us, followed by the closer *boom, boom* of antiaircraft guns firing at the bombers. The next day we were relieved to hear that the British hadn't done any damage, but a shock wave had been felt through all of Berlin.

"I don't know why everybody is acting so surprised," Frank said later as we were getting back into bed. "Berliners have been hoping peace is right around the corner. But how can you blame the Brits for bombing us after what the Luftwaffe is doing to London? They aren't going to take that kind of beating without fighting back."

"Do you think it's going to get worse?"

"If the Germans would stop, the Brits would," he replied. "But with all of the military victories the Germans have had, I don't think they'll stop anytime soon."

I shivered as I pulled up the covers under my chin. "Do you ever think about Stratford anymore and wish you were back there?"

"Not too much," he answered. "This is more exciting. It's like being on a great big adventure—much bigger than our old games back there."

"But don't you sometimes want to be back there?" I pushed.

"Well, maybe sometimes."

~

Our little Jungmädchen troop suddenly became involved in grown-up activities. We collected money for Winterhilfswerk, a winter relief fund. Like the other girls, Annemarie and I knitted socks for soldiers at the front and hauled coal for the elderly. We were told about possible poisoned gas warfare and were taught how to wear gas masks.

The block warden instructed the families in our building to place sandbags across the cellar windows. Heavy wooden poles were installed in the cellar to support the ceiling in case of a direct hit. There was a possibility that we would be spending long periods of time down in the cellar, so we tried to make it as comfortable and safe as we could. Like other families, we placed first aid kits and buckets of water in the cellar. Mother and I stored emergency food rations. Some families put old mattresses and canvas chairs in their area of the cellar, but Father built and installed a bunk bed in ours.

War preparations were going on everywhere in the city. I began to realize just how dangerous the bombings could be. Occasionally the air-raid siren went off, and we all raced for the basement. But thankfully, we still saw no signs of damage in Steglitz.

When I went to downtown Berlin with Mother, I noticed that some of the streets were being camouflaged with netting to simulate forests. Frightening signs were going up all over the city, on advertisement pillars and in subway cars, warning us about crimes against the state. "Listening to foreign broadcasts is strictly forbidden under Penalty of Death!" declared one. Another showed a picture of a parrot with a noose around its neck and read, "This is what happens to the parrot that talks!" "Careful! Enemy Listens In!" another poster screamed, showing a pair of eyes looking in both directions.

"Why is listening to foreign broadcasts forbidden?" I asked Mother one night.

"Because we're not supposed to hear outside accounts of what's going on in the war."

"But who is the parrot that talks?"

"Eleanor, those posters are trying to discourage people from giving information to Germany's enemies," Mother said impatiently.

I was too afraid to ask my other questions. *Who is the enemy? How will I know who not to talk to?* I feared being killed for doing something wrong. I decided to keep my mouth shut tight.

When school started again in the fall, air raids were infrequent and occurred only at night. Often we didn't even go into the cellar when we heard the bone-chilling howl of the air-raid siren. For us kids it meant that we could sleep an hour longer the next day before going to school. After an air raid Frank and I searched for flak, antiaircraft splinters. He took our prize finds to school to compare sizes and trade them with the other boys.

That winter, Berlin had a coal crisis. Families were put on a ration of coal, so Mother set the heater lower, and we all wore extra layers of clothing to keep warm.

Coal wasn't the only shortage. Many factories were being mobilized to produce war supplies instead of manufacturing clothes, shoes, and household goods. "This new soap is hideous," Mother complained bitterly. The grainy, pale-green bars were full of grit, produced few suds, and melted away in no time flat. Toilet paper was another hard-to-get item, and what Mother and I could find in the stores was rough and scratchy. The government decreed that we were all to have two meatless days per week, and shortages of coffee, dairy products, and fruit became more frequent. It seemed as though every day brought a new shortage.

~

In April 1941, the newsboy at the U-Bahn entrance screamed another headline: "Germany invades Yugoslavia and Greece!"

After listening to the news that night, father rubbed his head. "My God!" he exclaimed to Mother. "The man is an idiot! We're heading for another world war, I'm afraid!"

All I could think about was returning to the United States. "Are we still going back to Stratford at the end of this year, as you promised?" I asked fearfully.

He shrugged. "I don't know! I don't know if we can!"

That evening Mother took me aside and firmly held my arm. Her eyes were not angry, but serious. "Listen carefully, Eleanor," she said. "I don't want you to discuss anything that is said in this household with anyone outside." And with an especially penetrating look, she added, "Not even to Annemarie. Don't tell *anyone* what we say about the war, or about Hitler. It would be very, very dangerous and could have serious consequences for all of us."

I nodded but remained silent, wondering what the "serious consequences" might be. *Will we be taken away by the Gestapo?* I felt a chill run through me.

That spring Father tried again to get us back to the United States. The German government granted Father, Frank, and me exit visas. But Mother had never gotten around to changing her citizenship when in the United States. She was still a German citizen and so was denied permission to leave. When Father and Mother told us that we couldn't return without leaving Mother, I was devastated and cried myself to sleep. *I hate Germany and I hate Father for bringing us here.* My growing disappointment that we would not return to the States soon, as Father had originally promised, overwhelmed me.

Although by the spring of 1941 we had lived in Germany for close to two years, school continued to be a struggle for me. I was constantly worried about my slow progress. I was facing an entrance exam into the Oberrealschule, the high school, that fall and I was afraid I wouldn't make it.

At the end of April my great aunt and uncle, Tante Mieze and Onkel Adolf, visited us from Stolp, in Pomerania near the Baltic Sea. Tante Mieze was Grossmutter Rump's younger sister. Onkel Adolf was the director of the bank in Stolp. Like Grossmutter Rump, dignified Tante Mieze enjoyed a certain amount of wealth and never had to want for anything. Onkel Adolf catered to his wife's every whim.

At the time of their visit, a few weeks before my eleventh birthday, I was miserable. The ever-escalating war preparations going on in Berlin made me anxious. Because I was in such fragile shape, Mother and Father agreed that Tante Mieze and Onkel Adolf should take me back with them to Stolp for a couple of months. I looked forward to seeing a new place and having a temporary break from Berlin. The idea of Pomerania reminded me of a very old folk song I had learned in school: "Ladybug, ladybug, fly, / Your father is in the war, / Your mother is in Pommerland, / Pommerland is burned down, / Ladybug, fly!" The lyrics weren't very encouraging, but I liked the melody.

The three of us took the train to Stolp, and from the window I watched the unfolding landscape of rural Pomerania, its softly rolling hills, its meadows, lakes, and forests. I already knew I would like it there.

Stolp showed no signs of war, and there was no shortage of food. I began to feel much happier and more relaxed. My aunt and uncle lived with their twenty-one-year-old daughter, Ruth-Margot, in a spacious apartment above the bank on Blumenstrasse. Their son, Karl Heinz, twenty-four, had just been drafted and was already off at basic training. A young Polish woman, Edit, cooked and cleaned for my aunt and uncle.

Tante Mieze believed in rigid distinction between the elite and the working class, so we had several unpleasant encounters about my friendship with Edit. To avoid conflicts with my aunt, I went into the kitchen to see Edit only when Tante Mieze was taking a nap, when she had her late afternoon coffee, or in the evening after she had gone to bed. I loved to sit on the edge of the kitchen table, my feet swinging, watching Edit work and listening to her talk about her lovers and her life in Poland. She told me that after the Germans took over Poland, she had been deported for labor into Germany and had to wear a yellow *P* on her coat. She talked about her family's farm in Poland, which the Germans had taken away from them.

"Edit, what about your family? Where are they now?" I asked.

Edit shrugged her shoulders. "I don't know."

"Oh Edit, how sad! I can't imagine being without my family. It must be terrible! Did you cry?"

Edit wiped her work-hardened hands on her apron and looked at me. "Yes, I did at first, but tears are useless. They won't bring the family back. What is, is. I'm trying to make the best of it. I was grateful when I was assigned to work for nice folks like your aunt and uncle. They're kind to me, and I have enough to eat. I could've been sent to a factory or to a farm to work outside all through the winter." Edit returned to washing dishes, clattering the plates more noisily than usual. "I'm going back to Poland after the war to find them," she said with quiet determination.

Then I heard Tante Mieze coming down the hallway and thought it best to get out of the kitchen. *Poor Edit,* I thought as I headed out the back door, *I know I would have cried—a lot. I'm such a crybaby.* Then I thought about my family. *Mother, Father, and Frank never cry. Frank doesn't even cry when Father beats him. It doesn't help anything to cry. From now on,* I told myself, *I'm going to try hard not to cry anymore.*

So much puzzled me about this war and how people behaved who were involved in it. Edit was always cheerful and friendly. She didn't appear to bear a grudge against anyone. I knew I would have been furious at the Germans if they had taken away my property and family and forced me to work for my enemy.

~

Shortly after I arrived in Stolp, I was enrolled in the local school to complete my last few months of grammar school. I continued to have doubts about my ability to pass the exam to enter the Oberrealschule in Berlin that fall, but I swore to myself that I would try hard to do it.

As it turned out, I adjusted rather easily to the Stolp schoolwork, because Onkel Adolf spent many hours patiently tutoring me in German reading and grammar and in mathematics. He never made me feel dumb. He always encouraged me and rewarded me for good work. If I had learned well, I found a piece of chocolate on my pillow at bedtime.

Onkel Adolf had a beloved parakeet, Peter, whose favorite place was on top of Onkel's bald head, where it perched and talked, much to my delight. Onkel often walked downstairs to his bank, completely forgetting that the bird was still teetering on top. It wasn't unusual for a clerk to point to the bird's dropping on Onkel's head, and for everybody in the bank to break out in laughter at the sight of the usually dignified executive with the bird on his head. Onkel took it all with good humor. Peter sat on Onkel's shoulder during our lessons and tweaked his ear for attention, then bobbed its head up and down. The parakeet often broke up our lessons as we laughed at its antics.

I loved to visit the bank with Onkel Adolf and sit on one of the high stools at the accounting benches. Sometimes he let me go into the vault, where the money was stacked in big piles. I pretended it all belonged to me. I fantasized I had enough money to get my family back to America and still have plenty left over to buy the Stratford house.

It was customary among well-to-do families to have separate sitting rooms. After dinner, ladies retired to one room, gentlemen to the other. I much preferred Onkel Adolf's dark drawing room because it was far more interesting to hear his views on politics and be talked to like an adult, than to listen to the boring conversation in Tante's room about children and household problems.

Tante Mieze constantly protested my choice. "You will never learn to be a lady," she predicted darkly. Then she added, "I don't know what they taught you in America, but it certainly wasn't good manners and deportment."

Onkel Adolf praised me often and always set aside time to talk to me and help me with my studies. I eagerly looked forward to these times and felt myself growing more confident. I brought home a much improved report card. For the first time, I thought I might have a chance of passing the entrance exam to high school.

In my Stolp school I made two new friends, Panky and Lieschen. The three of us spent many happy hours together outside of school. Panky came from a large family with lots of brothers and sisters. She lived in the poorer section of town, and I loved to go to her house. It was never a bother to her parents to have an extra child at the table. They shared whatever they had, which wasn't much. It was a noisy, friendly, chaotic household.

Lieschen lived with her family in a small apartment on the grounds of Stolp Castle, the local medieval castle where her father was the caretaker. The dark castle, which had been open to the public before the war, was closed now, and many of its treasures had been put in storage. Lieschen's father maintained the building and the grounds and prevented vandalism.

My greatest delight after school and on weekends was to be invited to play in the castle, which I imagined hid terrible secrets. Our favorite game was hide-and-seek played throughout the entire castle. Sometimes other children came and played too, which made it even more fun. We loved finding new hiding places in the gloomy corners of twisting hallways or on narrow staircases leading who knows where. The boys particularly liked to sneak up on the girls and scare us with bloodcurdling screams or fearful grimaces that caught the light slanting in from the lead-paned windows. One of the castle's rooms was a chamber filled with rusty tools of torture, among them a wooden chair covered with spikes, a cradle embedded with nails, and a thumbscrew. On the floor were dark stains that we knew must be dried blood.

Cold fear crawled down my spine whenever I stepped into the castle. The chilling stories of its ghosts burrowed deep into my imagination. The torture chamber was at the heart of this thrill. The scent of evil in the room both fascinated and repelled us. If any of us dared to hide alone in the torture chamber, that child was considered a hero. I got as far as opening the creaking door with Lieschen firmly beside me. When we imagined we heard groans coming from within, we fled, terrified.

~

On my eleventh birthday, May 25, 1941, Tante Mieze gave me a party, and she even hired a clown. I was very excited, especially since Mother had kept her word about not giving me another party after the disaster of my ninth birthday. Tante Mieze, always class conscious, had invited the doctor's daughter, the lawyer's daughter, the dentist's daughter, and so forth—all girls I didn't particularly like to play with despite Tante Mieze's tireless urging. I didn't care one way or the other that these girls were invited to my party, as long as my best friends were also coming.

But then Tante Mieze informed me, "I didn't invite Lieschen and Panky. They are not suitable company for you. You know I don't approve of them. They don't belong in our class."

I was furious. *How dare she judge my friends!* Lieschen and her family were quick to welcome me as one of them. At Panky's house, things were relaxed and happy. I didn't have to worry about spilling food on the plain wooden table or watch my table manners, which Tante Mieze was constantly criticizing.

When I heard that neither of my best friends had been invited, I stormed out of the house, shouting defiantly, "I'm inviting them anyway! It's my birthday!" I was determined to have my friends present. When Lieschen and Panky arrived some time later, Tante Mieze refused to allow them in the front door. She made the girls come up the back stairs, through the servant's entrance. I bitterly resented this insult to my friends. I hardly noticed the beautifully decorated table out on the terrace, the birthday cake, or the funny clown. I spent the day fuming at Tante Mieze.

≈

On June 22, 1941, the war found its way even to Stolp. One Sunday morning, Onkel Adolf asked me to buy a newspaper for him from the paperboy on the corner. I was surprised to see a crowd gathered around the boy, who was shouting, "Germany declares war on Russia!" His customers' faces looked grim. Silently they bought newspapers and dispersed quickly. But as one man passed me with the folded paper tucked tightly under his arm, I heard him mumble, "First Poland, then western Europe, and now Russia. Where will it end?" I bought my uncle's newspaper and hurried home.

I raced up the stairs and into the apartment. Tante Mieze and Onkel Adolf were sitting at the breakfast table in the early morning sun, sipping coffee. They were stunned when I showed them the headline.

"Russia!" Onkel exclaimed. "What does Hitler want with Russia?"

"I thought we had a nonaggression pact with Stalin," Tante Mieze said.

"That doesn't mean anything to a man like Hitler," Onkel replied. "It's never enough. My guess is he wants Russia's natural resources. He wants their iron and ore and oil for his damn war machines."

I had never seen Onkel Adolf so upset. It worried and depressed me. "What do you think is going to happen?" I asked.

"Another world war," he said grimly. "And it's going to get bad!"

He looked at the wall where a photo hung of his son, Karl Heinz. A short time later they received the news that their son had been sent eastward to the Russian front.

≈

At the end of June, school let out. I was happy to be returning to my family in Berlin, but I was sorry to leave Stolp. Except for the unfortunate birthday party, Tante Mieze had been good to me in her own fashion. And Onkel Adolf had taught me the multiplication table at last. I was actually beginning to like math just a bit because of him. I knew I would miss Panky and Lieschen, and also Edit and our grown-up talks. I hated saying good-bye. It seemed as if that's all I was doing lately.

CHAPTER FIVE

ENTRANCE INTO HIGH SCHOOL
SUMMER 1941–WINTER 1941/42

I RETURNED FROM STOLP late in June 1941, amid the daily reports of what the radio announcers kept calling the "crusade in the east," the invasion of Russia. Nobody had expected this new campaign. We had all thought Hitler would be satisfied with the lands he had already conquered. We had thought that the war would soon end. I could see a new tension in the faces of Berliners. Mother and Father talked in hushed tones after each broadcast.

Special announcements kept coming over the Wehrmachtbericht, the Armed Forces News, preceded by trumpets. "Quickly our divisions are moving forward according to plan, with great results. Victory is assured!"

"This can't end well," Father finally said to Mother.

Soon it seemed that anxiety about the future permeated everything my family did or said. I knew it was pointless to keep asking, "When are we going back to the States?" Stratford now belonged to another time, another era. It seemed as unreachable as the most distant star in the sky.

But in the middle of all the uncertainty, Mother had some surprising news. "I'm going to have a baby," she announced, beaming happily.

"A baby?" Frank echoed.

For once I was speechless. I hadn't thought of Mother in terms of being *able* to have a baby. I thought you had to be young to have babies, and here she was, thirty-seven years old. And Frank and I were practically grown up: he was now twelve and I was eleven. But after the initial shock, I was as excited as the rest of the family about a new child. Mother's slightly rounded belly already showed signs of new life.

The months that followed proved to be difficult for Mother. She was nauseated most of the time, so Frank and I had to pitch in more to help around the house. We also had to take turns waiting in line for groceries that were increasingly hard to get. Even potatoes, our main staple, were not easy to come by. Most of the farmers and farm hands were being drafted, and many women were being assigned to weapons factories, so no one was available to harvest crops left in the fields. We heard rumors that the Hitler Youth, especially the older girls, might be called on to work the farms and help bring in the harvest.

Frank and I spent some time that summer at Omi Ramrath's house in Eslohe. Omi, Frank, and I hiked over much of the Homert mountain range, which rose gently above Eslohe. We stopped often at the wooden benches placed along the trails, where we could catch our breath and absorb the scenery. From high up on the Homert, Eslohe looked like a collection of tiny houses down in the valley, shaded by the mountains all around. I loved this peaceful time with Frank and Omi.

On one of our hikes down a broad trail just out of the village, we came across some dark-skinned, gaily dressed men and women, some walking and some riding in their horse-drawn wagon. The women wore dangly earrings and bright red scarves tied around their long black hair. Children with dark, mussed hair and stained clothes chased each other around the wagon.

I was fascinated. Astonished by their clothing and looks, I asked, "Omi, who are they?"

"They're Gypsies," she replied. "We used to see a lot of them around here, but lately I don't see very many."

"Where do you suppose they went?"

Omi shrugged. "I don't know. Lately more and more people go away, disappear. Who knows where they go?"

Onkel Anton and Tante Burga, who lived in Ober Salvey, just over the mountain from Eslohe, invited Frank and me to spend a few days with them on their farm. Onkel Anton, Opa Ramrath's brother, was a quiet man whose face was permanently red and furrowed like the fields he had worked for a lifetime. Too old to be drafted, he ran his farm with the help of French prisoners of war. Tante Burga was a big, comfortable woman accustomed to hard labor.

There was always plenty to eat, like sausages, eggs, ham, and home-made bread with churned butter and jam from berries in the garden. Frank and I loved these wonderful meals and gorged ourselves. We ate at long wooden tables in Tante Burga's big kitchen, right along with the French prisoners and some older kids from the community who were helping out on the farm. The prisoners were good workers and lots of fun. We all laughed together at their attempts to speak German. They seemed to enjoy working the farm, and they obviously thought highly of my aunt and uncle. Onkel Anton treated the prisoners and the hired help just the same, even though the Nazis forbade fraternization with prisoners. Punishment could be severe if such rule-breaking were brought to the attention of authorities, but people in the community respected Onkel Anton too much to report him.

Frank and I were supposed to help do chores around the farm, but we weren't much help to Onkel Anton. After completing a chore in the barn, we sneaked up to the loft again and again to jump down from the barn's rafters into the soft hay below.

One day when Frank took a dive into the haystack, he smacked his chin on a wooden beam and his two lower teeth pushed right through his lower lip. Blood ran down his chin. With a shudder, he yanked his teeth free from his lip, moaning and sobbing softly.

Onkel Anton, Tante Burga, and the farm help were all in the fields. There was no doctor or hospital in the village, but Frank and I knew that he needed a doctor right away. We knew that nearby Eslohe had a hospital, but we had to cross a mountain to get there. We stopped some of the bleeding by putting cold water compresses on it. Since there was no other transportation available and no one to take us, we climbed on bicycles.

Frank, bleeding and in pain, somehow managed to stay on his bike while pedaling as fast as he could. I rode behind him.

We had finally arrived at the steep hill leading up to the hospital in Eslohe when Frank collapsed and fell off his bike, scraping his knee and beginning to bleed there too. I was terrified and screamed for help. People came running and gathered him up, taking him into the hospital. The doctors sent word to Omi, and she immediately came to be with us. Thankfully Frank was all right. He recovered quickly, with only a scar to remind him of his ordeal.

When we returned to Berlin a couple of weeks after Frank's accident, I prepared to take the entrance exam into the Oberrealschule that I had dreaded so much. This school was different from what I had understood an American high school to be. In Germany, high school was more like preparatory school or junior college, an essential step on the ladder to higher education. Students entered Oberrealschule at age eleven and then faced nine years of hard study, crowned by the Abitur, or baccalaureate, which was the passport to the university. Students had to earn good grades in high school, and parents had to pay tuition.

Most German children went to the elementary school for eight years and then instead of continuing to high school, they entered the Berufsschule, or trade school, where they learned both theory and job training. But our parents expected both Frank and me to go on to college. And besides, my best friend, Annemarie, was going to the Gertrauden Oberrealschule, and I wanted to be with her.

Somehow, with help from Onkel Adolf's patient tutoring the spring before and, I suspected, the care of the Invisibles, my special guardian angels, I passed the exam. I didn't see the results of the test. I only heard the tester telling me that I had passed. The only thing that mattered to me was that I was accepted.

That night, at the dinner table, I beamed and made my announcement to the family. "Guess what? I made it into the Oberrealschule!"

Mother and Father smiled at each other and then at me. "Your Father and I never had any doubt you would pass the exam," Mother said.

Well, I sure did, I thought to myself. *And I bet Father didn't really think I could do it either.*

In late summer, a few weeks before school started, Mother, Frank, and I made plans to visit our grandparents in Münster. When we arrived at the Berlin railroad station, it was crowded with soldiers and their families, all milling around a troop transport train. Women and children were crying as the soldiers pulled themselves away from their families and boarded the train. Out of the mob of people appeared the familiar face of Frank's favorite teacher from the previous year, Herr Dr. Schwenke, in soldier's field gray.

"Hello, boy," he shouted over all the noise. "What are you doing here?"

Frank simply waved and shouted back, "We're waiting for a train." Once the troop transport started to pull out of the station, Frank turned to Mother and me. "I couldn't admit to Dr. Schwenke that I was going on vacation while he was heading to the Russian front." He watched Dr. Schwenke's train until it pulled away and stared at the empty track after it had departed.

After a few days in Münster, we all went to the village of Wellingholzhausen to visit Onkel Willi, who was engaged to Tante Elsbeth and home on furlough from the army. Onkel Willi's family owned Hotel Dütting in the village, and we stayed there for the week. Another family in the hotel had children our age, Ruth Alm and her brother Bert. Frank and I explored the surrounding countryside with our new friends. We gathered mushrooms, called champignons, that grew around cow dung in the fields. The fields were generally surrounded by barbed wire to keep the cows in and children like us out, but we found our way in with little difficulty.

On one of our mushroom expeditions we were all carefully avoiding stepping in cow patties when we were spotted by a bull we hadn't noticed until then. For a moment after we realized our predicament, all of us froze. Then the enormous bull charged after us, horns lowered, mouth frothing.

"He's mad!" Bert shouted. "Let's get out of here!"

Dropping the mushrooms, we ran for our lives, frantically diving through the wire fence, ripping our clothes and scraping our skin. As the last one of us slipped through, the snorting bull skidded to a halt just inside the fence. Catching our breath, we stared at the thick horns that might have gouged our bodies. I thought I detected disappointment in the bull's small red eyes as he glared at us through the fence. Now safe, we made faces at him and broke out in uncontrollable laughter.

During that same week at the hotel, we heard sad news: a little girl in the village died of meningitis. Before burial, she was to be on view in one of the hotel rooms. I hadn't known the girl, of course, but I was curious to see what a dead child looked like. After the family and mourners had left the room, I cautiously opened the door and sneaked in, not sure what I would find. It took a few moments for my eyes to adjust to the semi-darkness.

And then I saw her, not in a casket, but lying on a table that was covered in white satin, surrounded by flowers and candles. She must have been around three years old. She was dressed in a long, white lace gown with a wreath of tiny pink roses on her head. Her blond hair cascaded down and around her shoulders, curling sweetly around her cheeks like silky white feathers. In her folded hands she held pink rosebuds. She was breathlessly beautiful. I couldn't take my eyes off her delicate porcelain face. Any minute I expected her to wake up, like the sleeping princess in the fairy tale. In the flickering candlelight she looked otherworldly, like an angel. And suddenly it dawned on me. *Yes, that's what happens when a person dies: she becomes an angel.* I was curiously pleased with the thought.

∼

In September of 1941 I started high school, where, like the other girls, I was treated as a lady and addressed formally as Fräulein. We now respectfully called teachers Frau Doktor or Herr Professor. The teachers didn't usually practice corporal punishment on us older students, much to our relief.

The school curriculum was tough, especially for me. It included Latin, English, physics, mathematics, geography, biology, German grammar, essay writing, drawing and painting, sports, music, and needlework. Instead of history we now had Gegenwartskunde, current events, a course filled with Nazi ideology and interpretation of German history. It was completely boring to me.

I did not enjoy needlework at all. It was too tedious and time consuming. An embroidery, according to our teacher, had to be as perfect on the reverse side as on the right side, but usually a lot of knots and long ends dotted the reverse side of my embroidery. Besides, all my handling gave the embroidered piece a dingy, smudged look, which was reason enough to pull down my grade.

I loved art class, but reading and writing were my favorite academic subjects. I dreamed about being a poet or a great writer someday. I began writing poetry of my own. In addition to writing essays and retelling stories, we had to memorize long epic poems by German romantic poets and by classical lyricists like Goethe and Schiller. World literature was strangely absent from our curriculum. The great writers from other countries whose books I found on the bookshelves in Annemarie's house and in our own home were never discussed at school. Instead, we studied Germanic hero mythology and German regional mythology.

Of all the myths we studied, I found the saga about Gudrun the most fascinating. This eleventh-century heroine accepted her fate with the faith that good eventually prevails over evil. I clung to this belief, and learned by heart Gudrun's long, bitter lament as she stood on the shore of the raging sea, washing the garments of the cruel king and queen who held her captive in a foreign land. She cried, "Even if I must die here, I will never give up my loyalty." I saw myself as Gudrun, a captive of dark, evil forces in a foreign land. Whenever I felt depressed, I soulfully recited her soliloquy and tears sprang to my eyes.

Like the Hitler Youth, the school placed a heavy emphasis on physical training. Our sports teacher was Fräulein von Brauchitsch, the daughter of an important Nazi general. She drilled us relentlessly in jumping over vaulting horses, climbing up ropes, broad jumping, and running. It wasn't easy for me to keep up with the others.

I struggled through endless running and jumping excercises, but I dreaded the vault most of all. My legs always slowed down just before I reached the vault, causing me to lose the speed I needed to clear the horse.

"Do it again!" Fräulein demanded. "Don't slow down."

I knew what I had to do and tried hard to follow her instruction. I made a great running start, but as I neared the horse, my legs heard another signal: *Slow down!* I envied Annemarie and the other girls, who flew over the horse with hardly an effort. It didn't seem fair. I hated my body; it never did what I desperately wanted it to do.

Sometimes we were divided into teams. I was usually the last one picked, even after Barbara Stantin, a heavyset girl, slow on her feet.

The argument between the two team captains was usually, "You take Eleanor. I had her last time."

"No, it's your turn to take her."

"All right, girls, let's not fight over me." I always laughed, trying to cover my humiliation.

My trouble didn't end when school was out. At home, Mother complained, "You walk like an elephant! You need to be more graceful." She tried to remedy my coordination problem by sending me to private gymnastics lessons.

The gymnastics teacher, Fräulein Peschel, did help me become better coordinated. I mastered the vaulting horse, and even learned how to do the splits, which I became quite proud of, and to dance the Russian Krokoviak, a wild folk dance that required me to squat and kick out first one leg, then the other. I would never be as athletic as many of my classmates, but at least I could now help my teams be a little more competitive.

Annemarie and I once again sat side by side in the classroom. I was happy and relieved to have a ready-made best friend at the Oberrealschule, and we always helped each other. She had a better ear for music than I did, so when the teacher instructed me to read music and sing an unfamiliar song, a difficult task for me with my tendency to sing off-key, Annemarie hummed the correct notes under her breath and I was able to repeat them correctly. And since I was good in drawing, I helped her with perspective and detail.

I also made some new friends. Renate came from a foreign country like me. Her parents had emigrated from Germany years before to

Guatemala, where they bought a coffee plantation and where Renate was born and raised. Attracted by Germany's economic recovery after the Great War, her family had returned to Germany.

Inge, the daughter of a prominent judge, lived just around the corner from me. She and I walked the two and a half miles to school together every day. On cold days, the trip took us about forty minutes. On warm afternoons, we tended to meander and find all kinds of things to look at, so the trip home might take almost an hour. On rainy days we took the subway.

And then there was Erika, a beautiful girl with wavy blond hair and sky-blue eyes. Oh, how I wanted to look and move exactly like her! She was graceful and sophisticated. Compared to Erika, I still looked like a kid, scrawny with straight hair and a front tooth that stubbornly refused to align itself with my other front teeth. Annemarie, Renate, Erika, and I became a clique. Erika knew that Annemarie and I had been best friends for several years, but wasn't above causing occasional misunderstandings by playing one of us against the other. When Erika tried to upstage me as her best friend, I became very possessive of Annemarie. I suspected at times that Erika enjoyed making me jealous. But most of the time Annemarie and I were wise to her games, and we didn't let her interfere in our friendship.

~

Frank continued his habit of riding the subway as far as it would take him for pocket change. But one day that fall he came home visibly agitated. "You can't imagine what happened today," he said to Mother and me. "You know how all Jews have to wear the yellow badges?"

Mother narrowed her eyes and nodded. I nodded as well.

"Well," he continued, "I was riding the subway to Unter den Linden, and soon all the seats were taken. At one stop an old woman got on who had a yellow star stitched to her sweater, with *Jude* written in the center. I got up and offered her my seat.

"Suddenly a man from the other end of the car stomped up to me and started yelling. 'You! What do you think you're doing?'

"I was surprised. I didn't know what he was talking about. 'You mean getting up for the old lady?' I asked stupidly. 'I always do that for older people,' I told him. 'My mother taught me good manners.'"

Mother nodded, pleased.

Frank continued. "The man glared at me. 'Well, that doesn't go for Jews,' he said as the subway pulled into the next station. I was so scared, I quickly got off and went into a different car."

After a moment, Mother said, "I'm proud of you, Frank. You did the right thing." She looked at each of us. "Sometimes we have to do what's right, even if the society we live in tells us to do otherwise."

"But Mother, why don't the Nazis like the Jews?" I asked. "They blame them for everything. But the Jews I've seen on the streets look just like us except for the yellow star they have to wear."

"It's hard to explain prejudice and hatred," she said. "There's often no real reason for it."

"Yeah, it's irrational," Frank added. "I bet if you had asked the guy on the subway why the old woman shouldn't be offered a seat, he wouldn't have had a halfway reasonable answer. He's just been told to hate Jews, so he does."

"Yeah, what did that old woman ever do to him?" I asked indignantly.

"The other day I saw some people wearing white cloth Os on their jackets," Frank said.

"What does that mean?" I asked.

Frank replied, "I heard that it identifies captive laborers Hitler is forcing to work in German factories and on German farms. O stands for Ostarbeiter, workers from the east.

"They're Russian civilians," Mother explained.

"It's like Edit in Stolp who has to wear a yellow P because she's a Polish captive?" I asked.

Mother nodded.

It made me so sad that people were singled out and humiliated that way. Although the subject confused and disturbed me, I liked these conversations among the three of us. They made me feel grown up and a part of the family. But when Father was home, Frank and I were reluctant to voice our opinions. We knew he would criticize us with his usual sarcastic remarks.

~

My family was Roman Catholic, but my parents had never encouraged us to attend church. My friends, who were all Protestants, went to church on Sundays, but we never went.

In late fall Mother surprised Frank and me by announcing, "You children are going to church."

"To church?" we echoed, not sure if we had heard right.

"I want you enrolled in religious instruction," Mother said in a tone of voice that allowed no argument. "Next year you will receive your first communion."

I suspected that Mother's mother, our religious Münster Grossmutter, was behind this sudden decision.

Religious instruction was given by pastors who came to our school after hours, with the Protestants in one room and the Catholics in another. These instructions were allowed by the regime as long as they didn't interfere with a Hitler Youth event.

I soon hated the Catholic priest who taught us catechism, religious doctrine that we were expected to memorize. He wore thick glasses and had short, stubbly gray hair that stood straight up on his head, like quills on a porcupine. He slowly walked up and down the aisles, fingers laced behind his back. Then, with no warning, he stopped abruptly in front of a terrified student, pointed a fat finger, and called out a question. "Seven sacraments!" he shouted. The girl he pointed at had to rattle them off quickly. Each of us dreaded the moment he stopped in front of our desks.

During the last class before Christmas vacation, we took our revenge on the priest. Before he arrived, we drew a heart with arrows in thick white chalk on the seat of his chair. After he had stalked his daily victims, he retired to his chair. We held our breath and tried hard to cover our grins when he settled down on the seat. After class, we all followed him out to the streetcar, admiring our artwork on the backside of his black pants. He kept glancing at us, clearly wondering why a bunch of giggling girls was following him to the street car.

In addition to catechism at school, Frank and I were instructed at the Marienkirche, Saint Mary's Church, in Friedenau in preparation for our first communion, which was scheduled for the following April. I enjoyed that class a lot more than catechism. We learned about the saints and how they suffered and endured pain and torture for their beliefs. The martyrs we read about reminded me of the heroes of mythology, brave like Gudrun.

I also studied with interest the life of Jesus, in awe of his suffering on the cross. And I liked Mary, Jesus's mother, because she was kind and gentle; she was easy to pray to.

I had suspected for a while that the God in the Bible was a Wotan god, a warrior god who had no mercy, and now the story of Jesus confirmed my theory. God let his own son die and made no attempt to save him. Sometimes I saw this powerful, merciless God in Father's uncompromising face. Sometimes I was frightened to see this God in the rigid face of Hitler, whose picture was plastered on the walls of every city building and classroom.

I never, ever prayed to this God. Instead, I believed I was surrounded by my Invisibles, the angels who protected me, and I sent my thoughts to them. If I closed my eyes I could picture them clearly. They were magnificent creatures in white dresses. Often I thought I could hear the fluttering of their golden wings.

On Sundays, when I watched the priests reach into the tabernacle and take the monstrance—the golden cup that held the Host—and lift it up like a sun, when I heard the sanctus bells ring out three times, I knew something mystical was happening at the altar. I sensed the presence of an invisible being unlike the warrior god I had imagined, a being higher than my invisible angels. Its presence filled me with indescribable joy. This feeling, intensified by the music, the chanting, and the Latin mumblings of the priests, seemed so wonderfully mysterious to me. The mythology I had learned in school and the Church's teachings jumbled together in my mind. I didn't know where one began and the other left off, but all seemed to point to the existence of an invisible world inhabited by angels and spirits, and that suited me fine.

I never shared these visions for fear I would be ridiculed. My parents had repeatedly made clear to me that they did not appreciate what they called an overactive imagination. "Stop that fairy-tale nonsense," Father ordered. "You're too old for that. Do your homework."

I knew they measured my worth by my scholastic achievement, by how I measured up to others. They showed no interest in what was inside me. I struggled with their expectations, wanting desperately to please them. But I always felt that I failed. My report cards were never good enough.

"You can do better than that if you work harder," Father often criticized.

Mother would say, "Why can't you be like so-and-so? You are such a stubborn child!"

I was reminded of those detested relay games. Desperately I wanted my team to win, and I would put every ounce of effort into winning the race, only to let my teammates down time and again.

∼

On December 8, 1941, horrifying news came over the radio. "Yesterday, the Japanese, Germany's ally, bombed Pearl Harbor." *Oh no,* I groaned, *now America is being attacked!* Frank told me that now the United States would be drawn into the war. He was right. Three days later, we heard the devastating news that Germany and Italy had declared war on the United States.

America's involvement in the war sent me into a tailspin. *How bizarre!* I thought. *The soldiers of the country where I was born, the country I love, will be told to kill me, my family, and my new friends. And the soldiers of the country of my ancestry, of my beloved Omis, the country where I live, will be told to hate and kill Americans. Where do I stand in all of this? Who should I be loyal to?* I felt pulled in two between America and Germany.

Frank turned to me and grinned. "Do you know you're an enemy alien now?"

"We're going to have to be even more careful now that America is in the war," Mother warned, pointing her finger at each of us in turn. Frank stopped grinning. "There'll be people out there watching us. Remember to keep your mouths shut." She flashed a look at Father in particular.

That night I worried about our new status in Germany. *An enemy alien? What does that mean?* When I went to school the next morning, I was afraid I would suddenly look like an enemy. As I stepped into the classroom and walked down the aisle to my desk, I held my breath. I exhaled when the only exclamation I heard was, "Oh no! Another geography test today by old Stammer-Schreiner." Nobody took notice of my enemy alien status.

That Christmas, my family tried to celebrate as we usually did. The government allowed everyone extra rations of margarine and flour, and Mother was able to bake some traditional Christmas cookies. The usual Christmas package arrived from our Münster grandmother. Onkel Franz, Mother's brother from Hamburg, came for the holidays with his wife, Tante Trudel, and our baby cousin Ursula. I enjoyed playing with the little cousin and looked forward to my own little brother or sister due in January. Frank and I found a tree, brought it home, and decorated it with wax candles and homemade ornaments, made from aluminum strips found on the streets after air-raid attacks. The aluminum was used by British aircraft to foil the antiaircraft radar. By international agreement there were no air raids Christmas evening. We walked through the new-fallen snow to church.

The gifts we gave to each other were simple, mostly homemade. Frank got a few more fish for his tank, and I received wool leggings that Mother had knit for me.

After washing and ironing my first school embroidery project and clipping the offensive dangling threads, I had decided that it didn't look too bad after all. I proudly gave it to Mother. She smiled and seemed pleased with it. I gave Father a pair of socks I had knit. Unfortunately, one was shorter than the other.

New Year's Eve we decorated the living room with festive streamers and a big paper moon. Tante Trudel dressed in Mother's beautiful gold lamé dress, but poor Mother had to cut up two dresses and sew them together to make one to fit over her extended belly. All of us wore silly paper hats, and we toasted the New Year at midnight. Even I was allowed to have a glass of wine. We lit the remaining stubs of candles on the tree.

Everybody tried to be jolly, but the happiness felt forced. Onkel Franz murmured about "a storm brewing over Germany of catastrophic proportions." *What does he mean by that? What does he think the new year will bring?* I looked at the tired smile on Mother's pale face. *What is she thinking?* I puzzled. *Is she wondering about the new baby, about us? About the terrible storm Onkel Franz is predicting?*

CHAPTER
SIX

FIRST COMMUNION AND
EVACUATION TO BANSIN

JANUARY 1942–FALL 1942

THE 1942 WINTER MONTHS in Berlin were bitter cold, with many days below zero and frequent snow and ice storms. Coal for heat was increasingly hard to get. We wore more and more layers of clothing indoors. When it was too cold in the school building for classes, we had Kohlenferien, coal holidays. Of course, my friends and I didn't complain about missing school. Even though our homework was doubled to make up for the lost days, we somehow still found time to go sledding in the Grunewald or to spend an afternoon at the movies.

Air raids were more frequent now, but the targets were mostly war industry and government buildings. Only occasionally did a stray incendiary bomb hit an apartment house in our area, burning out the attic and perhaps the upper two floors. Sometimes a stray bomb left a crater hole in a street or in somebody's yard.

When this happened, Frank and I ran with other kids to the sites, inspecting the damage and looking for bomb shrapnel. We compared our twisted pieces of shrapnel with those that the others had found.

Generally, however, the bombings happened somewhere else, not in our neighborhood. Steglitz was in the suburbs, while the government buildings were located in the center of the city.

Air raids meant interrupted sleep and nighttime excursions into the cellar. I hated to leave my nice warm bed only to sit for an hour or two in the cold, damp basement. Usually we were all half-asleep, too tired to speak. I sometimes dozed off sitting in a chair, while Mother lay uncomfortably on the bottom bunk. Her stomach was quite large, and I knew the baby would be born soon. I wondered how our basement nights would change then.

Occasionally, we heard the distant drone of engines overhead, followed by volleys of antiaircraft guns from the streets and rooftops of Berlin. I was always glad when the all-clear sounded, so I could finally slide back into bed and snuggle down under a toasty feather comforter, trying to pick up the broken threads of a dream.

At last, on January 18, 1942, Mother went into labor. She preferred to have the baby at home because she was afraid of the bacterial infections that plagued the hospitals. Father and a midwife tended to Mother's needs, and just before the delivery, a doctor arrived to assist with the birth. Frank and I listened to the sounds coming from our parents' bedroom: soft voices interrupted by shrieks from Mother. Father and the midwife ran back and forth between the bathroom, kitchen, and bedroom without explaining what was happening. I was scared for Mother.

"Why isn't the baby coming?" Frank and I asked each other. "What's happening?" It was taking forever. Mother screamed in agony.

After a difficult delivery, the baby was finally born. "It's a boy!" Father announced. "Thomas Joseph!"

I had hoped for a girl, but when I saw how adorable my new brother was, I forgot about my wish. When I held him in my arms, I found myself pretending to be his mother.

I felt a strange competitiveness with Mother. I had always admired her and wanted desperately to please her, but I resented her ability to nurse the baby. I wanted Thomas to depend on me instead of on her.

I also began to admire someone else. On the top floor of our apartment house lived the Gadows, a chic couple without children who moved in opera and theater circles and went out on the town a great deal. Although I don't think anybody knew what Herr Gadow did professionally and how he had managed to stay out of the war, somehow he and Frau Gadow always looked and acted as if the war didn't exist for them. I sat for hours on the stairs of the apartment house just to catch a glimpse of the two as they swished by me on the way to an engagement, leaving behind a trail of expensive French perfume and cologne, which I inhaled with a thrill.

Other times the Gadows spent evenings with my parents, talking deep into the night or until an air-raid alarm interrupted the conversation.

On those evenings when the Gadows came over, Mother primped longer than usual and sometimes even wore her beautiful gold lamé evening gown—now that she could fit back in it. When Herr Gadow fixed his eyes on Mother or gazed at her when she spoke, Mother's cheeks flushed and her eyes sparkled the way I rarely saw them. In those moments she was at her most charming, almost like a young girl again.

Just after little Thomas was born, Omi came to stay with us for a few weeks to care for Mother and the baby, and I loved it. I was sad when she left for Eslohe.

Then a girl named Lucie came to live with us to help Mother. Teenaged girls who were not aiming for a career or university degree had a choice of working in a household or in the war industry, and Lucie came to our apartment. We all liked her, and she became a great help to Mother. She worked hard and quickly learned Mother's magic of preparing tasty meals out of limited rations.

We soon discovered, though, that Lucie had two big problems. First, we occasionally caught her wearing one of Mother's necklaces, Mother's angora sweater, or whatever struck her fancy. Although when caught, Lucie was quick to explain that she only wanted to borrow these things, not to keep them. In the cellar Mother kept vegetable and fruit preserves she had put up during the summer for the winter ahead. These disappeared one by one until Mother finally discovered the culprit. Tearfully, Lucie promised never to do it again. "Please don't let me go!" she begged.

It was hard to get household help because most teenage girls were opting to work in the munitions factories. And Lucie was cheerful and helpful. It was hard to stay mad at her. Mother always felt sorry for her and let her stay. My family secretly nicknamed her "the thieving magpie."

Second, Lucie had quite an appetite for sex. Sometimes I overheard her talking to Mother about her many lovers and her meetings with them after hours or on her free weekends. Mother felt that whatever Lucie did outside of our home was her business. She made clear, however, that she would not tolerate any of Lucie's lovers in our house.

Sex was a taboo subject in our household—for that matter, in most German households. Our Münster Grossmutter wouldn't even allow Frank and me to talk about what she referred to as the "unmention-ables"—underwear. She never hung these intimate items out on the clothesline where anyone might see them.

Most of my friends got their information about sex from other friends. But I was lucky to have an older brother to educate me. One Sunday on the way to church, I announced to Frank, "I know for a fact that a woman doesn't need a man to have a baby."

Exasperated, Frank replied, "You're wrong, Eleanor! I told you a million times, it takes a man and a woman to make a baby."

I shook my head vigorously. "I know what you told me about the man putting his thing into the woman and all that disgusting stuff. I just can't believe that."

"Would I lie to you? How do you think our little brother got here?"

"No way! Not Mother and Daddy!" I protested angrily, punching him.

Frank rolled his eyes and quickened his pace, "You're so unbelievably naive!" he exclaimed.

"Wait!" I cried. "I want to tell you something!"

Frank stopped. "What? Some more nonsense like your theory that babies come out of belly buttons?"

Breathlessly I caught up with him. "You remember Frau Umhau?"

"Of course. She's Mother's friend who lives on the Ku'damm. What about her?"

"Well," I said, "she just had a baby!"

"So, what's so important about that?"

"Everything, you idiot!" I shouted. "Don't you get it? Her husband has been missing in action for over a year, and she just had a baby anyway!" I could feel my face glow with triumph. "You see what I mean?"

Frank shook his head. "That doesn't mean a thing."

"Yes, it does. A woman doesn't need a man to make a baby. She had no husband and still had a baby."

Frank just rolled his eyes and walked on.

After that day, he tried a different method of teaching. Lucie had told him that she had some photos of herself in intimate positions with her lovers. Frank tried to find the photographs in her room when she was out, but she had hidden them well. He tried talking her into sharing them with him, but she refused. Then one day he bribed her with his chocolate rations. Frank knew how Lucie loved chocolate.

Naturally, he told me about the pictures. "I want to see them too," I begged.

"I'll show them to you only if you give me your next chocolate ration."

Even though I loved chocolate and savored the small amount I received, I was ready to sacrifice it for this greater cause.

When Frank showed me the pictures, he said, "You see? That's how babies are made."

I was shocked and repelled and swore I would never do this thing called sex. I regretted giving up my precious chocolates for such vulgar pictures.

After that I watched Lucie closely to see if a baby was coming, but nothing further happened. Mother, of course, was unaware of the photos and our wheelings and dealings. Had she known, I'm sure Lucie would have lost her job, and Frank and I would have faced a nasty whipping.

Because Lucie lived with us during the week, Frank gave up his little room and moved into the other bed in my room. He was good company. It was comforting to talk to Frank about many things, but the main topic of our conversation was our Father. I felt like we were co-conspirators against him. We always had long discussions at night, mainly about

Father's rules and the harsh consequences we suffered if we disobeyed them.

Frank and I still had to walk a fine line to avoid punishment. But Frank, who was now taller than Father, often defiantly baited him. Then, when Father beat him, Frank refused to cry because he didn't want to give Father satisfaction.

"How do you keep from crying?" I asked him one night. "Even though I try not to cry, I shake with fright and am already crying by the time Father yells 'Come here!'"

"I just keep telling myself, Don't cry," Frank replied. "I pretend to be a saint martyred for a great cause."

Mother, as usual, never interfered with Father's discipline. Sometimes she narrowed her eyes, looking upset when Father hit us too hard, but she never stopped him.

For Father's birthday in February, I tried once again to please him. I wrote a poem about him: Although I was afraid that he might not like my creation, I knew he might like the attention, and I took the risk. I spent many days writing and rewriting. Then I went to the breakfast table on his birthday with flowers in hand and recited my poem, which rhymed and poked a little fun at his habits, like smoking cigars and pipes and drinking schnapps brandy. Afterward when he smiled and hugged me warmly, I felt that all my efforts had been worthwhile.

That winter and spring, air raids continued. When the alarm woke us at night, Mother, Father, Frank, Lucie and the baby, and I scrambled down the stairs to the cold basement. We waited, cranky and half-asleep, until the long note of the all-clear signal, and then we climbed upstairs again. We could never get a good night's sleep.

At night, Frank and I resumed the Pudel adventures we had started in Stratford. Pudel's predicaments were now more complicated and dangerous than before. Sharing stories brought us closer together again. I had missed Frank. Each of us had been concentrating on making new friends and adjusting to life in Germany.

On April 12, 1942, Frank and I went to our long-awaited first Holy Communion. Our Münster grandparents came for the special occasion, as did Tante Mieze and Onkel Adolf. Mother was able to scrounge up some white material and had a seamstress transform it into a dress for me. On my head I wore a wreath of white baby roses, which reminded me of the dead child I had seen the year before in Wellingholzhausen. I felt holy.

Before church, Grossmutter Rump gave Frank and me each a wood carving of Jesus nailed to the cross, and she gave me a watch with a tiny red ruby on it. Tante Mieze presented me with a silver cross necklace, and I was also given a print of a painting of the Madonna by Botticelli.

Because we had joined the church so late, Frank and I were much older than the rest of the communicants. Most of the kids were around nine, whereas I was almost twelve and Frank was thirteen. Frank towered over the other children, and I was at least a head taller. We felt more than a little embarrassed.

All of us were given long white candles to carry in the procession into church. The Saint Bernard Church in Dahlem was new and modern with shiny marble inside. The pale blue dome over the altar was guarded by a golden angel on either side holding red vigil lights. The bishop in his red and gold finery sat on a chair near the altar, godlike.

We walked to the pews, carrying the lit candles in front of us. Girls were seated on one side and boys on the other. Then we were to rest our candles in wooden holders.

Approaching the altar in my holy state, I hoped I might actually be able to see this invisible being I had felt on Sundays during communion service. But then a terrible thing happened. The girl beside me got sick and retched red vomit all over my beautiful white dress. I was horrified. The stench was nauseating. I gagged, close to throwing up myself. I thought about running out of the church. But just then it was my turn to walk up to the altar, and I could do nothing but put one foot in front of the other like a zombie.

I knelt in misery at the altar rail while the bishop gave me communion and rested his hand briefly on my bowed head. All I could think of was my ruined dress. The joy and anticipation I had felt earlier were gone. I was convinced that I didn't see the holy being because I was unacceptable in its sight. When I returned to my seat, the world turned dark, and I fainted. As I keeled forward, my head hit the candle in front of me and with some satisfaction I heard the crash of a whole row of falling candles.

~

That spring the bombings became more frequent. One day the director at my school announced, "Due to increased air-raid activity, the students of this school will be allowed to evacuate to safer areas." The children land evacuation program, the KLV, offered students at my school, the Gertrauden Oberrealschule, the option of being sent to Bansin on the island of Usedom in the Baltic Sea. Those students who chose not to go would continue with classes in Berlin.

For days after the announcement, my class buzzed with speculation about who was going and who would room together.

"You, Annemarie, Rena, Erika, and I can all room together," Inge said. "And just think, we can go swimming every day. We'll only have school in the mornings."

My parents urged me to go. During the day I felt excited about the prospect of going away with my friends, but at night in bed, doubts and fears crowded in on me. I realized that I was afraid to be without my family. And the chubby new baby—we'd nicknamed him Möppi—was getting cuter every day. I wanted to stay home to watch him grow. I feared that when I returned home, whenever that would be, he wouldn't know me anymore.

I told Mother of my worries. "We'll write to each other," she promised, patting my shoulder. "I'll tell you all the new things Möppi learns. I know he won't forget his big sister."

I decided to go after all, but Frank chose not to go away with the students from his school. "I want to stay here, where the action is," he said. I was worried about him. *Who will be there for him when he gets into trouble with Father? Who will he share Pudel stories with? Who will he argue with?*

To make matters worse, Renate and Erika decided not to go. Then at the last minute, Annemarie couldn't go either. Her mother had missed the deadline for filling out the necessary papers. She promised that she would try to get to Bansin by midsummer.

With all the busy preparations for the trip, packing, and last-minute details like sewing name tags into all my clothing, I was able to bury the ache of leaving my family. But on the day of departure it overwhelmed me.

My deepest worry was one I could hardly admit to myself. *Will my family still be alive when I return? What if a bomb hits our house while I'm gone?* I held back tears as I said good-bye to my family.

Inge and I boarded a ship called *Summer Tales,* a name that conjured up images in my mind of summer magic and fairy tales, and sailed along the Hohenzollern Canal and the River Spree to the town of Eberswalde near the Oder. There we stayed overnight in a gym, waiting for girls from other schools to join us. I was starting to feel homesick, but the next day my spirits lifted as we boarded *Summer Tales* again. All of us girls got caught up in the excitement of our voyage. We laughed and sang folk songs as our ship moved down the Oder River, then through the Peene Canal to Bansin.

In Bansin, a famous vacation spot, elegant hotels stretched along a flower-lined beachfront promenade. The government had confiscated the hotels that year to house schoolchildren from the big cities that were being bombed more and more often. The island was covered with forests, lakes, and hills. Sea Castle Bansin, where my school was quartered, was an old Victorian hotel.

Inge and I were adamant about staying together. We were overjoyed when we were both assigned to room 34, which had a glassed-in veranda facing the ocean. We shared the room with three more girls from our school. I didn't know Gönna, Brigitte, and Uschi very well, but soon we all became close friends.

The five of us had an endless string of parties in our room, which included pillow fights and jumping from bed to bed. More than once we got in trouble with our BDM floor leader for being so noisy. Our floor leader, Storch, accused us of being the loudest room on the floor.

We had strictly programmed days in Bansin. Wake-up call was at seven o'clock. We had one hour to get ready before we stood at attention in front of our beds for room and personal inspection. Each girl was expected to be washed, dressed, combed, with nails clean and beds made, room spotless and orderly. If anything wasn't correct, the culprit received a demerit and a warning. Too many demerits resulted in a visit to the director, who scolded and sometimes humiliated or punished the girl.

Meals were served buffet style in a large dining room. Grace before dinner was not allowed. Instead, we had to hold hands and recite, "Before dinner and after dinner and while we eat dinner, never forget the torture of hunger. That's why we say, *eat, eat, eat!* Begin!" I thought the saying was silly. I had never suffered from the torture of hunger, and I was sure that nobody else in the room had either.

After breakfast, we had classes from nine to noon and then an hour of homework before dinner. Then came the best part of the day: mail call. We all suffered from homesickness, and everybody waited feverishly for news from family and friends. From two to three was rest time. We could read or write, but no talking was allowed—a rule we always ignored. We whispered to each other and then feigned sleep when Storch checked in on us.

In the afternoon, weather permitting, we went on long walks along the water or through the forests of the island. Sometimes I took along my colored pencils and paper and sketched a tree or a solitary mushroom. I had not yet learned how to swim, and the wide, endless expanse of ocean intimidated me. I preferred to walk along the beach, letting the cold water swirl around my ankles, and collect the treasures the sea offered me, like a shiny pebble, a shell, or a piece of driftwood floating in on a wave. I often thought about the walks I had taken with my family along the New Jersey shore, collecting shells in the warm sun all afternoon.

On one cool, blustery day, with rain threatening, we took a long hike along the beach, singing songs, enjoying the marching and the brisk air. After some time at a fast clip, we rested on the sand and ate our snack— a piece of bread with what was supposed to be cheese, but didn't look anything like it. It was some kind of yellowish gelatinous stuff with lots of caraway seeds in it—an ersatz, substitute, cheese. "Everything is ersatz these days," I grumbled.

As we ate, we watched a man standing chest-deep out in the water. The man appeared to be waving to us and we obligingly waved back.

"I wonder why he's just standing there," one of the girls said. "He must be freezing."

"If he's freezing, then why doesn't the idiot come out?" another one observed.

Suddenly he began to leap through the waves heading for shore. As he emerged from the water, we were shocked to see that he was completely naked. He tried to cover his private parts with his hands as he dashed past us openmouthed girls and quickly vanished behind some scraggly bushes on the embankment where he had left his clothes.

We exploded into laughter. We held our sides and rolled around in the sand. No words from Storch could stop us. "It was either freezing to death for the poor man or exposing himself to you silly girls," she scolded.

Our laughter lasted well into the evening as we told and retold the story to others. I imagine it was the first time that most of the girls had seen a grown-up man's private parts, although I remembered when Annemarie and I had had the uncomfortable experience at the Gypsy Promenade some time earlier. The hearty laughter was a welcome relief from the constant, sick feeling in my stomach and the worry about my family.

Sometimes we went on shopping trips to the nearby towns of Heringsdorf or Ahlbeck. Mother sent me some spending money for incidentals like soap or hand cream or safety pins. But I preferred to use my money to buy things to send home: a toy for Möppi or food items for Mother that I knew were hard to get in Berlin. Almost everything was rationed, though, so I could only occasionally find something edible that didn't require a ration card.

Eight o'clock was bedtime, and eight-thirty was lights out. But with the darkness that settled in around us came the homesickness and worry, invading our room like unwelcome ghosts. In the moonlight we shared letters and cookies from home, shed tears, and discussed our fears. Broadcasts from the barely audible radio hidden under a bed kept telling us that all the major cities in Germany were suffering more frequent air raids.

"Did you notice Marianne hasn't been in class for two days?" whispered Gönna one night.

"I know," said Inge. "The director called her into the office at dinner the other night."

"Why?" I whispered back.

"They say her parents and little sister were killed in an air raid!" Brigitte answered.

"I heard she was sent to her grandmother's in Bavaria," Uschi whispered. We were silent after that, each of us wrestling with her own demons of fear.

One night we were awakened by the distant *boom, boom* of antiaircraft guns and heavy explosions.

"What's that?" a voice cried in the darkness.

"Let's see what's going on!" I said, throwing back the covers.

Shivering with worry, all of us jumped out of bed and ran onto the veranda. From there we could see across the isthmus to the mainland. With both fascination and horror we watched the fantastic fireworks of a heavy air attack on what we presumed to be Peenemünde, near Stettin.

"I heard they make rockets in underground factories there," Uschi said.

"I'm sure that's what the British are after," said Inge.

We witnessed the spectacular sight of enemy planes caught in a web of searchlights, then the fireballs as they plunged to the ground or the sea. When it was over and the smoke cleared, when the stars were once again visible in their rightful places in the night sky, we slipped back into bed, subdued and anxious. It took a long time to get back to sleep, each of us wrapped in a cocoon of worries.

We began living from one mail delivery to the next, always awaiting news that our families were safe. My mother wrote often.

Steglitz, Berlin
June 12, 1942
My dearest Mäti,
Frank went to Hamburg for a visit with Onkel Franz and Tante Trudel. He was there for that terrible raid on Hamburg. Onkel Franz

writes that incendiary bombs exploded in their house, but they were able to put out the fires. A blockbuster went down close by and killed eight people in the house. Everybody from Lubeck shops in Hamburg because Lübeck was so badly destroyed.

How is the vegetable situation there? Here we have not been able to get fresh vegetables for the past 14 days. Cigarettes are virtually impossible to get. And the bars and theaters all close down by 10 p.m.

Recently the bombings have been more severe here. The Commerce bank at Hauswogteiplatz was completely destroyed, and the State Opera House is now completely burned out. In Lankwitz 246 houses were damaged. These new English bombs are supposed to have greater detonation power than the old ones.

The other day Möppi put the pacifier in his mouth the wrong way so he could not close his mouth. He screamed terribly in anger and frustration. He sends you a wet kiss. He does this by licking your cheek.

Mother

Steglitz, Berlin
June 18, 1942
My dearest Mäti,
Thank you for the stuffed animal you made for Möppi. It's so cute and he loves to play with it. I have some leftover oilcloth. Perhaps you could make another one which can be washed. This afternoon your red cabbage head arrived. I will cook it tomorrow, and when we eat this feast, we will think of our Eleanor. We look forward to your return before long. Lucie just took Möppi for a walk. He only wants to stand now in his carriage so he won't miss anything. When you come home, you can take him for a walk in the park.
Mother

Occasionally I received letters from friends. Letters detailing living conditions in the cities made me worry even more about my family and friends. Sometimes I heard from Ruth Alm, my friend from Wellingholzhausen, where the mad bull had chased us.

> *Osnabrück*
> *June 23, 1942*
> *Dear Eleanor,*
> *In the night of June 19, a lot happened, as you probably heard over the armed forces news. The entire inner city burned. We went up the Westerberg and from there we watched through binoculars as burning beams plunged to the ground. The whole sky was blood red. The next day we couldn't go to school because all the streets were blocked with debris. We helped people carry stuff to safety from houses that threatened to collapse. I fell down the stairs while carrying glass preserves and hurt myself. I'm still sore today.*
>
> *The main street in town doesn't exist anymore. The Michaelskapelle and many, many stores and family homes are gone, almost all the houses downtown. Oh God! I can't enumerate everything. It was awful to watch people sit at the street curbs with the few possessions they could rescue. Some didn't even have the necessities to wear. Horrible! Streetcars don't work.*
>
> *The Tommies [the British] dropped leaflets saying that they would attack Osnabrück again on the seventeenth and twentieth. And they did. Now they have thrown down fliers announcing that they will come again on the twenty-seventh. They said that they are going to bomb our Bishop's seat because we bombed theirs in Birmingham. For this reason Heide and I went to our aunt in Oldenburg. I go to school here. Please write to me.*
> *Ruth Alm*

> *Osnabrück*
> *June 1942*
> *Dear Eleanor,*
> *It must be nice where you are. Here we have air-raid alarms almost every day, sometimes even twice. Once even four times and at*

night too. Our baby Stefan gets scared and cries. We then hold our hands over his ears so he won't hear the noise. He is so cute and smiles a lot. How is your little brother? Please write.

Ruth Alm

I could feel from my mother's letters that she missed me. When I was sick, I looked forward even more eagerly to the letters from her.

Steglitz, Berlin
July 1, 1942
Dear Mäti,

Yesterday your card came with the news about your throat infection. When my package arrives, the two peaches are for you and the cookies you may share with your friends. I can't send you much since I had to give up your ration cards to the KLV. When you feel better, you won't be so terribly homesick anymore.

Mother

Steglitz, Berlin
July 22, 1942
Dear Mäti,

Many thanks for all your cards. Have many children come down with scarlet fever? What is the matter with your arm? Why is Inge in the hospital? I was happy to learn that you have become orderly and hope it continues when you come home. I'm sending tooth powder, because toothpaste is no longer available. I'm also enclosing more cards. Envelopes are hard to come by.

Möppi is getting so big. You won't recognize him anymore. On Sunday Father and I will take him to the Grunewaldsee swimming. He already has a nice tan just by being out on the balcony in the sun. Sleep well, dear Mäti. Be brave and good.

Also a kiss from your Father. We are all envious of you that you can be at the seashore sunning yourself.

Mother

Annemarie wrote to tell me she wouldn't be coming to Bansin, as we had hoped. No more beds were available. She was sent to her aunt's in Zicher instead.

Each day, as more children were called into the director's office with bad news from their families, and as disturbing letters arrived from parents and friends, we became more anxious. It seemed that we were always sick with one illness or another. Some of the girls contracted scarlet fever and had to be quarantined for a while in the hospital.

By the end of summer, it was clear that the KLV was a dismal failure. It was costing the government a tremendous amount of money to keep us children healthy and out of the hospital. Nobody had considered how we girls would react emotionally and physically to the separation from our families in stressful times like these.

In early September, the camp was dissolved and we returned to our families. I was thrilled to be going home. I couldn't wait to see my family and friends again. I even missed Father. We took the train to Stettin and there boarded a boat called *Winter Tales* for home.

In Berlin, as I walked to the subway from the train station, burnt-out buildings and rubble heaps greeted me where houses and buildings had once stood.

I raced into the apartment to hugs from Mother, Frank, and even Father. Möppi had grown into a strong child while I'd gone, always crawling around the apartment or pulling himself up. He squealed when I grabbed him and squeezed him.

Although I was overjoyed to be back home, I soon saw that life in Berlin had become harder. We had air raids now almost every night, and our ration cards limited us to even less food than before. Food items like meat, coffee, and eggs were becoming harder and harder to get, and when they were available we had to wait in long lines for them. Sometimes at the butcher shop near us, the line of housewives with their brightly colored fishnet bags snaked all the way down the block and around the corner to the next block. Some of the older women took folding stools to sit on, and they knitted as they waited. Their children shoved and wrestled, impatient and desperate to do something more interesting than stand in line.

Even in these grim times, I frequently heard people poking fun at things that made their lives hard, often ignoring the fact that they were putting themselves at risk with the Gestapo. One day when I was standing in line, I overheard one woman whispering to another, "Did you hear the latest?"

"No," said the other. "Tell me."

"Two men were walking down the street. One man accidentally stepped into a pile of dog doo-doo. He turned around and smartly saluted it: 'Heil Hitler!' Puzzled, his friend asked, 'Why on earth did you do that?' The first man replied, 'Well, don't you know? The rule is when you step in anywhere, your greeting must always be "Heil Hitler." That's the law!'"

Often while we waited hours in a breadline, people also exchanged important stories and information.

"Can you believe it?" one woman said. "We can have meat only once a week from now on."

"Yah," said another woman. "And the portions won't fill a hollow tooth, never mind a family."

But one day I heard three women discuss their neighbor's son, Jürgen, a Hitler Youth who had been chosen to be part of Hitler's elite corps, the SS.

"Jürgen himself told me how proud he was to be sent to training. He couldn't wait to serve the Führer."

"I would never want one of my sons in the SS!" one of the women exclaimed, crossing herself.

"Well, he was sent home in disgrace, not the same nice boy, but a physical and emotional wreck."

"What happened?"

"Jürgen's mother found out the boys were being drilled in killing and learning how to suppress their emotions." Everyone around me was silent, listening to the woman's words.

"The boys were given dogs to train," she continued. "They were warned not to become emotionally involved with the dogs, but a number of boys like Jürgen became attached to their animals. One day, the boys were ordered to line up at attention with their rifles in hand, and their dogs beside them. Then they were ordered to shoot their dogs!"

"No!" the woman's friend exclaimed.

How horrible! I thought.

"Yes. No wonder the poor boy went insane." She cupped her mouth with her hand and whispered angrily, "And those are the brutes that are leading our country today. What's going to become of our young people, of us?"

After I picked up my loaf of bread, I trudged home. *Why make a boy kill his dog?* Nothing made sense anymore.

Everyone had to be careful when talking about Hitler and his regime. The woman I'd overheard was taking a big risk, criticizing the Nazis that way. Most people who felt negatively about the Nazis tried to be very careful about expressing their thoughts.

Father told us that some of his coworkers considered him an enemy alien and watched him closely. He had a difficult time keeping his opinions to himself, however, and one day a secretary at the office overheard Father criticizing the regime, saying that with both Russia and America in the war, there was no way Hitler could win. All German citizens—including Hitler Youth, like us—had been instructed to report such remarks, and the woman promptly denounced Father to the Gestapo. The Gestapo lost no time in summoning Father to its headquarters.

Father came home subdued and meek. He finally told us about the experience after dinner. "My legs turned to jelly," he admitted, "when I entered that building of horror on Prince-Albertstrasse. I wondered if I would ever see all of you again. I knew that the Gestapo was imprisoning, torturing, and shooting to death Germans and non-Germans alike for a lot less than what that woman reported about me. Fortunately, Doktor Biermans, my boss, stepped in for me. He discredited the secretary and denied that I had ever made such a remark." He wiped his brow.

I was shocked to see Father shaken like that. "What did you say, Father?" I asked.

He stared at me. "I denied everything." He exhaled slowly, then continued. "They...they interrogated me for most of the afternoon. After I swore never to say anything against the Führer or the regime, they finally released me."

"This shows that our status as American citizens makes us vulnerable," Mother said. Her face was pale. "We must not bring attention to ourselves," she reminded us, looking at Frank and me, then to Father. "We must be very careful what we say or do outside our home. We must live as anonymously as we possibly can."

But despite these problems, I was happy to be back together with my family in Berlin. I felt as if I had been gone for years, when in reality it had been just three months. Baby Thomas, our precious Möppi, was eight months old now and had learned many new things in my absence. I proudly took him for walks in his carriage. And wherever we went he used his cheerful disposition to make friends. He was a ray of sunshine in our gray and dreary lives.

Father doted on Möppi, spending a lot more time with him than he ever had with Frank and me. But I didn't mind. This special baby deserved all the attention he could get.

～

On Saturday nights, when I didn't go over to Annemarie's, I often went next door to the Schmidts', who had two little girls, Sigrid and Inge, and a boy named Frieder. I loved to give them their weekly bath. We called it the bath festival when all three children crowded into the same tub, with lots of splashing, laughing, and fun. Herr Schmidt, tall and handsome, was an anthropologist. Just before the war, he had been part of a German expedition to Tibet and had often told us stories about the trip. Early in 1942, though, he had been drafted into the SS. Now I was wary whenever I saw the skull and crossbones on his officer's cap. I didn't know what his position was in the SS, but he was always kind to me and to our family on the rare occasions when he was home on furlough.

Frank spent many evenings working on his aquarium and often traded fish with his school friend, Georg. But one night one of the fish he received from Georg killed all of Frank's fish. After that, Frank gave up on aquariums.

On October 3, 1942, our beloved Onkel Franz, my godfather, died of cancer at age thirty-five. It was the first time a family member I'd known had died. It made us all feel sad. We remembered him as such a vitally alive, handsome young man from those early years in America when he shared our home with us. His death was particularly hard on Mother, who had been so close to her brother. It was heartwrenching for me to see Mother, who so rarely cried, break down.

Mother could not attend the funeral because she was pregnant again. I could tell by her listlessness and the pallor of her skin that she was anxious and depressed.

The news of the new baby had shocked and angered me. *How could she? What we don't need is another baby. How can I explain this to my friends? It will be so embarrassing!* I could see my having to baby-sit more often encroaching on my time with Annemarie.

Then again, I felt ashamed of my negative feelings. Gradually I began to think more positively about the new baby. *Möppi will have someone to play with,* I reasoned. *And anyway, won't it be fun to have a little sister?* I never considered the possibility of another boy. We had two in the family already and that settled the matter for me.

My greatest concern was Mother's health. I felt sorry for her, throwing up all the time and constantly looking tired and worn out. I was afraid she might not be able to tolerate another difficult delivery. The year 1942 ended on a somber note, with new worries looming ahead.

My family, summer 1939, in Stratford, New Jersey. I (age 9) am with Frank (age 10 ½), Mother, and Father.

Our house in Stratford as seen from the side yard. The apple tree is on the right. Mother, Frank, and I are waving from my bedroom window.

On board the S. S. Hamburg, September 3, 1939, in the middle of the ocean. To take our minds off the war that England and France had just declared against Germany, the captain threw a party for all passengers. I am holding the umbrella.

Frank and me on deck the S. S. Hamburg en route to Germany.

Our Berlin apartment building at Breitenbachplaz 15 in the Steglitz district. Our apartment was to the left on the ground floor.

In 1940, before the war reached Berlin, Steglitz was bustling and prosperous.

The Brandenburg Gate, looking west from Unter den Linden toward the Tiergarten. The Pariserplatz is in the lower left corner. The pillar from the Siegesallee and the dome of the Reichstag are in the upper right corner.

Berlin. Blick vom Adlon auf den Pariser Platz, Tiergarten, Siegessäule und Reichstag

Berlin-Steglitz

Grossmutter and
Grossvater Rump
in 1939.

Going to church
with Frank for our
first communion
in 1942.

Our Eslohe Omi
with new baby
Tommy, Frank,
and me,
March 1942.

New Year's Eve 1941, just before Tommy's birth. Onkel Franz, Father, Tante Trudel, and I are in the back row. Frank and Mother are in front.

In summer 1942, I was evacuated with many other school girls to Bansin, on the Island of Usedom in the Baltic Sea. From left to right, Brigitte, Storch (our BDM leader), Inge, and me. I am wearing Brigitte's dress and she's wearing mine.

CHAPTER
SEVEN

CHILDHOOD LOST
JANUARY 1943–MARCH 1943

BY EARLY 1943, Germany's eastern campaign against Russia had turned sour. Daily we heard reports that the fierce Russian winter, lack of supplies, and tenacious resistance of the Russian soldiers proved too much for the German soldiers, weakened by hunger and cold. At the beginning of February we heard a stunning announcement over the radio: "General Paulus has surrendered his Sixth Army at Stalingrad." More than 300,000 German soldiers had lost their lives in the battle of Stalingrad. The Soviets were beginning to take back their country.

Special reports on the radio no longer bragged about Germany's successes. On the "Weekly Review," a news program that was shown before every movie, we no longer saw pictures of triumphant, victorious soldiers draped in flower garlands, proudly marching into foreign cities and countries. Instead we saw sad, dull-eyed, emaciated men in tattered uniforms with dirty bandages, shuffling or limping through heavy snow, seemingly directionless. Many soldiers were freezing or starving to death. Others were dying from typhus, dysentery, or infected wounds. The newspapers in Berlin were full of death notices. Again and again I read "Died for Führer, Nation and Fatherland," in announcements in the long obituary columns. On the streets I noticed many people wearing black armbands, indicating that one or more of their loved ones had died in the war.

Our own extended family did not go unscathed. Tante Mieze and Onkel Adolf lost their son Karl Heinz. Tante Anne (Tante Mieze's sister) and her husband Leo (Onkel Adolf's brother) lost their son, also named Karl Heinz, at Stalingrad and then a few months later their son Leo in Yugoslavia. Onkel Leo refused to put "died for Führer" in the obituary notices. He simply stated, "Our beloved son died for his family and the Fatherland."

Annemarie's father was reported missing in action. I had learned that "missing" often meant a soldier had been killed but couldn't be found and identified. Annemarie and her family agonized as they waited for news about Herr Tesch's fate. Papa Petke became a surrogate father to Annemarie and her brother Christoph, and a strong support for Frau Tesch, who had to cope somehow with the children, the big house and garden, and the two old ladies.

In school we could tell by the sad faces around us who had lost a father, a brother, a friend. We also heard that Lehrer Lautsch, our grammar school teacher, had died in the battle of Stalingrad. But we couldn't muster many sad feelings for that cruel man. I looked at my hands. The bruises he had left on them were long gone, but I remembered well how angry and hurt he had made me feel.

Our Hitler Youth troop was frequently required to visit army hospitals. We were supposed to bring good cheer to the wounded soldiers by giving them flowers and singing patriotic songs. But I didn't feel much like singing when I saw those young men, some without legs or arms, some with holes in their chests, charred faces, or empty sockets where eyes should have been. Some of the less wounded smiled. Others turned their heads to the wall or lay motionless. The political songs seemed like a mockery to me. I wished I had the courage to run away. Instead I just stood there like a wooden statue, with the notes stuck in my throat like dry clumps of cotton.

The deadly British bombers began flying over Berlin more often and leaving dead bodies in their wake. We took the almost nightly raids more seriously now. Although nothing had happened in our area of Steglitz, we were always afraid.

～

Frank, who had received a camera from Father at Christmas, started his new hobby with a passion. He eagerly read all the books he could find on photography and created a darkroom in the bathroom. He took pictures of the family and of his friends, and some of the bomb sites. Then he rushed home and closeted himself in the bathroom.

"Frank! I need the bathroom," I yelled. "Open the door."

"Don't come in! I'm developing my pictures."

Tired of hearing us shout at each other through the door, and often needing the bathroom herself, Mother finally told Frank, "Make sure you check that no one else in the family needs the bathroom before you commandeer it for your photos. And clean up afterward! That smell makes me queasy."

～

It seemed as though my whole life in the cold winter months revolved around standing in long food lines, going to school, and mending socks. It was my job to mend socks and stockings for everyone in our family, a chore I intensely disliked. Mother had taught me how to use a wooden mushroom. I stretched the offending hole over the mushroom and then wove the thread over and under, over and under, to make a smooth patch.

Our stockings were ugly, dark brown, scratchy things. Mother insisted that I wear them for warmth. To keep them up, I had to wear a garter belt with dangly straps with hooks and eyes on the ends. The elastic straps stretched out fast, allowing the stockings to sag and twist around my legs. Like many of my friends, I preferred to freeze in the white knee socks with fashionable tassels that we wore with our BDM uniforms, or even plain old socks, rather than the repugnant stockings.

The stockings were a constant source of friction between Mother and me.

"You are so incredibly stubborn and so vain!" she scolded. "You'd rather freeze to death than wear these warm stockings."

"But they're so ugly, Mother!" I wailed. "Nobody wears them in school."

"I'm not going to take care of you if you get sick," she finally yelled in exasperation.

I glared at her, then stomped back into my room and put on the hated things. I knew Mother rarely made a threat she didn't keep.

Socks and even those hideous stockings were almost impossible to come by anymore. All supplies were going into the war effort. At times even darning thread was hard to find, and expensive. And often the thread didn't match the color of our socks, so we ended up with an odd assortment of colorful patches. The worn socks piled up. Just when I thought I had made a dent in the pile, more were tossed on top. They became my enemies, pursuing me relentlessly.

Sometimes, instead of carefully weaving the thread, I angrily pulled the holes together and made a big lump. I didn't dare pull the holes together in Father's socks. But when I bunched up Frank's socks, I always heard about it afterward.

"I have a blister on account of you," Frank complained.

"Why can't you mend your own socks?" I replied, annoyed.

"That's your job!" he said, tossing the sock at me.

Fuming, I flung the entire disagreeable pile at him. He threw it back at me. Before long it was outright war. We threw the socks and stockings back and forth in a frenzy of yelling and name-calling until Mother came in.

"Stop this fighting at once, both of you!" she cried.

After Frank left the room, it took me a long time to find where all the socks had landed and to match them up again. But it was worth it.

To get away from the drudgery of everyday tasks, Annemarie and I escaped to the movies whenever we could. I told Mother, "I'm going to Annemarie's to do homework." Instead, we met Renate and Erika and headed for the movie house to see the latest Marika Röck film. She was our favorite female movie star. Marika usually starred in musical revues, like *The Woman of My Dreams.* We learned all of Marika's popular songs by heart and sang them when we were together.

Marika was beautiful and talented. She could dance and sing, and she always captured the love of her handsome leading men. I imagined that I was that gorgeous creature dancing my life away. For a time, sitting in the darkened theater, watching the glitz and enchantment of a musical, my friends and I forgot the dreary business of war with all its ugliness and fears.

Books were another escape for me. I now felt pretty comfortable reading in German, which opened up an exciting world that I could explore on my own. I read everything I could get my hands on. Of course, I had already devoured *The Treasures of German Mythology* and in our home library the novels by Sigrid Undset, the 1928 Nobel Prize winner for literature.

I read books by Josefa Berens-Totenohl, who wrote about the stoic people of the Sauerland, where Eslohe is. Life was often harsh in that region, and the many months during the year of dark, cold, rainy weather made its residents feel isolated and depressed. I admired the people for their strength and sympathized with their sadness.

I also read many volumes by Karl May about *Winnetou, Chief of the Apaches,* as told by Old Shatterhand, Winnetou's white friend and blood brother. Those adventures about bravery, human dignity, and love and peace fascinated me.

Books gained such a hold over my imagination that I got lost in them. To me they were no longer fiction, but reality. I became the characters I read about. I was another person far away in another land, another life. I came back into the real world only when the book was abruptly slammed shut and I felt a stinging blow on my cheek.

"Eleanor, you will *not* disobey me!" Mother shouted.

"What did I do?" I rubbed my cheek, smarting from the slap and from the unfair accusation.

"I said, set the table please. *Now!*"

Sometimes after school I went over to Inge's house. Her mother was always kind and loving and insisted that I call her Inge-Mutti. She always laid out cookies after school for Inge, her younger sister Karin, and for any visitors they brought home. Inge-Mutti was interested in everything we had to say, and I was eager to share my problems at school. Because Inge's father was a judge and a member of the Nazi party, Inge's family was privileged to a lot of delicacies my family couldn't get anymore, like coffee, butter, ham, and eggs.

But what I admired most at Inge's was a dollhouse that belonged to both sisters. It was a magnificent four-story Victorian home, almost as tall as I was, with every miniature detail imaginable, including tiny pots and pans in the kitchen and miniature chamber pots under the canopied beds. It was exquisite. An entire doll family of mother, father, children, grandparents, and servants lived in the house. We played with this doll-house, rearranging the furniture, relocating the occupants, and making up stories about them. I found this little make-believe world as enchanting as the movies or the books.

It didn't take Inge long to find out the main reason I enjoyed playing at her house. She soon came up with rules that controlled the use of her dollhouse. Our Hitler Youth troop urged us to collect as many old papers, rags, clothing, bones, and scrap iron as possible to be used for the war effort. Inge was an avid member of the troop. She fervently believed in the cause and was eager to please our BDM leaders.

"You can play with my dollhouse this afternoon," Inge sometimes announced to me on the way to school. "But you'll have to collect a wagon full of old stuff for me first. No load, no play!" Dutifully, I trotted off after school, pulling an old wagon behind me, ringing doorbells, always with the idea of the dollhouse as my goal. Inge got to be a good Hitler Youth, and I got to play with the dollhouse. Other times she required me to do her homework in order to play. I didn't resent these arrangements one bit. It seemed fair, and it worked for both of us.

That year my friends and I began to create Poesie albums, or poetry albums. Almost every girl had one. We exchanged albums, asking each other to write a favorite poem or saying inside. To be asked for a poem was an honor, and this honor was not taken lightly. I searched for just the right lines for my friends' books. These poems about happiness and the goodness of man were two of my favorites.

> *Oh human heart*
> *What is happiness*
> *But a mysteriously born,*
> *Barely greeted, never repeated*
> *Moment.*
> > —Nikolaus Lenau

> *Noble be the man*
> *Helpful and good*
> *Since that alone*
> *Differentiates him*
> *From other living species*
> *We know.*

> > —Johann Wolfgang von Goethe

Often we made up our own poems. It was easier for us to express our deeper feelings without actually speaking the words out loud. Poetry opened up a new door of expression for me.

～

On March 2, 1943, I woke to a clear, blue sky, not the usual dreary cloudiness. Early signs of spring were beginning to emerge. Tiny crocuses pushed their little heads through the partially frozen ground in the courtyard out back. The snow had melted, except for patches lingering in shady corners. Knobby brown buds appeared on the branches on the big chestnut trees across the street in the park. I could even smell spring in the air, like the fresh, clean scent after a rainstorm on a hot summer day.

I was in a joyful mood when Inge stopped by for our walk to school. The signs of spring teased me with summer dreams of swimming and canoeing on the Wannsee, hiking in the Grunewald, and playing in Annemarie's garden.

"You know what a clear sky means?" Inge interrupted my delicious thoughts.

I nodded. "Of course. We'll probably have an air raid tonight. The Tommies always come when the sky is clear."

"The better to see you with, my dear," Inge joked.

A vague anxiousness invaded my summer dreams. In the afternoon I took Tommy out in his carriage. He was now thirteen months old and walking, but his little feet couldn't keep pace with my big ones, so it was easier to push him in the carriage. Though harnessed in, he stood, viewing his domain. I took him to a little park close by with a mushroom-shaped gazebo and played with him there.

Frau Rossmeyer arrived with her twin toddlers, a pair of adorable little girls sitting side by side in their carriage. We often saw Frau Rossmeyer or her husband proudly pushing the girls in their carriage down the street. I could never tell one twin from the other. Tommy, of course, was thrilled to have company close to his age, so he chased the girls around the benches, shuffling after them until he couldn't run anymore. I plopped him back in his carriage, and he soon fell asleep.

At home, poor Mother looked tired and stressed, big and heavy with the new baby due in two months. She was often irritable and difficult to please, no matter how hard I tried.

After supper and homework, it was bedtime. As we had for months, that night we laid out all our clothes in precise order on the chairs next to our beds before going to bed so we could find our things in the dark.

"It's clear," Frank observed, looking out at the stars. "I bet we'll have an alarm tonight for sure."

"Maybe they won't come," I replied wistfully. I looked out the window at the bright moon and stars and the dark, silent trees across the street. A tune came into my head, a beautiful evening song by Matthias Claudius. I knew the words by heart.

The moon has risen
The golden stars shining
In the sky so light and clear
The forest stands black and silent
And from the meadow rises
The white fog so wondrous.

Chilled, I quickly jumped into bed and snuggled down beneath my feather comforter, with only my nose peeking out. It always took a while to warm up the comforter because of its bulk. But once my body heat created a warm pocket, the down kept the heat in for hours, even after a stint in the cellar. Above my bed hung the Botticelli print of the Madonna, looking protectively down at me. I often spoke to her about my fears and anxieties and believed without a doubt that she heard me. In fact, I could keenly feel the Invisibles' presence. Soon I drifted off to sleep.

The piercing howls of air-raid sirens ripped through me like a knife. I was instantly awake. "Oh, no, not again!" I groaned, groping for the warm wool leggings and throwing on a sweater and shoes. The screaming sirens always set my teeth to chattering. I could hear Frank getting dressed in the dark across the room from me. "You were right," I said into the blackness. Even though our windows were covered by blackout paper, we weren't allowed to switch on the lights. The bombers overhead might spot the light seeping between the cracks.

"Hurry up!" Mother called. "Eleanor, get the baby."

From the start of the sirens to the time the bombers were expected to arrive, we had only seven minutes to get ourselves ready and into the cellar. Once we dashed out of our bedrooms, we could then turn on a flashlight or light a candle. Each of us had duties in the mad rush of those minutes. It was my job or Lucie's to dress Tommy, as it was too difficult now for Mother to lift the heavy child. Father and Frank were responsible for carrying into the cellar the blankets, baby carriage, emergency luggage, and important family documents, including the irreplaceable ration cards.

When I ran into my parents' bedroom, Tommy was already standing up in his crib, arms outstretched, ready to be lifted out. His little face was flushed with sleep, blond hair rumpled and blue eyes sparkling at the prospect of another midnight adventure. "More boom, boom," he crowed, jumping up and down, making my job of dressing him more difficult. I finally gave up struggling with him and just wrapped him in a warm blanket while Lucie grabbed his clothes.

We hurried down the two flights of stairs into the air-raid shelter, where most of the cellar clan had already assembled. Everybody was dressed in odd assortments of hastily thrown-on clothing. Old Herr Stier from the second floor apartment, usually so dignified, wore a worn housecoat covering a pair of baggy, red-striped pajamas, hair standing on end in little white tufts, like crests on a stormy sea. The Gadows from the third floor, still in dinner clothes, had probably just returned from some gala affair, although most public places in Berlin closed by ten. Frau Schmidt and her children, Inge, Sigrid, and Frieder, were also there, as were Herr and Frau Kries, a childless older couple who lived just above us.

Herr Kries, a retired police officer, had been assigned to be the air-raid warden for our cellar. He was charged with enforcing rules and regulations governing conduct in the cellar during an air raid. He made sure buckets were filled with water, gas masks were handy, and occupants behaved in a civilized manner. In case of a direct hit, he was to try to prevent panic.

After greeting the others, my family settled in our room in the cellar, into our bunk bed and old canvas-covered lawn chairs. The one small window just above street level was covered by burlap bags filled with sand. In the middle of the small room stood Tommy's big basketlike carriage with the hood up and the back toward the window. Lucie and I dressed Tommy and then harnessed him into the carriage, where he bounced up and down. Then, ignoring Mother's plea that I lie in the bunk bed, I sat with Lucie on the edge of my red snow sled. I was too keyed up to sleep, listening to any sounds that might be coming from outside.

Frank and Father and the other men in the building had gone upstairs to stand at the entrance of the apartment building, scanning the skies for signs of aircraft.

"Please, Mother, may I go upstairs too?" I begged. She nodded and I dashed upstairs to be with Frank. Outside it was a peaceful, very cold, star-studded night. No light shone anywhere except for the occasional glimmer of a cigarette. Men from the neighboring apartment houses were also standing out front, their murmuring voices a little eerie in the deathly quiet of the night. I wasn't afraid anymore.

"If anything was going to happen, it would have happened by now," Frank said. I thought I detected a note of disappointment in his voice.

The cold penetrated my loose clothes, and I was just about to return to the cellar when I heard the distant drone of a single engine, interrupted by the *tack-tack* of antiaircraft guns. I looked up and saw a plane, caught in spotlights from the antiaircraft stations, as it approached our area. It appeared to be circling right above us. Soon fluttering down on our neighborhood were what looked like hundreds of tiny Christmas trees, weaving gently back and forth toward the earth in a choreographed dance. *How graceful,* I thought.

"Oh no!" one of the men yelled. "Those are flares used by reconnaissance pilots to identify areas for the bombing squadrons that follow!"

Then the distant roar of what sounded like a thousand engines shattered the quiet night. Somebody screamed, "This is it!" We tumbled down the cellar stairs in wild confusion. Fear clutched my throat as I crowded next to Lucie on the red sled. Frank perched on the edge of the lower bunk bed, while Mother and Father sat in the canvas chairs, Tommy's carriage between them.

Lights in the cellar suddenly flickered, followed by a piercing whistle and a deafening blast. I placed my forehead on my knees and wrapped my arms around my legs. Screaming bombs and explosions erupted all around us. The whole foundation of the building shook. Plaster rained from the ceiling, enveloping us in ghostly white. The pole in the center of the room shook. It had just been pushed under the ceiling and wasn't attached to anything. *Please, please,* I begged the Invisibles, *let it hold up the ceiling.* Waves of intense air pressure surged through the room, pressing on our lungs and eardrums. Somebody in one of the other rooms shrieked, "We're going to die!"

Suddenly a powerful rush of air was followed by an explosion so loud, it shattered the light bulb above me and blew out the sandbagged window, showering us with particles of glass. A sliver lodged in Father's nose and he began bleeding.

"Are we hit?" a voice yelled from somewhere.

I looked up at the ceiling. *Will it collapse and bury us?* Lucie and I clutched each other. The baby cried.

"Please let me hold him," I begged.

Mother placed him in my arms. I felt Tommy's warm little body pressed against mine, smelled his sweetness, and rubbed my face in his silky hair.

Please don't let us die, I called to the Invisibles again. I imagined that I could feel their powerful wings as they surrounded us. Tommy stopped crying and settled down on my lap.

Bombs continued to fall and explode all over Steglitz. Every time I heard the screaming of an approaching bomb, I held my hands over the baby's ears. Acrid smoke filled the cellar, making it hard to breathe. Barrage after barrage pounded the neighborhood for minutes, hours, an eternity.

After the bombs had stopped for a short while, Frank, Father, the air-raid warden, and Herr Gadow ventured up the cellar stairs to see what had happened to our building and the neighborhood. I could hear their steps crunching on broken glass and debris.

A horrified voice cried, "Oh my God! Everything is on fire!"

I then became aware of an intense heat in the cellar. *Is our house burning?* I had to see. Lucie took Tommy, and I ran up the stairs to the outside. I couldn't believe my eyes. Everywhere I looked, all that had been familiar had vanished in a pile of rubble or was burning. Swirling green phosphorus, flaming trees in the park across the street, and gray smoke clouded what only a few hours ago had been an untarnished landscape. The entire apartment block next to us, where Klugs' grocery store had been, was gone. Flames roared wildly from attics in some of the buildings still standing.

I turned around to look at our building. It was still intact, although all the windows had been shattered so they looked like dark, empty eye sockets. Some areas of the front wall were covered with a glowing green substance. I recalled from my Hitler Youth lessons that phosphorus was terrible stuff, and very dangerous. It attached itself to walls and streets and became highly flammable in sunlight, and was deadly to humans. The smoldering phosphorous pellets embedded themselves in skin and, as soon as the victims came into daylight, the pellets burned and the victims died a slow, torturous death.

Again, the roar of engines approached. A new wave of bombers. Back into the cellar we ran. Another barrage of screaming bombs fell. The air in the cellar was stifling. I thought about death. *What is it like? Does it hurt? Is it dark, or is it gold with sunshine? Would I become an angel after all? Or maybe a star in the sky? Would I see the Invisibles?*

The all-clear siren interrupted my thoughts, and I suddenly noticed that except for the crackling flames, it was silent outside. I looked around at the faces of my family in the flickering candlelight and sighed with relief. We had made it. I refused to think about the dangers to come tomorrow.

Outside the sky was blood red. Heavy smoke burned my eyes. Somebody had opened up a fire hydrant, and people in the neighborhood had begun to form a bucket chain. Frank and I immediately joined the group and tried to put out the fire in the attic of the building next door. Father and other members of our cellar clan were trying to scrape off the phosphorous from the front of our building. Others were scrambling to reach people buried beneath the rubble of demolished buildings. Survivors ran frantically back and forth. Everything was a jumble of humans and debris.

After the attic fire was put out, I went home to Mother, totally exhausted. She was struggling to put the overexcited Tommy to sleep. He was fussy and kept fighting her attempts to calm him down. The apartment was a mess, with broken glass everywhere, window frames at crazy angles, the front door blown off its hinges and lying in the corridor, cracks running down the walls, and chunks of plaster from the ceiling strewn about. Mother looked bone weary, with deep circles under her eyes. I put my arms around her. Part of me wanted to be her little girl, and another part of me wanted to comfort her.

"What's going to happen?" I cried.

"You're going to have to be a big girl now," she said, firmly untangling my arms from around her. "I need you to be strong for me." Her dark eyes looked into mine. "Bad times are coming. And with the new baby on the way, I have to be able to depend on you." I nodded with a sob, feeling anything but strong, but proud that she needed me.

Frank and Father returned home, black with soot. Father looked around at the mess in the apartment. "What are we going to do?" he wailed.

Mother lost no time in shoving a broom in his hands. "Here!" she said. "Sweep!" To the rest of us, including Lucie, she commanded, "Shake the glass out of the beds! Get rid of the debris in front of the beds! Then we're all going to get some much-needed sleep!" We did as we were told. It was clear who was in charge. Ever-practical Mother knew what to do.

I hadn't realized just how exhausted I was until I finally sank into bed. Amazingly, underneath the feather comforter a little warmth still lingered. I felt as though we'd been away forever. Just before drifting off to sleep, I glanced up at the painting of the Madonna above my bed and found her missing. I jumped out of bed and searched on the floor. There she was, a scratch across her green robe, the gold frame chipped but otherwise whole. I returned her to her rightful place on the wall above my bed. Shadows danced eerily across the Madonna's face in the red glow from the burning trees across the street.

I became aware of an overwhelming, heart-wrenching sadness—of something irretrievably lost. I knew in that moment that nothing in my life would ever be the same again. Gone forever were the Stratford days, my childhood days, buried beneath the rubble of this one catastrophic night. The war was now part of my life. No longer somewhere else, but right here in my own neighborhood. I realized that all of us were as vulnerable to death as any soldier on the front line. The battleground was no longer out there, but right here on our doorsteps. *Today we survived, but what about tomorrow?*

The next morning I wrote these words in my Poesie album:

> *Oh, if only I could have the*
> *Courage of a hero.*
> *I would conquer the fear of death.*
> *Instead I cry.*

The next few days we cleaned up—sweeping, washing, repairing, and boarding up windows with cardboard. Glass was almost impossible to get, with so many windows blown out all over the city. Anyway, it was fruitless to replace windows, since the next air raid would just shatter them again—and we knew there would be more air raids. There was no time to go to school, no time to visit with Annemarie or Inge.

The big apartment building next to ours had received a blockbuster hit. It was a giant pile of rubble. Horribly, we could hear desperate knocking from survivors trapped under the ruins. Rescuers struggled to reach them. Leaks from broken gas lines threatened to poison the rescuers as well as the buried people they tried to reach. Heavy cranes were needed to remove the giant concrete slabs that were blocking the entrance to many of the cellars. But there were not enough cranes and earth movers in the city to take care of all the emergencies.

Unfortunately, more people than usual had been in the cellars of the bombed-out building that night. Three doors up from our house was the Lida movie house. When the alarm siren had sounded, people had fled the movies to seek shelter. Many of them had chosen the cellars of this building.

The constant knocking was terrible to hear. I even thought I could hear voices calling from deep within the ruins. All of us outside stood around, frustrated and helpless. What could we do? Picking at stones and twisted steel with naked hands was an exercise in futility. All the victims near the cellar windows that had not been completely blocked by tons of debris had already been pulled to safety. We just couldn't get to the others.

Had the blockbuster bomb landed a hundred feet to the right, I realized with a shudder, *we would have been the ones buried, knocking for help that never came.* After several days, the knocking stopped.

The apartment house at the end of our block, next to the bombed-out one, was declared structurally unsafe to live in and had to be evacuated. Frank and I, along with other neighbors, helped residents carry out their belongings. Up and down the creaking stairs we trotted, carrying clothing, furniture, dishes, and suitcases, always aware that ceilings could collapse anytime.

One woman asked me to carry out her preserves from the cellar. The cellar was dark, and I wasn't sure which section of the cellar the preserves were stored in. I tried to find a light switch by groping along the wall, not sure if the electricity was working, all the while feeling spooked. As my eyes adjusted to the dark, I saw a faint light coming from one of the cellar rooms. I thought the preserves must be in there.

A single candle flickered in the room, casting a huge shadow of myself on the wall behind me. A terrible stench of something decaying hung in the air. There were bunk beds along two walls where people were sleeping. As I stepped closer, I froze in horror. The bunk beds were piled high with grotesquely disfigured corpses. I screamed and ran up the stairs and out of the building. Later I found out that these were bodies of some of the victims taken from the rubble next door. They were being stored there until they could be properly buried. The bombed-out ruins of the city became the grave for many others.

Frank and I explored the streets beyond our own neighborhood. No structure was untouched. Many of the apartment houses, villas, and other buildings had been completely demolished, including the new Saint Bernard Church in Dahlem, where a year earlier Frank and I had received our first communion.

One morning, a few days after the attack on our area, I ran into Gabrielle, a girl who lived around the corner from me.

She greeted me with a somber question. "Did you hear about the twins?"

"No, what happened?"

"A phosphorous bomb flew through their cellar window and exploded right in front of the little girls, covering them with that dreadful stuff."

"Oh God, no!" I gasped. "How awful!"

"I heard one of the neighbors say that the only thing they could do to stop the burning was to put the girls into a tub of water."

"But what happened after that?" I asked, shaken to the core. "They couldn't keep the girls in the water forever."

Gabrielle shook her head sadly. "No. There was no hope for them." She paused, her eyes downcast. Then she took a breath and looked back up at me, her eyes wet. "Their father shot them."

CHAPTER
EIGHT

A SPECIAL BIRTHDAY PRESENT
AND BACK TO STOLP
SPRING 1943–FALL 1943

IN SPITE OF THE INCREASED air raids around Berlin, each of which brought destruction and hundreds of deaths, daily life in my family continued with a weird kind of normalcy. After every air raid, we followed the same routine: sweep the debris from the floors, nail cardboard back into the windows, shake dust and plaster from bed linens, stuff cracks and holes with paper. For days we could hear hammering and repairing from every household in the neighborhood. People whose homes had been bombed out searched through the rubble, looking for anything they might salvage.

The families in our building converted the rose garden in the backyard into small vegetable garden plots. My family planted string beans, tomatoes, lettuce, and cabbage, using the seeds that we had dried from earlier crops. Since living at Omi Ramrath's in Eslohe, I had liked to watch things grow, so Mother put me in charge of our plot. Sometimes Frank helped. I watered faithfully when necessary, which wasn't often since it rained a lot in Berlin.

When Bolle, the dairyman, passed by with his horse-drawn buggy, Mother, Frank, and I kept our eyes open for horse manure, as did all the others in the apartment house. As soon as the horse left his treasured manure, we all scrambled to the street. The one fastest out the door with

paper and shovel was the one to get the precious stuff. It made great fer-
tilizer when shoveled into the earth; the vegetables grew bigger and better because of it. When scooping the smelly manure, I reminded myself
of how proud I would feel when I could pluck the first ripe tomatoes or
a cabbage head in the summer.

Lately, because of the debris flying from the air raids, the new little
plants pushing through the ground were in danger of being crushed
before they could flower or bear their precious fruits. I worried about
them and hovered over them daily, pulling away shrapnel, dusting off
tiny leaves, and replanting those seedlings that had been ripped up.

After that first big air raid over Steglitz, we no longer ran into the cellar for shelter. Now we ran across the street and into the subway station.
Father believed that if a bomb hit just above us while we were in the station, we would be killed instantly. But if it smashed onto the other end
of the subway station, the hole created by the bomb would allow the air
pressure to escape sufficiently to prevent death at our end. He reasoned
that instant death was preferable to being buried alive under tons of
debris from the apartment building. Ever since the blockbuster destroyed
the apartment house down from ours, being buried alive had become my
personal terror. In my nightmares I could still hear the terrible knocking
of the victims trapped in the cellars.

The disadvantage of being in the subway, however, was that we heard
the screaming and detonating bombs more intensely than we had in the
cellar. The terrible noises echoed along the walls, often coming from
both ends of the station. When the bombs fell, a rush of air like a tremendous windstorm swept through the station, creating painful pressure in
my chest as though my lungs were ready to burst. With each pressure
wave, I tried to gasp for breath but only ended up inhaling and coughing
out the clouds of dust blown into the station from above. My mouth
tasted as if I had licked the sidewalk. We soon learned to take damp rags
with us to cover our mouths and noses.

It was cold and gloomy in the subway—*like a gray cement tomb,* I
thought. Many others joined us from neighboring apartments. After the
wild scramble across the street and down the stairs to the station, we sat

huddled together on our suitcases, wrapped in blankets, trying to keep warm. Air raids lasted anywhere from one to three hours, and some nights we were hauled out of bed several times as the bombers came in waves.

I developed a routine that helped me control my constant fears for a little while. At the first sound of the warning siren, I summoned the Invisibles and imagined I could feel their presence. Then, the moment I settled on the floor of the subway, waiting for the bombers to attack, I pictured myself back in Stratford. I would walk through the front gate and into our house, pull down the shades, and curl up on the velvet sofa in the living room, feeling protected. While the bombers droned overhead and bombs rained on Berlin, I deliberately looked at every object in the old living room, recalling the details of those happy years. No matter how often the story played in my head, it was always fresh and new.

Sometimes the story was interrupted by whirls of fiery sparks spinning through the subway station from one end to the other, trailing yellowish black smoke. Other times my ability to immerse myself in a book, when there was enough light, helped with the monstrous fear tugging at my gut.

Even while the story was playing in my head, I kept an ear out for the all-clear signal. Often my efforts to concentrate on my peaceful inner scene were interrupted by the other part of my mind, pleading for the sound of the all-clear siren, the long wail that told us no more bombers for now. Each time I heard it, my first thought was *We made it again!* My relief was even greater when we climbed out of the subway station and saw our apartment building still standing. As long as I had a home, I told myself, I still had some sense of security, of belonging somewhere in the frightening, chaotic world. *Please, please, keep our home safe,* I prayed to the Invisibles as I watched the hundreds of people who roamed the streets after a night of air raids, pulling wagons or pushing baby carriages piled high with dusty clothing, pots and pans, and blankets, trying to find another place to live.

School became sporadic. Many classmates and their families fled the city to safer areas or to relatives in the country, traveling alone or with their families. Teachers often had difficulty finding transportation to school when bus lines or subways were hit by bombs. Students were often too tired to concentrate after a night of constantly interrupted sleep. Yet, whenever possible, school, like other daily routines, went on in these strange times.

~

And so May 25, 1943, arrived. My thirteenth birthday! The day I had long looked forward to, the day I became a teenager. Mother had warned me a few days before, "Now don't look for a present. I'm in no condition to try and find something." And I understood that.

Even though Mother had kept her promise about not giving me another birthday party, she still had a way of making me feel special on my birthday. When I came to the breakfast table on the morning of my birthday, she often circled my plate with flowers and placed a gift to the side. Everybody in the family congratulated me and I felt important.

When this morning dawned, I hoped that just maybe there would be a little something for me—at least flowers. But no flowers were around my plate, no gift, and no congratulations were offered. Mother didn't even mention my birthday. She looked especially tired and nervous that morning, not even getting out of bed to see Frank and me off to school. Hurt and disappointed, I hiked off to school with Inge.

"Just think," I fumed, "not even a 'Happy Birthday' from Mother."

"Well, here's some good news for you," Inge said, smiling importantly. "My mother wants you to come over to our house after school today. She's going to have a party for you."

"A party? Wow! With real cake?" I asked, brightening considerably.

"Yes, real cake! It'll only be you, Karin, and me."

Soon the disappointment of the morning was gone in anticipation of the afternoon.

The cake was covered with apple slices and buttered cinnamon crumbs, the way Mother used to make it in Stratford for our immigrant friends' Sunday visits. Luxuries such as cakes, cookies, and sweets were almost impossible to come by now, even with ration cards. But Inge-Mutti had managed to find the precious ingredients, perhaps through her husband's connections. Inge, her sister Karin, and I sat down at a festive table covered with an embroidered tablecloth and set with Inge-Mutti's fine bone china. In the center stood a bouquet of lilies-of-the-valley, my favorite flowers. The cake was delicious, rich and sweet. I truly felt honored and almost forgot the sting of rejection I had felt at home. To top off the afternoon, Inge let me play with the dollhouse.

In the late afternoon Frank came to the door. "Hurry up! Come home!" he said with a grin. "Mother has a birthday present for you."

"A present for me?" I cried, surprised. *So Mother hasn't forgotten my birthday after all!* "What is it?" I begged. "Tell me."

But Frank just grinned. No amount of pleading could get the secret out of him. *He can be so stubborn,* I thought, exasperated. I thanked Inge and her mother and ran home behind Frank.

As we entered the hallway of our apartment, I could see bloody sheets on the bathroom floor. For a moment my heart stopped. *Mother! What happened to Mother?*

But then I heard what sounded like a kitten mewing. In a flash I knew the baby had come. I rushed into Mother's bedroom.

"Congratulations," she greeted me, looking tired, but pleased. "Your birthday present!" she said. "A baby sister!"

And there she was, Hildegard Elizabeth, cuddled in Mother's arms. She was so tiny, so pink, so perfect, with a mop of dark hair. Right away I loved her desperately. I was allowed to give her her first bath. She was so small and looked so fragile, I was afraid she might break. But she was a true war baby. I knew she would become a tough little girl who would survive against terrible odds.

The almost nightly trips into the subway became even more complicated with two babies to get ready—a wiggly and cranky fifteen month old, who no longer enjoyed being awakened in the middle of the night, and an infant. On weekdays Lucie was there to help us, but on weekends, when she went home to her parents, we were on our own. It took all of our coordinated efforts to transport into the subway the babies, the baby carriage, the luggage—which included a change of clothing for everybody and even more diapers—medical supplies, wet cloths to keep ourselves from inhaling the smoke, and crucial papers like passports, identity papers, and ration cards. If we lost our identity papers, we could be imprisoned or even executed. If we lost our ration cards, we would die another way, by starvation.

The rhythm of life in the city was now dictated by a cable radio that was attached to our regular radio. *Tick-tack! Tick-tack!* it went when enemy planes approached. Its bulletins gave at regular intervals the exact position, number, and type of enemy aircraft heading for Berlin. "Achtung!" Attention! the announcers alerted us. "Enemy airplanes are on an east-southeast course by way of Hanover-Braunschweig in direction of the capital city. Berliners can count on a bombing raid in approximately twenty minutes. Be ready to seek shelter!" And the mad rush into the subway, bunkers, or cellars began once more.

All public events, like concerts, movie houses, and plays as well as many restaurants now closed by seven. Everybody went to bed early. Many people lined up at public shelters or bunkers by late afternoon or early evening to stake out a place for themselves. Often they stayed the whole night. Some mothers took their children to underground bunkers, where the children slept overnight, and picked them up again in the mornings. But more and more frequently, a child was not picked up because its mother had been killed in the nighttime air raid.

Mother did not consider the option of sending her children—four of us now—to the bunkers. She felt that if we were to die, the family would all die together. I would have refused to go, even if she had insisted. The thought of my mother not being there in the morning was too unbearable. Despite our sometimes difficult relationship, she was the one person who anchored me and gave me some sense of security. Sometimes after an air raid I begged to sleep in her bed. I was terrified of a time bomb lurking in the bushes outside my window. Time bombs detonated hours after the all-clear signal, just when we least expected an explosion.

Occasionally Mother gave in to my pleading and let me crawl into bed with her, but since it made Father angry, I was usually sent back to my bed.

"A big girl like you," he scolded. "You should be ashamed of yourself."

I was ashamed of being such a coward. *Where are my good intentions of being a hero?* I wondered, *I long to be like Joan of Arc, or Gudrun or Brunhilde in the myths, or Frank, who never seems to be scared.*

∿

When school was over in June, my parents decided that Frank and I should leave Berlin for the summer. I was to go to Tante Mieze and Onkel Adolf's in Stolp, while Frank was to go to Eslohe, to Omi Ramrath's. I was pulled between wanting to get away from the air raids and not wanting to leave Mother and the babies. I had promised to help Mother, and now I felt that I was running away. Added to this was the constant worry that something might happen to my family. I knew this fear would be worse when I wasn't home with them.

Mother saw me struggling. "Look," she said, patting my shoulder, "with you and Frank gone, I'll have two less people to worry about." Seeing my still-skeptical face, she added, "You'll be more useful to me when you come back rested and less nervous and upset all the time. Anyway, Lucie is here to help me with the little ones."

I nodded, somewhat reassured. I had to admit that it might be nice to get away. All my friends were also leaving the city. Annemarie was going to her aunt's in Berchtesgaden, Bavaria. Erika, Renate, and Inge and her sister were all going to relatives in the country. I decided to go.

Father took me by subway to the Anhalter Bahnhof, the train station. We couldn't believe the devastation downtown. Many buildings were just shells, with their outer walls still standing and the insides burnt out. Some had been sheared in half, with bathtubs hanging at crazy angles, iron radiators teetering on the edge, ready to crash down, mirrors still intact here and there on the walls. In some places, shreds of pink and yellow flowered wallpaper provided a touch of color to the gray ruins. I spotted an armless teddy bear sitting forlornly in the debris. I wanted to rescue him, but I realized that Father would think it was silly.

Streets and parks were piled high with twisted metal and rubble, obstacle courses to get through. The once-beautiful city of Berlin was no more. At the Anhalter Bahnhof, with its glass dome shattered, we ran into hordes of people, mainly women and children with armloads of baggage trying to catch any train as long as it was headed out of the city. I became panicky when I saw the crush of people, afraid I would lose Father in the shuffle. He held on tightly to my hand, though, and by pushing and shoving we managed to get close to the tracks.

"I don't want to go," I yelled over the din. But just then a train thundered into the station, and my protest was lost in the screeching brakes of the locomotive.

We were fortunate. The train with many soldiers on board was heading east through Stolp. The crowd stampeded to get on the train. And before I could say good-bye, Father pushed me and my suitcase onto the steps of the train. Bodies crushed behind me. I was terrified of being trampled to death. Somebody shoved me into an already-filled compartment, but seeing that I was alone and close to tears, the inhabitants kindly made room for me. I managed to look out the open window and wave good-bye to Father.

When I saw him standing there, so forlorn in the pushing, shoving crowd, I was overcome with love for him. *Will I ever see him again? Mother? Frank? My baby brother and sister?* As the train pulled out of the station, I watched Father's receding figure through a blur of tears, waving to him until he was just a speck in the distance. I sat down, feeling utterly alone and abandoned. As the train moved through the devastated city, I closed my eyes. I didn't want to see anymore.

Once out of the city, the scenery changed. There was no sign of war anywhere. The peaceful pastures outside the train window soothed me. I found myself perking up as I watched the last rays of sun change the ordinary fields and grazing cows into a Renoir painting with brilliant strokes of gold and emerald green. *Is this the work of the Invisibles?* Everybody in my compartment, soldiers and civilians alike, stopped talking and looked out the windows. I didn't realize until then how empty of color my life had become. I had learned to see the world around me only as shades of gray.

Poor Onkel Adolf had spent practically the whole day at the railroad station, not knowing which train I would be on. The big bald man welcomed me with a broad smile and a bear hug. I was safe.

The city of Stolp had not been ravaged by war. Everything appeared to be the same as it had been two years ago.

Yet, upon closer inspection, I noticed big changes. The city was now flooded with thousands of refugees who had fled from Berlin, Cologne, Hamburg, and other cities that had been bombed. They all tried to find places to live, but housing for these evacuees had become scarce. Many local families were required to take them in, whether they wanted to or not. Changes had also taken place in the apartment above the bank. Ruth-Margot, Tante Mieze and Onkel Adolf's daughter, had moved out. They were still mourning the death of their son, Karl Heinz. But Edit was still there, taking care of the two old people.

My life soon settled into a comfortable routine. Tante Mieze insisted that I go to confession every Saturday evening before receiving communion on Sunday. But I could never think of enough sins to confess to make it worthwhile. I took confession seriously and wanted to be sure that I had indeed remembered all my sins. So I consulted Edit.

"What did I do that was bad this week?" I inquired during Tante Mieze's nap time as I sat on the kitchen table and dangled my legs. I kept my pencil poised over an empty sheet of paper.

"Well, for starters, you stole a cookie from the cookie jar the other day," she contributed helpfully. "I counted them."

"Actually, I took three," I said. I jotted down the sin. "What else?"

"I heard you talk back to your aunt," Edit reminded me.

"But she deserved it," I replied indignantly. "She didn't want me to see Panky again because she's poor. Panky can't help that she's poor."

"Still, it's a sin to talk back to your elders. You have a bad temper."

"Well, all right." I wrote, I lost my temper.

"And what about the kiss Joachim gave you behind the garage the other day?"

"That's not a sin!" I protested. "You do it all the time!"

"But at your age it's different," Edit insisted. "As a child of God, you should be pure and untouched."

Something rebelled in me. *No! Something that is so nice is not a sin. It can't be a sin.*

Hans-Joachim was the fourteen-year-old older son of our janitor. When I had visited Stolp two years before, we had barely greeted each other in passing. I didn't have much use for boys then, thinking they were generally a nuisance—noisy, always showing off, and ready for a fight. My world had consisted mainly of girls. The only boy I had liked was my brother.

But now something had changed. I looked with interest at Hans-Joachim—his good looks, his dark eyes, his sculptured cheekbones. We began to spend time together by tossing a ball to each other, going to the local swimming pool on a hot day, or just talking on the back steps of the bank. He proudly told me that he was no longer in the Jungvolk but now sworn into the Hitler Youth. He was learning how to load and shoot guns and how to throw hand grenades.

"I'm planning to join the Marine Hitler Youth," he said. "That's for guys who're going into the navy. I want to be a commander of a U-boat, a submarine," he declared. "I'll torpedo enemy ships," he added, eyes sparkling.

I told him about my plans of returning to the United States, and about my happy childhood days in Stratford, hunting arrowheads, stealing watermelons, and going on vacations in the Poconos.

One day, Hans-Joachim motioned for me to follow him behind the garage, where we were hidden from view. Somewhat awkwardly, he took me in his arms and kissed me. I was startled, but at the same time curiously pleased. The feel of his lips on mine made my insides quiver—it was not at all a bad feeling. In a flash I realized that something in my life had changed. His kiss somehow made me feel pretty. I had never thought of myself that way before.

After that kiss, we didn't see each other much. Hans-Joachim's Hitler Youth duties took him away from home for long periods, and we didn't have an opportunity to be alone with each other again. I savored the experience like a precious thing, unwrapping it and looking at it again and again when I was alone. I shared it only with Edit and in a letter to Annemarie. From that time on I began to look at boys in a different way.

I did not add the kiss to my confessed sins. Instead I borrowed some from other kids who were standing in line for their turn in the confessional. We all carried slips of paper with our sins listed and passed them back and forth. If I saw one I liked, I added it to mine to make the list more impressive.

The Hitler Youth demanded that when we were thirteen we get our free-swim certificate in preparation for entering the next stage of the BDM. The test included a dive from a five-meter board and at least a jump, but preferably a dive, from a ten-meter board. I enrolled in the swim program at the local pool, which was organized by Hitler Youth boys, and completed both the free-swim portion of the certificate and the dive off the five-meter board.

I prepared to jump from the ten-meter board, which the Hitler Youth considered to be a test of courage. Everybody ahead of me jumped without hesitation. It was my turn. I walked to the tip of the bouncing board and looked down into the dark pool below. I felt light-headed, as if I were standing on top of a skyscraper, looking down. I knew I couldn't do it headfirst. Everything inside me froze.

"I don't want to do this! I can't!" I sobbed out loud.

Below me kids shouted encouragement from either side of the pool. "You can do it!"

The young instructor waved his hands. "Don't be a coward! Don't give up!"

Help me do this, I pleaded to the Invisibles. And then from somewhere deep inside me came a spark of courage. I took a deep breath and jumped, hitting the water partially on my belly. Ignoring the sting on my stomach and face, I smiled to myself with relief and pride as I swam up to the surface. *I did it! I'm not a coward.*

As I surfaced, though, I sensed that something was wrong. The girls were giggling, their eyes downcast, and the boys were laughing instead of applauding as they had all done for the others. I felt a strange coolness across my belly. As I looked down I saw with horror what was left of my red bathing suit floating in the water. I was stark naked.

The impact of my body hitting the water had split the worn old bathing suit from top to bottom. I wanted to die. Somebody threw me a towel, and I struggled to wrap it around my body while treading water. Triumph over the jump had quickly been replaced by shock and embarrassment. I no longer cared about the free-swim certificate and didn't return to the swimming pool after that.

~

One hot day Tante Mieze let me go blueberry picking in the forest with Edit on her day off. The blueberries grew in short bushes and were hard to find and even harder to pick. My back soon ached from the constant leaning, reaching, and bending over. My hands worked the bushes back and forth, lifting and looking, but for each movement, I might be rewarded with only one or two ripe berries. Added to the pain of constantly bending down was the increasing heat, as well as the incessant buzzing and stinging insects.

Edit and I had all but stopped talking as we concentrated on our task. What kept me going was the thought of how surprised and pleased Mother would be when she received the blueberry preserves I planned to make with Edit's help. While I worked and sweated, I pictured the smile on Mother's face as she opened the package from me. *Even Father will be impressed with my efforts at contributing something to the family,* I thought, *and won't Möppi love the sweet berries. Even Baby Elizabeth might be ready to have a taste of juice.* I worked with hardly a break through the afternoon until my basket was finally filled with the treasured berries. I had really accomplished something. Edit promised that the next day we would make the blueberry preserves.

When we got back to Stolp, I put the basket on the kitchen table and took a long bath, nursing my many insect bites and sore muscles. Out on the terrace Tante Mieze and Onkel Adolf were entertaining guests. Later, when I walked into the kitchen to look for something to eat, the basket wasn't on the table. And it wasn't on the counter or in the pantry either. I became hysterical. *Where is it? Could I have misplaced it?* Frantically, I searched in every corner of the kitchen, sure that I had left the basket on the table.

Suddenly a dark suspicion took hold of me. I stormed out on the terrace, and one glance told me what had happened. I spotted the blue remnants of the precious berries in the grown-ups' dessert dishes.

"How could you do that to me?" I screamed. "They were not for you! They were for my family!"

Onkel Adolf tried to console me. "We didn't know the berries were meant for your family. We thought you had brought them back for us."

I glared at Tante Mieze. "I told you before I left that I was picking them for Mother!" I screamed. "I spent all day picking them! You could have asked me first instead of just taking them!"

"My dear, how selfish you are!" Tante Mieze replied coolly. "After all we've done for you. You should be ashamed of yourself. Where's your gratitude?"

I wasn't ashamed of myself. I stormed back to my room and slammed the door. I threw myself on the bed and sobbed uncontrollably, angry and frustrated. A little later Tante Mieze came into my room, bringing several half-eaten sandwiches.

"It's a shame to throw them away," she said. "I thought you might be hungry."

"I don't want them!" I replied. "They have somebody else's *spit* on them." I preferred to go hungry. Exhausted, I finally fell asleep.

Occasionally that summer I got together with Lieschen and her brother Fritz, my friends from two years earlier. They were busy, as both had become enthusiastic Hitler Youth members, involved in lots of organized activities. Whenever possible we played hide-and-seek in the castle. I was happy to find that now I could hide alone in the creepy torture chamber without fear. The real world had become a lot more threatening to me than the unreal world of ghosts and goblins.

One day, while seeking a good hiding place, I stumbled onto a tunnel in the castle dungeon. I had heard that the castle had a secret tunnel that provided an escape route for the castle inhabitants from invading tribes. Many such tunnels led to the sea, where in days of old a ship would wait to carry the feudal lord and his entourage to safety. This tunnel was spooky in the semidarkness, with long shadows cast by lights far behind me. It was very quiet. I could hear only the *drip, drip* of moisture running down the walls. I stood still for a moment, listening. *I'm getting out of here,* I thought.

Then I saw something move far ahead of me, deep in the tunnel. *Maybe it's one of the kids hiding there,* I hoped. Gingerly, I peered into the shadows and discovered five very thin, unshaven men in rags huddled together. I don't know who was more startled, they or I. My heart beat wildly. In the dim light the men appeared to be otherworldly. But then one of them whispered in broken German, his finger pressed to his lips, "Please don't scream! If you do, we will die!"

My thoughts raced. *They must be escaped prisoners,* I guessed. *But who are they? Poles? Jews? Russians?*

Just then I heard running footsteps in the hallway above me and voices from the kids who were looking for me. "Eleanor! Where are you? Give us a clue!" echoed through the halls.

Quick! What should I do? For a second I agonized. *Should I scream?* Then I shook my head. "I won't tell!" I whispered. Trembling, I backed away from the men and ran up the stairs to prevent the kids from finding me there.

I told no one about what I had seen, though I knew my decision wasn't without grave risk. These were dangerous times. Posters and radio announcements constantly reminded us that we were forbidden, under penalty of death, to harbor fugitives or to help them escape. Every Hitler Youth was sworn to report to the Gestapo any information about prison escapees.

My biggest fear was that somebody would discover my secret just by looking into my face.

"Your face is like an open book, Eleanor," Mother had said once. "It tells me everything."

Can others, like the Gestapo, read my face as well?

I pushed the memory of this strange encounter deep down into the dark interior of my being, where I covered it up with all kinds of other thoughts and happenings. There it remained as something ghostly, something barely remembered and never touched. After that experience the castle appeared sinister to me. I didn't want to play there anymore.

~

Onkel Adolf, because of his position as Reichsbank Director, had certain privileges. One was to have a table in the dining room at the railroad station hotel permanently held for him. A reserved sign always sat in the center of his table; nobody else could use it. He often sat there with colleagues or with city leaders, discussing important issues. Sometimes he used the table to invite private or business guests to dinner. Other times he just liked to sit there with a glass of beer and enjoy a cigar.

On occasion he invited me to join him at the table. I loved those times. As the grandniece of the Reichsbank Director, the maître d', the waiters, and even Onkel's guests treated me with all the respect and attention of the privileged. I felt quite grown up. Through the window by the table I could watch the activities of the busy railroad station.

One afternoon late in the summer, I had just finished eating with Onkel when a colleague of his entered the restaurant. The man sat down at our table and soon the two were deep in conversation, ignoring my presence. I knew it would be a while before Onkel was ready to go home, so I excused myself and walked out onto the train platform. It was teeming with refugees, irritable mothers and cranky children sitting on suitcases, soldiers, old men, and women standing four or five rows deep, impatiently waiting for a train to arrive. If the trains originated in heavily bombed cities, there were often long delays. I wondered where these people were going. Everybody looked stressed and unhappy.

Two years before, I recalled, the scene had been different. Happy people had thronged the platform then. Children had jumped up and down at the sight of visiting grandparents, aunts, and uncles, and people made tearful good-byes, waving handkerchiefs and blowing kisses to those leaving or going away on vacation.

The mournful wail of a locomotive whistle interrupted my thoughts. Immediately life jumped into the waiting crowd, and the pushing and shoving began. Everybody was trying to get closer to the train. As the engine thundered toward the station, a man in soldier's uniform standing next to me suddenly pushed his way through the crowd and ran out onto the tracks. I heard a scream and shouts from the people closest to the tracks, and I stood on tiptoes and stretched my neck to see what was happening. As the throngs shifted some more, I caught a glimpse of the man as he knelt down and put his head on the tracks. The brakes gave a terrible screech. The engineer tried to stop, but it was too late. The locomotive ran over the man's neck and severed his head from his body. I stared at the side of the monstrous black locomotive as it moved past us, seeing the words that were then painted on all trains, WHEELS MUST ROLL FOR VICTORY. But incredibly, on this engine, someone had crossed out the word WHEELS and replaced it with HEADS.

For a long time after that, the man's mangled head stared at me in my dreams, as though it wanted to tell me something. I brooded endlessly about the man. *Why did he take his life when I am trying hard to stay alive? Did he lose his family? Why die in such a grisly way? Is he an angel now, even without his head?*

The danger of war had reached Stolp, my refuge. I dreaded the daily reports on the radio of heavy bombings over major cities in Germany. Of course, I was particularly attuned to the mention of Berlin. "All areas in the southern part of Berlin heavily damaged, Lankwitz, Südende, and Steglitz," the merciless voice blasted.

My anxiety became unbearable. Life in between broadcasts and news from home was torture. At night, especially, my imagination worked against me. I saw Mother and Father crushed beneath the house, Baby Elizabeth suffocated from the dust and debris, and Möppi crying because he was alone. I cried myself to sleep over these terrible images and begged Mother in letters to let me return home. But she told me to stay at least until the end of August.

My constant worry and anxiety took its toll. I became listless and depressed, not interested in anything. Then one day, toward the end of August, I heard that Dr. Goebbels, Minister of Propaganda, had commanded a mass evacuation of women and children from Berlin. All schools were to be closed. The work force, however, was ordered to remain in the city at their jobs. Immediately I pleaded with Tante Mieze and Onkel Adolf to invite Mother, Frank, and the two babies to Stolp.

"Look," I said, trying to sound as convincing as possible, "if you don't have your own flesh and blood live with you, the authorities will put perfect strangers in your apartment. Do you want that?"

They knew very well that it was only a matter of time before the government would confiscate a number of their rooms to meet the housing needs of the ever-increasing number of refugees. I understood that it wasn't an easy decision for these two old people to make. Five extra people would bring noise and disruption into their home. But they finally agreed. *I must be the happiest girl in the whole world*, I rejoiced, and hugged them gratefully.

On the day when Mother had written that they would arrive, I went to the railroad station early, determined not to miss a single train. I didn't know which one they would find room on, but I was so excited that I didn't mind waiting. I paced the platform, deliberately not looking at the spot on the tracks where the man had lost his head. Several trains later, Mother emerged from the train carrying a clothes basket with three-month-old "Bassi"—as Möppi called her because he wasn't able to say Elizabeth—and a delighted Möppi jumping off the train into my open arms.

Mother and our babies were with me, safe, away from all of the bombs. And Frank was due to arrive in Stolp from Eslohe in the middle of September. Mother looked thin and tired. I knew it had been hard on her to leave Father to cope with the cooking, shopping, and loneliness that was sure to come in our absence. Added to this, of course, was her constant worry for his life. I vowed to be more helpful to Mother now and less selfish than I had been before.

Although she worried about Father, Mother relaxed a little in Stolp, often sitting and talking to Tante Mieze and Onkel Adolf while I happily entertained the babies. The grown-ups never talked now about winning the war. Their conversations were more about how and when it would end and what horrors were in store for everybody after that.

CHAPTER NINE

MOVE TO WALDENBURG

WINTER 1943–SUMMER 1944

WHILE FALL GAVE WAY to winter in Stolp, an Allied round-the-clock bombing offensive began over Berlin. And as air raids over Berlin intensified, so did our fear for Father's life. We were safe in Stolp, but he had to remain in Berlin, living in our apartment and going to work all the way over in Oberschöneweide, in the southeastern part of Berlin.

Whenever possible, Father tried to visit us on weekends. But train travel was becoming more and more difficult as so many train tracks and stations were being bombed. It often took many days to repair the damage. Those trains that were running mostly transported troops to the front line and brought back the wounded and dying.

After a time Father's visits became fewer and fewer. But when he did come, I felt as if we were a family again. We took long walks in the parks around Stolp, and for a brief time we forgot that we were in the middle of a raging war.

That winter I took a class in doll making. Mother gave me an old dark brown woolen stocking that had been mended too often to wear anymore, and Tante Mieze offered some colorful rags. I threw myself into the task of making a doll for Bassi for Christmas. I followed a pattern to cut out the doll, then stitched the pieces together by hand and stuffed it with rags. The result was a funny little chocolate brown dolly. It had a wild mop of bright yellow wool hair, blue stitched eyes, two black dots for a nose, a pouty red mouth, and a blue checkered dress covering a square little body. I was proud of my masterpiece and couldn't wait until Christmas to see Bassi's expression when she saw the gift. I named her Gretel, after a doll the Münster Grossmutter had sent me for Christmas years ago in Stratford.

I also began to keep a diary, and I took up painting in watercolors. I went to school and made new friends, but I had little free time to play with them. I now had to spend much of my time taking Tommy, who was almost two years old, and baby Bassi for walks after school to give Mother a break.

One day, after a snowfall, the temperature remained below freezing. Before our walk, I wrapped Bassi warmly in a blanket and put her on a sled. Unfortunately, in my zeal to protect her from the cold, I wrapped her up so tightly, with her arms tucked inside the blanket, that when the sled shifted over a bump in the street, Bassi couldn't keep her balance. She toppled over backward and smacked her head on the frozen ground, screaming bloody murder. I was terrified that she might have a concussion and die. I picked her up and held her in my arms, trying to soothe her. *Oh, it's all my fault!* I agonized. *She'll die because I was so careless.*

By the time we got home, Bassi had stopped crying. I didn't say anything about the accident to Mother for fear she would be angry and disappointed with me. Anxiously I hovered over the baby that evening, feeling guilty for not telling Mother and for causing the accident in the first place.

Bassi slept in her crib next to my bed, but I didn't sleep at all as I lay listening to every whimper from her. I knew that not telling Mother was a kind of lie, and I agonized over it. "Lying makes the angels cry," Grossmutter had told me once. When I did sleep I saw the Invisibles as they covered their faces and wept on account of my recklessness and deceit, their wings drooping in sadness. When Bassi stirred and woke me up in the night, I thought about the heroes I had so wanted to be like. I decided that I would be courageous and tell Mother. I only hoped that she was in a good mood.

The next morning I was overwhelmed with guilt about not confessing the incident. But Bassi was standing in her crib, jumping up and down, ready to be lifted out. She didn't even have a bump or bruise to show for her fall from the sled. *Bassi's okay!* I rejoiced. *She's not hurt. Boy, am I lucky.* But I approached Mother anyway as she was dressing Bassi. "Mother," I said timidly, "I have something to tell you."

She looked up at me as she placed the baby on the floor. "What is it?" she said, bracing her hands on her back and straightening up. "Stop fidgeting like that, Eleanor. Out with it."

I told her the whole sad story: the accident, the sleepless night, and the terrible guilt I felt. She listened with an occasional glance at Bassi, who was trying to reach a toy. Mother's eyes, I was surprised to note, showed no anger.

"I'm glad you told me," she said mildly. "Accidents happen, but you must always tell me about them." She paused and looked at me. "I see you've learned your lesson, so we don't need to talk about it anymore."

I nodded, then flung myself at Mother and hugged her. I was so relieved. *Bassi seems fine, and I haven't failed Mother.* I loved Mother so much, it was easy to promise that I would never again keep something like this from her.

Things were not going well between Mother and Tante Mieze. Tante Mieze wasn't used to the unrest and chaos that children—four of us now—brought into her well-ordered life. She complained a lot and was constantly correcting our manners. Mother couldn't do much to ease the tense situation. She was often irritable herself and short-tempered with us, her eyes flashing danger signals. Frank and I tiptoed around trying to avoid her wrath.

Because of Tante Mieze's constant complaining, Mother began to take us to eat our meals at a local soup kitchen for refugees. Buses and streetcars were often overcrowded with the many refugees in the city, so walking to the soup kitchen often seemed the better choice. It wasn't easy to get everybody dressed in warm clothes and to walk three times a day through ice and snow with the babies, but we did it.

Once we arrived at the soup kitchen, we had to stand in endless lines to get food and find enough seats at the long, narrow wooden tables. The little ones became fussy with impatience and hunger. It seemed that everyone at the canteen, the servers and refugees alike, was irritable and in a bad mood, pushing and shoving and yelling at each other. The air in the room was rancid with the smell of unwashed bodies, wet overcoats and shoes, and the strong odor of cooking cabbage. I could tell by Mother's wrinkled nose that she hated the place. Going there did nothing to improve her dark mood.

Despite the constant tension in the household, my usual excitement and anticipation of Christmas, my favorite holiday, would not be squelched. For weeks I had been busy making little gifts, singing Christmas carols to myself, and telling Tommy stories of how our Münster Grossmutter had a special relationship with Heaven and how she helped the angels bake at Christmastime. To prove it, I showed him the orange sky at sunset.

On the sixth of December, St. Nikolaus day, I put Tommy's shoe on the windowsill with a piece of dry bread in it. I explained to him, "Tonight, St. Nikolaus will ride by on his donkey. The bread is for the hungry donkey." Tommy's eyes grew wide. "If you are a good boy," I went on, "St. Nikolaus will leave something very special for you." I took him on my lap and hugged him. "And we all know you are a good boy. Right?" He nodded vigorously. I didn't tell him about the switch St. Nikolaus leaves for bad boys. I always hated that part of the story. Tommy's squeal of joy the next morning when he discovered a small piece of chocolate in his shoe reminded me how much I had missed fun and laughter.

I made an advent wreath from pine boughs I broke off trees in the park. On the four Sundays before Christmas, we lit a candle on the wreath. During those weeks I also scanned the stores for Christmas gifts. I had little money, and the stores offered little merchandise. But in one store I saw a white porcelain elephant that shimmered in all colors of the rainbow when held up to the light. I thought it was the most beautiful thing I had ever seen. *Wouldn't Mother love this?* I thought. It cost all the money I had, but I didn't mind.

The best part of Christmas 1943 was that Father managed to be with us. With his arrival, Mother became much happier. She rarely even complained about the soup kitchen. When Christmas Eve arrived, it carried the same sense of mystery I had always felt. After church, we gathered around the tree that Onkel Adolf had managed to find for us and that Frank and I had decorated with Tante Mieze's ornaments and wax candles. We sang "Silent Night" slowly, reverently. I heard the whisperlike flutter of the wings of the Invisibles. They were so close that I felt I could reach up and almost touch them.

As I looked around the room at everybody I loved, safe, out of harm's way, I thought I would die with sheer happiness. There wasn't a single worry lurking inside me. A tremendous, smothering burden had been lifted, and I could breathe freely once again.

Mother was delighted with the glazed elephant. "It's truly the best present I ever had," she said, stroking the silky finish.

And Father was pleased with the poem I wrote for him. He put an arm around my shoulder and squeezed it. "You're getting so big," he said.

I was proud that he thought I was growing up. I didn't know if anyone besides me had noticed.

I gave Tante Mieze a stitchery. Unfortunately, it turned out bumpy and uneven on the reverse side. I knew my needlework teacher in Berlin would not have been pleased with it, and I'm not sure Tante Mieze was either.

But the most rewarding event of that Christmas was Bassi's delighted giggles as she reached for the funny little brown doll. To her the doll had no flaws.

Filled with so much happiness, I wrote in my Poesie album:

> *Love is an invisible angel*
> *Who lives inside me.*
> *She shines through me and*
> *Brightens the dark world.*

A few days later Father returned to his job in Berlin. Shortly afterward, he wrote to Mother.

> *Dear Mathilde,*
> *This city is a terrible place to be. It's cold and dreary and hopeless, with ruins everywhere and so many sad, homeless people shuffling down the streets with bundles on their backs and no place to go. Our apartment house, thank God, is still standing. For how long, though? The nightly air raids continue. I don't know when I'll see you again. I miss you so much.*
> *Joe*

The peace I'd felt at Christmas vanished. My old fears of losing family members—this time, Father—burrowed deep in my gut once again.

Just before New Year's, changes began to happen rapidly in our family. We were moving again. Our relatives the Mettners had a small apartment in Waldenburg in Silesia. Waldenburg was not far from the border of Poland to the east and to the west it was near the Sudetenland, which Hitler had annexed in 1938. The Mettners were leaving the apartment because Herr Mettner had been drafted into the army, and Frau Mettner wanted to take their children to Breslau to be with her mother.

We could not go to live with Grossmutter and Grossvater in Münster or to live with Omi in Eslohe because neither house had room for us. Other relatives were already living with them. Since vacant apartments were quickly snapped up by refugees from other bombed-out cities, Mother knew she had to quickly accept the Mettners' invitation for us to live in the Waldenburg apartment. It was the solution to our problems with Tante Mieze. Even though the apartment was small, it would be a place of our own.

To avoid losing the apartment, we left Stolp on New Year's Day 1944. Somehow we managed to squeeze on a train in the direction of Danzig, through the Polish corridor, to Breslau, and eventually arrived in Waldenburg. A trip that would not have taken more than four hours in peacetime took all day, with many stops and delays.

It was freezing cold when we arrived, below zero and with a biting wind. We were on the very edge of German soil, where winters were known to be harsh and relentlessly cold. Waldenburg nestled near the foot of the Schneekoppe, the highest point in the Riesengebirge, a mountain range named for its giant peaks, famous before the war for its winter sports. I recalled from my studies that the main city of Silesia was Breslau, a large, important industrial and cultural center. Mother's cousin, Maria Koppe, lived there with her husband and two children.

Waldenburg was a small coal-mining town, isolated by mountains and forests on all sides. Most of the houses were built on mountainsides, with schools, stores, and the hospital below in the valley. From the railroad station we struggled up a steep hill through snow and ice, carrying Bassi and half dragging Möppi and all our luggage to the house on Pflugstrasse 13. The house had two apartments. The landlady lived in the lower one, and we had the upper one.

It was a tiny place—with one bedroom, a dining room, living room, kitchen, and bath—but it was ours. And we no longer had to listen to Tante Mieze's complaints. Off the living room was a small fenced-in balcony with a view of the forest climbing up the slope behind the house. It would serve as a perfect playpen for Bassi once the weather grew warmer. From the front windows we could look down into the valley and at the mountains beyond. The property had a garden in the back where Möppi could play with his new friend, Giese, the landlady's little daughter who was the same age.

We were forever walking and carrying in Waldenburg. Every morning either Frank or I had to go down into the valley with a milk can, stand in line for milk, then lug the heavy can back up the hill. It was the same for groceries. And trudging through the valley and up another hill to school was exhausting, especially when the weather was bad. The freezing wind whipped through my worn jacket, and my wool stockings weren't much protection. Heavy snow often slowed us down, but the cleared roads were just as difficult, with icy patches making it very hard to go up or down a hill. Some of the children, if they were lucky, went to school by sled or on skis.

After we had become settled in Waldenburg, Frank went to Berlin to see Father for a few days. When he returned he told us that Father had gotten himself into trouble again. "During an air raid," Frank explained, "Father and I ran into the subway station with lots of other people from our building and the neighborhood. Everybody was cranky. Father began to grumble, 'This whole thing is so stupid. The war is lost anyway. Why keep on with it?'"

Mother put a hand to her mouth and sat down hard on the kitchen chair.

Frank continued. "A Gestapo officer appeared out of nowhere. He stood in front of Father and barked, 'Papers!' Father turned pale and, with shaking hands, gave his identification papers to the officer. After studying them for a long time, the Gestapo officer said, 'I'm arresting you for defeatist talk.'"

"Oh no!" Mother moaned, her face very pale.

"Herr Kries and his wife stood up next to father," Frank said. "Frau Kries spoke quietly but firmly. 'My husband, who is retired from the Berlin police, and I know this man very well, officer. He's no defeatist. He's depressed because his wife and family are gone. He simply wasn't in control of himself when he made those remarks.'

"'Yes,' Herr Kries added, looking right into the officer's eyes. 'We can vouch for him.' The Gestapo officer hesitated, glaring at Father. We all held our breath, wondering if he would take Father away. The officer thrust the papers back at Father and without a word turned on his heel and strutted away. Father, the Krieses, and I looked at each other, and collapsed on our bags."

Mother stood up quickly, her eyes flashing. "When will he *learn?*" she said, then grabbed the bag of potatoes off the table and carried them to the sink, her back turned to us.

～

I finally resigned myself to the fact that although I often desperately wished for things to remain the same in my life, nothing ever did. This was my sixth school change in five years. Adjusting to the new school in

Waldenburg wasn't any easier than it had been at the previous schools. The old feelings of inferiority followed me here too. Each time my teacher and classmates discussed things that were unfamiliar to me, I realized how many gaps existed in my education because of my many school changes.

I was forever afraid that I might have to repeat a grade. When it was time to receive report cards, I became anxious. I didn't want to disappoint my parents. Even though I continued to study as hard as I could, my grades still never met their expectations. But somehow, thankfully, I always managed to squeak through into the next grade.

At school I met a new friend, Helga. She was a refugee from Hamburg. Her father had been missing in action for some time, and now she and her mother and sisters, Renate and Iris, lived in one room at the police headquarters in town. Many of the rooms at the police station had been confiscated to house the ever-increasing homeless population.

Helga and I met two boys our own age, Hans and Ernst, brothers who lived in the police building and whose father was the janitor of the building. Hans became my boyfriend and Ernst was Helga's. It was exciting to have a boyfriend. When I was alone with Hans, I felt the same kind of strange delight I had with Hans-Joachim in Stolp. After hours, when the police headquarters closed and most of the lights were turned off, we raced through the endless maze of corridors, hiding under staircases and in dark corners, stealing a kiss here and there.

Iris, Helga's baby sister, was the same age as Bassi. We liked getting the two little girls together to play. Bassi was quickly growing into a rugged little girl, almost a year old now. She was a serious child and didn't laugh very often, but when she did it was a reward worth waiting for. She also had an incredibly stubborn streak. One warm, early spring day I took Tommy and Bassi to the park. When it was time to go home, Bassi refused to leave. She threw herself screaming on the ground, and no coaxing or threatening could make her stop. When I picked her up, she made herself stiff as a board. Red-faced and embarrassed, I carried the stiff, screaming child through the streets, while pushing the stroller and dragging Tommy along.

Bassi always slept with a mangy-looking stuffed dog. Through so much love, the animal had lost most of its fur and stuffing and had gone from white to dirty gray. Mother wanted to wash it, but Bassi would not be separated from it long enough to wash and dry it. I had hoped the little doll I had made for her would take the place of the dog, but she was set on having that particular dog.

One night when I put her to bed, the dog was missing. She cried and cried and would not go to sleep. The whole family frantically turned the place upside-down looking for it. One of us hit on the idea that it might have dropped between the railings of the balcony to the garden below. It was dark and wet outside. Frank scoured the garden with a flashlight and finally found the missing dog in the bushes, soaking wet, covered with mud, and half frozen. He carried the dog to Bassi, holding it between thumb and forefinger. When she saw it, she broke into one of her rare smiles. Eagerly she reached for the mess and pulled it close to her, dropping off to sleep with a final sob, still clutching the beloved dog. We looked at each other and laughed.

The Armed Services broadcasts continued to bring frightening news from Berlin. In May we heard, "British terror flights continue heavy attacks on the Reichs capital. Under protection of clouds, high explosive, incendiary, and phosphor bombs were dropped in great numbers. Many city areas were heavily damaged, particularly homes, churches, hospitals, and cultural centers. The population suffered severe losses."

Usually Father called or sent a telegram after a particularly heavy air raid. This time several weeks passed without news from him, and we became frantic, especially Mother. "What will I do without your father?" she agonized, pacing the floor. "How can I support us?" Then she announced, "I can't take it anymore. I'm going to Berlin to see if your Father is still alive." And before we could say anything, she continued, "Frank will go with me. Eleanor," she turned to me, "you will stay and take care of the little ones." I was speechless. I wasn't even fourteen years old yet, but I would be responsible for two babies.

I'm glad Mother trusts me enough to leave me alone with Tommy and Bassi. But what if something happens to Mother and Frank? What will I do? Quickly I pushed those thoughts away. Mother needed me now.

She handed me money and ration cards with the warning, "Whatever you do, don't lose the ration cards. They can't be replaced. Without them you go hungry. Understand?" I nodded, my mind a jumble. "We'll be back in four or five days. You have enough ration cards until then."

I tried not to cry when Mother hugged me good-bye. But as I watched her and Frank head for the train station, the tears flowed anyway. *Will I ever see them again?*

Now at least I didn't have to go to school. I threw myself into the task of caring for the babies, washing and changing diapers, cooking, cleaning, and marketing, always with one ear tuned to the radio broadcasts, which were devastating. "Last night another terror raid on Berlin by American bomber squadrons. The civilian population suffered heavy losses of lives and property." I was terrified. The Americans were pounding my city, my family, and my friends with deadly explosives.

The nights were the worst. I lay awake listening to the silence close in around me, broken only by the occasional soft hoot of an owl or the mournful whistle of a train passing through the valley below. Sometimes I thought I could hear the fluttering wings of the Invisibles. *Or is it just the wind in the pine trees outside?* When the loneliness became unbearable, I lifted the sleeping Tommy into my bed and cuddled up to him, feeling his breath on my cheeks.

A whole week passed and I heard no news from Frank or Mother. My money and ration cards were running out. I was beginning to panic. *Surely they have perished,* I fearfully reasoned. *Otherwise I would have heard from them.* I went downstairs to the landlady. "What will I do?" I cried. "I don't have any more ration cards. I'm almost out of money."

She tried to comfort me. "I'm sure they will be back soon, dear."

But I wasn't so sure anymore. After this outburst, I tried to remain calm as I figured out what to do with two babies, no food, and no money. *Under no circumstances will I allow anyone, not even my grandparents, to take the children away from me. I am solely responsible for my little brother and sister now. I'll raise them myself. I'll get a job, earn money. The Invisibles will help me, I'm sure.* Coming up with a plan helped me cope with my panic.

Several nights later, I heard pounding on the front door. When I cautiously opened it I saw a tall man standing in the doorway, covered with soot and dirt. He looked like a chimney sweep, hair singed in places, grinning broadly. Then his features began to look familiar. "Frank!" I cried, throwing myself into his arms, laughing and crying at once. "You're alive! You're here!"

Immediately reading my thoughts, he told me, "Mother and Father are both okay." I slowly exhaled.

"What happened? Why didn't I hear from you?" I cried, pulling him into the kitchen. "I was so worried."

He dropped himself down on a kitchen chair. I stared at his blackened face, amazed at how much he seemed to have grown since he left. *Or had I just not noticed it before?* I wondered. Here he was, just fifteen years old, and overnight he had grown into a man.

I knew he was hungry, so I heated leftover soup for him and spread a slice of bread generously with Mother's precious goose fat, a gift from Onkel Werner, her brother, on his last furlough. She used it only on special occasions and then sparingly, but I decided this was an occasion to celebrate. Frank wolfed down the food. When he finished, I demanded, "Now tell me everything. What happened?"

"Well, when Mother and I got down to the train station," he explained, "we had a hard time getting a train. We waited three hours, until finally we managed to squeeze on one going in the direction of Berlin. It was terribly crowded and we had to sit on our suitcases in the aisle. When we arrived in Berlin, the subway system wasn't working very well. It had been hit in many places. It would stop at a station and we'd all have to get out and walk to the next one." He drank a long gulp of water from his glass.

"And?" I prompted.

He swallowed. "We finally got to Steglitz and, miraculously, our building was still there, although damaged. Father was so surprised and pleased to see us. We helped him with repairs and cleanup and stood in long lines for groceries. In the meantime we had more air raids, even some during the day. The city was burning everywhere. We were without electricity, transportation, and mail delivery, so we couldn't contact you. The subways finally stopped altogether. Father couldn't get to work for a while."

Frank paused again, rubbing his red eyes. "It was clear to us that we couldn't make it back to Waldenburg on time as promised. Mother worried about you. She knew you needed money and ration cards."

I nodded, relieved that Mother had been thinking of me.

"Mother asked me to try to get through to Waldenburg somehow. We knew it wasn't going to be easy. I had to walk to the train station through the burning city, dodging crashing beams and crumbling buildings. The smoke was so thick in places that I could hardly see a few feet ahead of me. The heat and smoke burned my eyes and made me gag and cough. But somehow I made it to the Anhalter station.

"Lucky for me," he went on, "a train was just leaving for the east. It was bursting at the seams with people, but I still managed to push my way through the crowd and find standing room in the aisle." He stopped and smiled, his white teeth glowing in his blackened face. "And here I am! I guess I was just lucky." He placed ration cards and money on the table between us.

I grasped his soot-covered hands that were folded in front of him. We were silent for a few moments.

"I have to go back tomorrow," he suddenly announced.

"No! To Berlin? Why?"

"I have to get back to Mother. She'll need me to help her reach Waldenburg. She can't do it alone."

I knew he was right, but I didn't want him to go. Now my worries would begin all over again.

He tried to reassure me. "Look, in the last few days there haven't been any major air raids over Berlin. And I'm sure they'll have the subways working again by the time I'm home. They usually fix them in a hurry. It'll be a lot easier this time.

"If all goes well, we should both be back in a few days."

Frank stood up, ready to get some sleep before the return trip in the morning. He turned around at the bedroom door, his face troubled. "I haven't told you everything. A terrible thing happened."

A shiver of fear ran over me. "What?" I whispered.

"You remember the Basedow family with all the kids, the Americans?"

"Yes, of course," I replied. "What about them?"

He swallowed hard. "Just before I left Berlin I heard that their apartment house had received a direct hit. Both parents and nine of the twelve children were killed."

"Oh no," I gasped, trembling all over. *But the Basedows were so much like us,* my mind swirled. *We were all Americans. We talked in English to each other and about our desperate longing to return to the United States. That could have been us!* "How?" I sobbed.

"I don't know all the details," Frank explained. "But apparently the whole family was in the cellar, except for two kids who were away—I don't know which ones. The parents were pushing the baby through the cellar window to passing strangers when the ceiling collapsed, crushing the rest of the family to death."

"And the baby?"

"I think the baby made it."

I felt a dreadful stabbing pain around my heart. I was unable to cry. Nothing before had ever frozen my tears this way. Later I lay in bed, tortured by thoughts about the Basedows. *Did they die instantly? Did they slowly suffocate? Did they knock for help and nobody came? Are they now with the Invisibles in Heaven?* I finally drifted into troubled sleep.

Frank left the following morning for Berlin. I was so relieved just by seeing him again and knowing that Mother and Father were alive, that Mother would be coming home soon. I went back to my routine of caring for the little ones. After I heard what had happened to the Basedow children, Tommy and Bassi were more precious to me than ever.

Bassi's and my birthday came and went. I didn't have much food left, certainly nothing to celebrate with, so I just gave Bassi an extra hug.

Frank and Mother returned to Waldenburg a few days later, as promised. But the reunion was dampened by renewed worries over Father's life in Berlin and what tomorrow would bring.

Frank often listened to the BBC on a crystal radio set to find out what was happening in the war. Listening to foreign broadcasts had been strictly forbidden for years. Anyone caught doing this faced a punishment of either a stiff prison sentence in one of the concentration camps where the SS sent people to do backbreaking work, or even death. But the German radio stations and newspapers reported only what the regime wanted us to know, and more often than not, we were learning, German news was badly distorted. Everybody hungered for a connection to the rest of the world, for news, real news, not just the same old propaganda and the latest battle disasters.

On the morning of June 6, 1944, Frank emerged from beneath his blanket, where he had been listening to the BBC, and pulled the earphones out of his ears. He excitedly announced what he had just heard. "Guess what? The Allies have landed in Normandy!"

"Wow! The Allies are back on the continent! But what does it mean?" I asked.

"It means that this is the beginning of the end of the war!"

What wonderful words, "the end of the war." It seemed to me as if the war had been going on forever, but now there might well be an end in sight after all. A tiny voice inside me, however, cautioned, *Not so fast, Eleanor. It isn't time to celebrate yet.*

In mid-July, Frank decided to go to Berlin again to check on Father. When he returned, he was burning to tell us what had happened. "After I saw that Father was coping and that the apartment house was still standing, I went to look for my friends. I found Matthias still living at his uncle's house just outside of Berlin. He invited me to stay with him for a few days. Well, Matthias's uncle warned us that something big was going to happen on July 20 in Berlin, but he wouldn't tell us any more than that."

He cleared his throat, then continued. "So, eager to find out for ourselves, we got on bicycles that day and pedaled back into the city. We couldn't get into the center, though, because all the streets were blocked by soldiers with machine guns. The tension from all the military and civilians there felt like electricity crackling in the air."

"What was going on?" I asked.

"We didn't know, and nobody was talking," Frank replied. "So we returned to the uncle's house. That evening we heard on the radio that one of Hitler's own generals had tried to assassinate him! He had placed a bomb in a briefcase and set it next to Hitler in a meeting! The bomb went off, but Hitler was only slightly injured."

"So why were the soldiers guarding Berlin? Were they part of the group that wanted to take over the government from Hitler?" I asked.

"I think so. They wanted to make sure Hitler's supporters didn't resist the new government."

If only the assassin had succeeded, I thought, *the war would be over now.* I could see that Frank and Mother were thinking the same thing.

For weeks we heard reports on Frank's radio about arrests and executions. Those who had plotted against Hitler were quickly identified and executed. And thousands of their friends and relatives were killed or sent to prison. Hitler called these arrests and executions Säuberungsaktionen, cleaning-up actions.

As we listened to these reports, Frank worried, "What will happen to Matthias's uncle? I hope nobody finds out that he knew about the plot." Then he said, "What if they find out that he told Matthias and me?"

By the end of July an order from Goebbels was repeatedly broadcast on the Armed Forces radio and plastered on signs all over town. No more travel by civilians except with special permission! For us this meant that Father could no longer visit us, and Frank's travels to Berlin had come to an end.

CHAPTER
TEN

WALDENBURG
LATE SUMMER 1944 – WINTER 1944/45

BY LATE SUMMER 1944, we were no longer alone in the apartment. Mother's cousin, Maria Koppe, had been bombed out in Breslau, so she and her three children came to stay with us for a while. Frank and I groaned at the prospect of so many of us living so closely together, but we knew that we had to help our relatives by taking them in, just as Tante Mieze and Onkel Adolf had done for us. We were soon two adults and seven children in the one-bedroom apartment.

Our landlady offered Mother an attic room, which had been empty for a long time and used for storage. Much to our delight, Frank and I were told that we could live up there. We spent most of the day cleaning out dust and cobwebs, stacking the landlady's things in a corner, and generally fixing up the room to suit our needs. Then we moved in our personal belongings. Twin beds sat just beneath the eaves, and a window to the garden gave a fine view of the forest climbing up the mountain behind the house. We loved having the luxury of a room of our own. That night we snuggled down in our beds, happy about our good fortune.

Some time later I woke up itching here and there on my body. *Probably mosquitoes,* I thought, and dozed off again. But moaning and groaning from Frank's bed pulled me awake again. "What's the matter,

Frank?" I mumbled, thinking he might be having a nightmare, and flicked on the light switch. He was tossing and turning wildly, arms flailing. Just then I became aware of a flaming itch all over my body. *What on earth?* I jumped out of bed and ran over to Frank. "What's going on?"

Frank's face and body were swollen with huge red welts. He could barely see from beneath puffy eyelids. He was panicky, swatting everywhere. "I'm being eaten alive," he moaned. "Bedbugs! The room must be infested with them!" We took one look at each other's red, swollen bodies and faces, and right then, in the middle of the night, we raced downstairs to the crowded apartment below.

The next day Frank said, "*You* go and get our things! The bugs don't like you as much as they do me." I went back up to the creepy room to retrieve our belongings. I was relieved to return to the chaos and lack of privacy in the crowded apartment.

That summer, food was becoming scarcer. Whenever we could buy carrots, we made juice from them for Bassi and Tommy. We collected dandelions and made tea with them and gave it to the children for vitamin C. The dandelion greens were very bitter, so I was always amazed at how the little ones drank the juice without a murmur of protest.

By early fall we could see and hear signs of political changes everywhere. The eastern front was rapidly crumbling. The Soviets were smashing toward Poland, with Berlin as the ultimate goal. Radio reports told us that the Allies had landed in southern France and liberated Paris, Brussels, and Antwerp and that they were penetrating into Germany on the western front. Goebbels told us in one of his many speeches that he had asked the German people, "Do you want total war?" And they had supposedly screamed, "Yes, we want total war!" But I could not imagine who would have said such a thing. Everybody I knew was sick and tired of war. They wanted it to end one way or the other.

Even here in the small, secluded town of Waldenburg we were beginning to feel the storm of war fast approaching. Occasionally our town was strafed by low-flying Soviet planes. If we were outdoors when that happened, we quickly dropped to the ground while bullets popped around us. Fortunately, it didn't happen very often.

Boys from age seventeen and men over sixty were called up to the Volkssturm, People's Army, to defend Germany. They were given uniforms and drilled in shooting and in throwing hand grenades. Schools in Waldenburg closed. Boys from fourteen to sixteen were ordered by the Hitler Youth to report to the marketplace to be recruited to do their duty for the Fatherland. Frank and his buddies, including the landlady's son, were given physical exams and the next day were sent to a camp in Kleinulbersdorf, close to the Polish border, to dig tank trenches for Unternehmen Barthold, Project Barthold. Hans and Ernst of the Police Presidium were also called up. They all said that the work was backbreaking and food was scarce. Frank wrote to us that sometimes the boys stole potatoes from the farm fields and ate them raw. This theft was considered a crime, though, and the boys were severely punished if caught.

It was soon clear to Frank that this was a fanatical Nazi camp. He repeatedly heard things like, "If Germany is to win this war, we have to get rid of these ridiculous Christian inhibitions and restraints and take the Gestapo [the German KGB] methods as role models instead." Frank confessed to me that he suspected these radical leaders were about to give the boys rifles and grenades and order them to defend the ditches against the advancing Soviet Red Army. We knew that would be a sure death sentence.

Frank had no intention of giving up his life for the Führer, the Fatherland, and a regime he did not believe in. He was American, and his loyalty was with America. For days he struggled to come up with a plan to get out of this clearly dangerous and fruitless situation. One day he heard that one of the other boys was being sent to Berlin as a courier. Frank asked the boy, "Could you do me a favor and take along a letter to my father? He lives in Berlin." The boy agreed. In the letter Frank asked Father to send a telegram to the camp commander requesting a weekend furlough for Frank because Father was coming to Waldenburg for a visit.

The plan worked. A few days later Frank was called into the commander's office. Frank could tell by the unpleasant expression on the man's face and the way he barked at him and called him names that he was displeased. Frank thought perhaps he was mad at him for giving a sloppy Hitler salute, and was afraid the commander might not let him go home. So Frank quickly stepped outside the office again and re-entered, clicking his heels and saluting smartly, "Heil Hitler!" And with relief he noticed that the commander seemed to relax and become less antagonistic.

"Be back here Monday morning, early," the commander growled, eyeing Frank coldly.

Frank said, "Thank you, sir," saluted again, and left, relieved that he was going home.

Frank had to walk two hours before reaching a railroad station and then waited for hours for a train to appear. He had begun to feel very ill. By the time he finally made it up the steep hill to our home in Waldenburg, he was in bad shape. He was completely exhausted, undernourished, and had developed a high fever and chills. A scary red line crept up his forearm. Alarmed, Mother took him immediately to a doctor who was a friend of the family. Frank, it turned out, had developed blood poisoning in addition to severe allergies from sleeping at night on rotten straw in a barn. The doctor, a lung specialist, wrote out a medical certificate to the commander, stating that Frank was "under suspicion of tuberculosis" and could no longer work at hard labor. To our great relief he was exempted from having to return for duty.

However, after Frank's return to Waldenburg, he was conscripted to work in the I. G. Farbenwerk, a chemical factory, where most of his coworkers were captured foreigners. These people were mostly Frenchmen, Poles, Russians, Ukrainians, and Eastern Jews. There were few Germans. Every day these people were brought to the factory from a nearby work camp.

"Today for the first time," Frank told me shortly after he had begun working in the factory, "I saw with my own eyes the cruelty of the SS guards and how horribly they treat their prisoners." Frank shook his head. "One man accidentally marched left instead of right as he had been ordered to do. Maybe he was too tired to care. Anyway, a guard clubbed the poor man on his head with a rifle butt until he collapsed into a bleeding heap."

Frank was glad when the approaching Russians soon forced the factory to shut down.

In late fall, Mother received an alarming letter from Father.

> *Dear Mathilde,*
>
> *I'm sorry to tell you that the AEG fired me under orders of the Gestapo because of something I said. I saw a newspaper ad showing Reichsmarschall Herman Goering drinking soda water and I joked with a co-worker, saying, 'No wonder Goering is so bloated. I would be too if I drank that stuff.' Of course, I knew it is forbidden to make fun of any leader in Hitler's regime, but many of us speak that way in private. I forgot how public the office is. Someone in the office denounced me to the Gestapo as an American spy.*
>
> *The Gestapo arrested and interrogated me at its headquarters. I was petrified. But thankfully, Dr. Biermans again spoke up for me, and the Gestapo found no evidence supporting the spying charge. But the Gestapo insisted that Dr. Biermans fire me.*
>
> *All is not lost, though. Dr. Biermans has arranged for me to keep working, as long as I don't set foot on AEG property. I meet him at the gate a couple of times a week. He hands me work and I give him my completed projects.*
>
> *Actually, I'm rather pleased with this new arrangement because the air-raid damage to the streets and the subway has made it difficult to get to work regularly every day. I'm glad I no longer have to worry about air raids while I'm going to and from work.*
>
> *Joe*

After Mother finished reading, she became angry. "That man is going to land us all in a concentration camp yet, with his big mouth," she said with fear and disgust. "I don't know if he'll ever learn to keep quiet!"

Thankfully Father still had a job and income. We were lucky. Many other families had no money. Many had lost family members. I prayed to the Invisibles to keep watch over all of us, especially Tommy and Bassi, who couldn't look out for themselves.

Raising Tommy, who was now two and a half, and little Bassi, fourteen months old, continued to take most of Mother's and my time and effort. They were headstrong little children.

On one of our daily excursions to get food, Mother and I took along the two little ones in the baby carriage. Tommy was restless, so I took him out of the carriage and held him by the hand as he walked. Bassi was bouncing up and down in the carriage, safely harnessed so she couldn't fall out. We parked the carriage just outside a store while Mother, Tommy, and I went inside.

Suddenly we heard loud screams and shrieks, so we dashed outside. The carriage had tipped over, and Bassi had landed with her mouth on the carriage handle, pushing her lower teeth straight out. Blood was all over her lip and chin, and she was screaming. Tommy began screaming as well. People crowded around, and I began to panic, recalling Frank's similar accident years earlier. Little Bassi couldn't understand why she was feeling so much pain.

Mother calmly and quickly unfastened the baby and pressed her teeth firmly back into place, holding them there with her fingers. She ordered me to take Tommy and push the carriage home. Several hours later the four of us were seated on a train to Breslau to see a dental surgeon. Going to Breslau was risky. Because of its industrial importance, the city was being bombed regularly. But fortunately, the city was spared a bombing raid that day.

When we arrived, the dentist looked at Bassi and then turned to Mother. "You saved the baby's teeth by your fast action," he praised her. "There's nothing more I can do. Had you not pushed them back into place or if you had waited for a few hours to do so, the teeth would have died."

～

Whenever possible, Helga, Ruth Wilner—another new girl I had met—and I got together for what we called a coffee circle, only we didn't have real coffee because it was no longer available. Instead we drank ersatz made from bitter hickory nuts. We mended clothes while we talked. Our clothes, and those of our families, were falling apart and could not be replaced, so we had to repair every hole and worn spot.

The long brown woolen stockings had followed me from Berlin to Stolp and now to Waldenburg. Tommy's were the worst. He played roughly and was always falling down and scraping holes in the knees of his stockings. I was now mending what had already been mended at least twice before.

"I hate these things," I sighed to my friends. "Someday, when I'm back in America, I'm never going to mend anything again in my whole life."

"And I'm sick and tired of wearing the same old dresses," Helga complained. "I've gotten so skinny that they don't even fit me anymore."

"What I hate are the shoes," said Ruth, looking down at the wooden soles and ersatz tops that looked and felt like thin vinyl. "Clodhoppers!"

"Not exactly for ballroom dancing," we agreed and laughed at the image it conjured up. We talked about and dreamed of pretty new dresses, real leather shoes, silk stockings, and cashmere sweaters.

Helga became quiet. Then she asked, "Do you think we'll still win the war?"

"Hitler promised wonder weapons," Ruth replied.

I didn't say anything because I didn't want them to know I was rooting for the Allies. My friends had readily accepted me as an American, but still I preferred not to tell them my hopes that Germany would lose the war. Father's recent carelessness reminded me all too well how dangerous it could be to voice an opinion.

In November 1944, one of my family's worst nightmares came true: Frank received an induction notice from the military. Mother was aghast. It didn't take much imagination to know that the boys drafted so late in the war had little chance of survival— they were cynically called cannon fodder. The late recruits received little training and were no match against the Allies' seasoned soldiers.

Mother insisted on going along with Frank to Army headquarters, where young soldiers with arms and legs blown off were serving as recruiters. She bombarded the surprised soldiers. "This is an American citizen!" she shouted. "He can't be drafted. If the Americans find him in the German army, he will be tried and executed for treason. Do you want that?" she demanded. "And besides, he's only fifteen years old!"

This was a situation the startled recruiters didn't seem to have come across in their military training, and they weren't sure how to handle it. For lack of any guidance, they let Frank go. I liked to think it was because they wished to spare Frank's life. But I thought it more likely that Mother's manner too closely resembled that of the drill sergeants they had learned long ago to obey without question. Whatever the reason, Frank was spared involvement in the war. Had he been drafted, he would probably have perished.

By December it was clear that little could be done to stem the Soviet tide that was flooding westward into Germany and toward us. The war was quickly coming home to German soil. Refugees of German descent and those from eastern countries like Latvia, Romania, Hungary, and Poland who feared Communist takeover poured in great masses across the mountains into Waldenburg on their way west. They knew that if the Soviets caught up to them, they would be sent to prison camps or deported to forced labor brigades, or would be tortured or even executed.

The pitiful group of mostly women, children, babies, and very old people were half frozen and exhausted, pulling or pushing makeshift carts and baby carriages with all their belongings piled high on top. Many had walked hundreds of miles through icy wind and weather. They came with stories of being driven from their homes in the middle of the night, of farms and land burned, of hunger, of rape, brutality, and death. They were fleeing from the Russian hordes who often overtook them on the road.

School buildings in Waldenburg were confiscated to house and attempt to feed the great influx of people. We BDM girls were ordered to help. While tending to the refugees one day, I noticed a woman sitting on the floor, rocking her baby for hours. Her eyes looked vacant, and she seemed detached, beyond pain. Her baby never cried or made a sound. I walked over to her and offered to rock the baby for a while. She didn't protest as I lifted the bundle into my arms. When I opened the blanket I discovered that the baby was dead and already stiff.

I was surrounded by so much misery, I hardly knew where to begin to try and help. There was no adult to guide us, so we just followed our instincts. This child needed to be washed, this one fed, that one comforted. One little boy, perhaps three or four years old, ran around the room, crying, "Mama! Mama!" Somebody told me his mother had collapsed and died by the side of the road. Friends had taken the orphaned boy with them. "He doesn't understand. He keeps thinking he's going to find her," the motherly friend said when I took the crying child to her.

In every child I saw Bassi and Tommy. In every old person I saw my beloved Omi, Grossmutter, or Grossvater. On occasion I caught reassuring glimpses of Helga and Ruth across the room, absorbed in similar tasks. I knew I had to be strong. I worked all day, and at dusk I climbed the hill to our apartment. In the distance, somewhere eastward across the mountains, echoed the *vroom-boom, boom* of artillery fire.

At night, physically exhausted and emotionally spent, I crept into bed, glad to have Tommy or Bassi next to me to cuddle up to for comfort. Nightmares haunted me. I dreamt of frozen babies and of babies crushed beneath houses. I dreamt of children running through the streets crying for their mothers. Sometimes they looked like Tommy. And I woke up, heart pounding, relieved to find him asleep beside me. I made a final entry in my Poesie album.

> *To reach for happiness*
> *Doesn't belong to me anymore*
> *It belongs to the child*
> *And the child is no more.*

Winter arrived Siberian cold, made worse by the lack of coal for civilians. Almost all of the coal was now going to the war effort. Warm clothing and boots were almost impossible to get. We had mended every item of clothing that could be repaired, and most of our clothing was threadbare. Now I was glad I still had the warm wool leggings Mother had knit for me that Christmas a couple of years earlier. It felt as if decades had passed since then. Somehow the ugly brown stockings had grown with me, stretching enough to still cover my long legs. But the stockings warmed me only so much. The cold was so penetrating that even under a feather comforter it didn't go away. My bones felt as if they were permanently frozen.

Bassi woke up one morning with her rag diapers frozen to her body. Even though we had covered her with lots of warm blankets at bedtime, during the night she had kicked them off. For several mornings we had to defrost Bassi's diapered bottom in warm water in the kitchen sink, the only warm place in the house. She never complained, nor did she catch a cold. But after a few episodes of having to defrost her, she slept with either Mother or me. We were willing to put up with the possibility of smelling like soiled diapers the next morning to keep Bassi warm.

Mother worried constantly about Bassi's health. Mother's breast milk had dried up far earlier than it should have, and she was afraid Bassi might get rickets or other diseases from malnutrition. Poor Bassi was so small and thin.

All of us lacked meat and fat in our daily diet of potatoes, bread, and semolina. Occasionally we could get cottage cheese, and that was a feast. My favorite dish was Heaven and Earth, mashed potatoes and applesauce. Sometimes Mother sparingly put a dab of Onkel Werner's goose fat into potato soup or thinly spread it on bread slices for us. With a little salt, it was absolutely delicious. But salt had become another rare commodity.

Sometimes Helga and I went on hamster trips. We called them that because, like hamsters, we were trying to collect and hoard food. Our goal was to barter for food with the farmers on the outskirts of Waldenburg, who were less interested in money than in trade goods.

One winter day, the clouds on the horizon were dark and threatening. A big snowstorm was on the way. But Helga and I were sure that we could go on a secret hamster trip and get home before it hit. We had collected items to barter and planned this trip for days, and we weren't going to let a little thing like storm clouds interfere with our plan.

Since the food from this trip was to be a surprise, we didn't tell anyone where we were going. We set off on foot to the farming village of

Adelsbach, about an hour away. We were in great spirits, singing hiking songs as loud and off-key as we pleased. Our knapsacks were filled with treasures such as pieces of jewelry, outgrown baby clothes, home-knit mittens that no longer fit anyone in our families, toys, an old Army cap I had found somewhere, and other prizes.

It was growing colder and darker by the minute, and a cutting wind soon silenced our singing and slowed our progress. We finally reached the village and trudged from farm to farm, but most of the farmers were unfriendly and unwilling to barter. Some just slammed the door in our faces. We were growing more and more tired, hungry, and discouraged. I wanted so badly to take home food to my family, but we were having no luck.

At the last farm, just before returning home, we peeked into a barn and saw a woman milking her cows. We stood at the entrance, two shivering fourteen year olds looking longingly into the warm interior. She gazed at us for a moment, then motioned us in. Gratefully, we stepped inside. The barn smelled pleasantly of fresh hay, manure, and animal bodies, reminding me of Omi's barn. It was cozy inside, and happily we dropped onto a pile of sweet-smelling hay, stretching our aching limbs. The woman offered us each a scoop of warm milk directly from the cows.

When we had sufficiently recovered and were about to thank her and leave, she suddenly said, "Now let me see what you have with you." Excitedly, we opened our knapsacks and displayed everything we had collected. Wordlessly she picked up each item. We hung on her every move. *Will she barter? Will she send us away with nothing?* She was our last hope. Finally, after what seemed like an eternity, she said, "I'll take everything you have, and I'll give you each a knapsack full of potatoes and turnips." We looked at each other and beamed. "I'll even throw in some winter apples," she added.

"Thank you! Thank you!" we shouted, hardly believing our great fortune.

As we heaved the heavy loads on our backs, we were filled with renewed energy and didn't mind in the least stepping out into the blizzard that was now blowing full force. The driving snow obliterated farmhouses and fields from view. We leaned our bodies into the wind as it blew through our thin overcoats, and we concentrated on just putting one foot in front of the other. Outside it was freezing cold and stormy, but inside me was a warm glow of pride at having accomplished something so important for my family.

Halfway home to Waldenburg, just as our bodies were beginning to protest the strenuous effort of fighting wind and snow, a farmer passed us in a horse-drawn sled. "Hey!" he shouted over the howling wind. "Want a ride?" We gratefully jumped into the back of the sled. "Going into town?" he yelled.

"Oh, yes," we cried.

"So am I!" he said. And off we went. I could no longer feel my fingers inside my sodden wool mittens, but it was great fun standing in the back of the sled and letting the wind buffet me, no longer having to fight against it. I stuck out my tongue and let snowflakes melt on it. The sled slipped and slid over the rough road, and the lone horse whinnied occasionally as it struggled with the sled through the storm. I felt so alive, as if my heart was about to jump right out of my chest.

It was almost dark when the farmer dropped us off near the deserted marketplace in Waldenburg, and I still had to climb the hill home. Mother was waiting, but any lecture she might have prepared about my being late, wet, and tired was forgotten when she saw the treasures I had brought home. She made my favorite dish that evening, Heaven and Earth. I was blissful, as proud as if I had personally grown the potatoes and apples for this meal.

Christmas that year, for the first time in my life, held no magic for me. In fact, the holiday came and went without any of us really noticing it. We concentrated on finding food and trying to keep our family alive and safe.

One day just after New Year's, after standing in line for bread down in the village, I took a different route home. Through the trees I spotted a tall barbed-wire fence that I hadn't noticed when the leaves were still on the branches. I stepped through the trees to get a closer look. On the other side of the fence, emaciated men in torn, thin clothes shuffled around in a daze. *What is this place?* I wondered. *A prison camp? Who are these people? Are they the ones who work in the factory?* I stood at the edge of the trees.

One of the ghostlike men spotted me and shuffled through the deep snow up to the fence. His gray, grisly, hollow face and deeply recessed eyes gave no clue of his age. *He could be eighteen or eighty,* I realized. He started to cough and then couldn't seem to stop. In between coughing attacks he tried to speak to me, holding out his hands, but I couldn't understand what he was saying. I felt sorry for him and utterly helpless.

I also realized that I was in plain view and began to fear that a guard might see me. I knew it was strictly forbidden and extremely dangerous to talk to prisoners. People who were caught were instantly shot by the guards. Heart pounding, I quickly stepped back into the woods and ran to the road.

Frank told me later that the camp I saw was a slave labor camp for captured foreigners who were forced to work for the Third Reich. I felt guilty about letting the sick man down. I couldn't get him out of my mind. I managed to find a few slices of extra bread and snitched some cough syrup from our medicine cabinet. A few days later I dared to go back to the same spot. The man was not there. When I was sure no guards were around, I slid the bread and medicine through the fence and left. *It seems as if the whole world is filled with nothing but sad, suffering people,* I thought.

〜

In early 1945 we heard rumors that the Soviets were launching a huge offensive, pushing north to Danzig, west to the Oder River, and south to Kraków and Breslau which, of course, would include Waldenburg. Mother faced a terrible dilemma. If we remained in Waldenburg, we faced being cut off permanently from Father in Berlin, and we would inevitably fall into the hands of the Russians. Any chance of returning to the United States would be completely lost. If we attempted to flee across the mountain ranges through ice and snow under subzero conditions, we risked the lives of Tommy and Bassi, who were too small and fragile to withstand such an ordeal. Trains ran irregularly, but when they did they were crushingly full and any passengers needed special permits. We had lost all contact with Father in Berlin. Mother was tormented about what to do.

Just in case we were forced to leave, she and I began sewing sacks from sheets for flour and potatoes. We hoarded whatever food supplies we could find. Whenever I had the opportunity in between searches for food, I slipped into the Waldenburg church. Its timeless rituals calmed me. In church I felt more strongly than ever the reassuring presence of the Invisibles.

As we were trying to decide where and when we should leave, Cousin Maria and her kids moved to another apartment. Then Frau Mettner with her two children and her mother moved back from Breslau to get away from the bombings, and they came to live with us. Now we were nine people living in quarters meant for two, adding additional strain to the already existing anxieties. I don't know how Mother and Frau Mettner managed.

We were always bumping into each other in the small space. Meal-times for so many people required shifts. We took turns cooking in the tiny kitchen, which was barely large enough for two people to move around in. But privacy was my biggest problem. There wasn't a corner where I could sit quietly and write in my diary, so I gave up trying. The only place I could find a moment to myself was on the toilet, and even there one child or another shattered the quiet by banging on the door. Most of the time I just tried to stay out of the house.

One day, trying desperately to decide whether or not to try to get to Berlin, Mother said, "I'm going to church today to ask God to give me some kind of sign about what to do." I stayed at home and tried to straighten the house. But while Mother was at church, I began to feel ill. By the time she arrived home, I had developed a high fever and had broken out in a rash. Mother and Frank wrapped me in blankets and loaded me on a sled. Together they pushed and pulled me down the mountain to the hospital, where I was diagnosed with measles. After that, one after the other of the little ones came down with the disease, and any thought of leaving was out of the question. "Well," Mother concluded grimly, "there's my sign."

By mid-January 1945, temperatures regularly dropped to minus twenty degrees. Grisly rumors circulated around town about thousands of refugees from the east freezing or starving to death on country roads or in the mountains. Some people said that the police had even sealed off train stations to civilians in some cities. The trains were to be used only to deliver soldiers to the eastern front and to return with the wounded. The steady *boom, boom* of artillery grew ever louder. Everybody lived in a kind of limbo. Nobody knew what to do or what was happening. News over the Armed Forces radio, Frank reported, was sparse and inconclusive.

Soon after, we heard that Warsaw had fallen to the Soviets, and the German army was in full retreat on the Eastern front. It would be only a matter of days before the Russians would reach Kraków and then Breslau. Waldenburg was about to be encircled by the Russians. Our need to return to Berlin was now critical, but the direct train route from Waldenburg to Berlin through Lauban had already been broken by the Soviets. Frank thought for a time that perhaps we could go through Jena and Dresden, but this route seemed to be too complicated. Later we heard that if we had taken that route, we would have found ourselves in the middle of the Allied fire bombing of Dresden and we all certainly would have perished.

Then two things happened. Lauban, the city that connected Waldenburg to Berlin, was recaptured by the Germans, during which time Father somehow managed to hop on a train and arrive in Waldenburg. In the meantime, the father of one of Frank's best friends, a doctor, was able to obtain a special permit that entitled our family to leave on a Red Cross train heading west.

We hardly had a chance to be relieved and pleased at Father's sudden appearance. He urged us to pack only what we could carry and to dress the little ones warmly. Then we immediately left for the railroad station. Throngs of refugees like us were waiting and milling around the station on the outside chance that a train would appear. After many hours, a Red

Cross train overflowing with wounded soldiers pulled into the station. The crowd stampeded to the train. The conductors who blocked the doorways were backed up by soldiers brandishing their rifles. They shouted to the crowd that space was limited and that only families with small children and special permits were allowed to climb on board. Mother held Bassi and Father carried Tommy, while Frank and I dragged the suitcases. I tried hard to stay on Mother's heels, terrified that I might lose her in the shuffle. Frank stuck right behind me.

Somehow we all managed to get on board and squeeze into an aisle. Filling the seats and most of the aisle were dull-eyed soldiers in tattered uniforms, wrapped in bloody bandages and covered with frostbite, staring listlessly out the windows. The stench of unwashed bodies, dried blood, and pus immediately made me gag. I had to swallow hard to keep from losing the potatoes I had eaten early that morning. We were wedged in like sardines, with barely a breathing space between us. Whenever possible we rested on our suitcases. After a long wait, the train finally chugged out of the station with its overload of human cargo, leaving behind many more people than had managed to get on. Desperate faces looked at us from the platform, hands clawed at the train, and mothers lifted crying babies up to the windows, begging someone to take them. My tears wouldn't come; they remained frozen in my throat.

As we passed through Lauban, Soviet planes circled the train and swooped low along the railroad tracks. Ignoring the big red crosses on the roof and sides of the train, they fired round after round at us. Windows shattered, and glass and shrapnel flew through compartments and aisles. Everybody lay as low as possible, often on top of each other. The train stopped frequently, sometimes in the middle of an open field, where we felt even more vulnerable to attacks. At last, however, the train chugged into a heavily damaged railroad station in Berlin.

When we peeled ourselves apart from one another and stepped out onto the platform, I immediately saw, tucked into the corner of the station and open to the elements, a large wooden cart with old-fashioned wooden wheels. Piled high on the cart were children's frozen corpses. I recalled the little dead girl I had seen at the beginning of the war, who looked like a sleeping angel. Since then the faces of death had changed.

We had no sooner arrived in Berlin when we were greeted by the terrifying howl of the air-raid siren. *Welcome back to Hell,* I thought as we raced for shelter. I could feel the familiar, ice-cold grip of fear creeping back into my chest. I had almost forgotten it in Stolp and Waldenburg.

The next day, we heard that the Soviets had taken back Lauban from the Germans and that they had reached Breslau. Waldenburg was now in Russian hands. Our timing was perfect. If we hadn't gotten through exactly when we did, we would have been cut off from the rest of Germany for good.

CHAPTER ELEVEN

A DYING BERLIN AND THE LAST BATTLE

JANUARY 1945—APRIL 1945

I HATED BEING back in Berlin, where I constantly feared for my family's lives. I missed the pristine mountain beauty of Waldenburg, which had been relatively unaffected by war, despite the occasional strafings from Russian aircraft and its incoming floods of refugees.

I worried about the approaching Russians. Could they be as bad as the refugees said they were? The refugees had talked of rape, brutality, and death at the hands of the Russians. I hoped they were exaggerating.

My dream of returning to the United States had almost vanished. Everything in my life quickly returned to the dreary shades of gray they had been before I left Berlin for Stolp eighteen months earlier. I felt dull, numb. The color had gone out of the landscape and out of life itself.

The city center was in far worse condition than when I had left. The beautiful dome of the Saint Hedwig's church had been hit, the cross on top shattered. The old Kaiserhof, the Hotel Bristol, and many of the stately embassy buildings were now completely bombed out. Unter den Linden, the promenade where our family had walked on warm summer Sunday afternoons, was now pocked with ugly bomb craters and covered with debris. Many of the once-proud linden trees lay splintered and charred, dead or dying in the heaps of rubble. The massive Berlin Cathedral was heavily damaged, its stone carvings and statues lying in fragments. The giant spire on the old Kaiser Wilhelm Memorial Church was the only part still standing, and the big department stores along the Ku'damm were now just hollow shells.

Fires still burned where incendiary or phosphorous bombs had hit, adding thick smoke to the dust that blew everywhere and settled on everything. The city looked as if it were part of another world. It was the way I imagined Hell to be: hopeless and ice cold amid all the flames.

Steglitz had fared better than the inner city. While many buildings were destroyed or made uninhabitable, quite a few were still livable. Often the upper levels had been burned out by incendiary bombs, but the lower levels remained intact. In many of the beautiful old villas, wisps of charred wallpaper fluttered from empty window sockets. Wherever possible, families still lived in usable rooms or in the basements of their bombed houses or apartment buildings.

Fortunately, our apartment house was still standing, albeit without glass in the windows and with cracks and holes in the walls. It was still there for us. *But,* I always questioned, *for how long?*

I didn't know if I should laugh or cry when I first walked into my room, crunching across the accumulated debris to look at my bed, my wardrobe, and the table in front of the window. This furniture that I knew so well no longer looked familiar. I had been away for over a year, and in that time I had grown and changed. My room had changed too. It had suffered from the war.

A glance at the empty wall told me the Botticelli Madonna was missing again. By now I knew where to look for her, so I crawled under the bed to retrieve her. *Who knows how long she's been lying there,* I thought. *Perhaps she was waiting for me to put her back in her rightful place.* Carefully I wiped the dust from her serene face and hung the painting back in its place above my bed. Despite all that had happened, I had great faith in the Madonna's protective power and in the Invisibles who I hoped— and still sometimes felt—were hovering nearby. After I cleaned up as best I could and put everything back into its proper place, my spirits lifted. I felt less like a stranger in my own room.

All schools in Berlin had been closed or moved out of the city to safer areas. Frank and I spent our days wandering around the city looking for food or fuel. I walked through Dahlem to see how my school had fared. It was still mostly intact, and it was now serving as a refugee center. The Saint Bernard Church, where Frank and I had gone to first communion, had suffered a direct hit and was reduced to a giant pile of bricks, crumbled concrete, twisted steel, and shattered glass.

On the eastern front the Russian army continued to crash toward Berlin. Air raids were now coming not only during the night but also during the day. Often there was no time to make it across the street into the subway before the bombs hit, so we grabbed the little ones and rushed madly down the stairs to the cellar with armloads of babies and supplies.

The bombings now sounded different and were even more intense than I had remembered. The first bombs of an air raid exploded in the distance, but then they rapidly came closer and closer, like the rumbling of a thundering train, until they fell all around us.

"What is it? Why is it so different?" I cried over the roar.

"Carpet bombing," Father yelled back. "It's saturation bombing. They're blanketing whole areas of the city with bombs."

At every crash the walls and ceiling of the cellar shook and trembled, and mortar poured down on us. The center post supporting the ceiling swayed crazily. The whole building shuddered above us. *Please, please,* I prayed to the Invisibles, *let the ceiling hold.* The noise was deafening, and the heavy air pressure from the explosions surged into the room and made my ears feel as if they were about to burst.

We all breathed a sigh of relief when we finally heard the bombers continuing over us and sensed that the planes were heading to another part of the city. We didn't have the energy to worry about the poor people who were the targets for that raid.

Now the Royal Air Force bombed Berlin at night and the U. S. Army Air Corps bombed during the day, which meant that sometimes as many as seventeen air raids occurred in twenty-four hours. The terrifying drone of a thousand super fortresses thundering over the city burned itself into my memory and echoed in my head, so that I often thought I heard the bombers even between air raids.

In the daytime we could see the American bombers flying high over us, like giant silver birds. White tufts—tiny clouds—marked the areas in the sky where the bombers unloaded their lethal cargo. And then, moments later, the earth shuddered, even when the bombs fell miles away from Steglitz.

The nights were far worse than the days, though. Four or five times a night we were awakened from exhausted sleep, our hearts pounding as we jumped out of bed, pulled together belongings with trembling hands, and raced to the cellar.

Everybody's nerves were constantly on edge. Bassi and Tommy were continuously fussy, crying and wriggling out of our arms, refusing to be calmed. The rest of us had no patience with each other. Father erupted in anger at the slightest provocation. Mother was short-tempered with all of us. Frank looked more tired than anything else, but he was quick to challenge anything Father did or said. I felt as if my insides—my stomach as well as my mind—were made of the thinnest glass, ready to shatter into a thousand pieces. Struggling to hold myself together, I tried to remember what quiet nights were like, with a moon and brilliant stars shining over green meadows and dark forests. I longed for clear blue skies filled with swooping, chirping birds, not dangerous steel ones.

After every air raid, smoke, soot, ashes, and the stench of broken gas lines permeated the air. During the day the sun rarely penetrated the dense haze that hovered over the city. On rainy days, and there were more of those than sunny ones, the thick ashes on the street turned to dirty, gummy glue that stuck to our shoes. Mother made us scrape the sticky stuff off before entering the apartment.

In between the constant bombings, Mother insisted on a certain routine and orderliness in spite of the chaos around us. As always, she made us clean up after every air raid, even if we had to do so seventeen times a day.

Each time we returned to our apartment after an air raid, I thought it looked as if an angry giant had blown through it. Doors were broken, window frames were ripped out, mortar and glass shards were strewn across the room, venetian blinds hung at crazy angles, and shredded blackout paper drifted everywhere. When we complained about having to clean the apartment again, Mother scolded us. "No matter how unciv- ilized the world around us is, as long as we are still alive," she said, "we will live like civilized people."

She still made me set the table with tablecloth and napkins whenever possible and, when necessary, polish the silverware. Somehow she came home occasionally with fresh flowers for the center of the table. "It isn't enough to feed the stomach," she claimed. "You also have to feed the soul with something beautiful." She insisted on grace before dinner and good manners at the table.

Electricity and gas were often interrupted for many hours at a time. We never knew when either one would come on again. When it did, everybody in our building, including Mother, hurried to get a meal cooked before it shut off. Dinnertime was directly tied to the availability of gas and electricity and the arrival of enemy aircraft. We were always racing to get something warm in our stomachs before the next air raid, and before the electricity was cut off again. If the alarm siren screamed before we had a chance to eat the soup that Mother had just finished cooking, then Mother quickly tucked the pot under a feather comforter to keep it warm. It was a wonderful treat after spending hours in the cold basement or subway to come back to a warm bowl of soup.

Bit by bit, the waterworks were being destroyed. But Mother insisted that we be neat and clean even though water was becoming increasingly hard to get. So when we could, each person in the family took a turn in the same tub of water, then we used it for washing diapers afterward. When the water was turned on again, we refilled the bathtub, sink, buck- ets, and any empty containers we had on hand.

Food became scarcer and scarcer as the farms in the agriculture-rich eastern provinces fell into Russian hands, until finally deliveries stopped altogether. We took turns standing in endless food lines when- ever we heard something was available. Frank and I stood in different lines, trying to improve our odds of getting food. Sometimes I waited in line for hours, enduring the strafing of low-flying Russian or American fighter planes, only to see the person ahead of me get the last loaf of bread for that day. I went home hungry, hoping that Frank had had better luck.

Father went to pick up and deliver work at the AEG once a week, despite the obstacle course he had to navigate to get there and the constant danger of being overtaken in the open by an air raid. Subways were damaged often and ran only partway. Buses and streetcars no longer ran at all. Father often rode his bicycle, which took him many hours of going and returning. Mother hated it when he was gone, and we worried about him.

Mother urged Frank and me to stay close to home when we were not standing in line for food. She kept repeating, "If we have to die, we're dying together as a family." She didn't want us to be orphans, like so many children who were now roaming the streets, homeless and without families.

Annemarie had returned from Bavaria to be with her mother in Berlin. Her brother Christoph was still with his school in Auersberg in Posen, which the Soviets had captured. Her family worried constantly about him. She and I had little time to spend together; so much was happening so fast.

Newspaper headlines screamed, "Save Germany from the Bolshevist Hordes!" "Fight to the Last Berliner!" "The Hard Spirit of the Front Rules Berlin!" *What's going to happen?* I wondered, not daring to speak my fears even to Annemarie. I thought of the myths I had studied in school. *Is this the twilight of the gods, when the whole world will go up in flames?*

One day in late March, heading home after waiting in line for potatoes, I saw Renate. I hadn't seen her since the spring of 1943—two whole years ago.

"Rena!" I cried, happy to see a familiar face. We embraced and sat down on a curb to talk. "What's new with you?" I asked.

"Our apartment was so badly damaged, we had to move to another one," she said. "It's much smaller, but it will have to do." She shrugged. "Anyway, we're leaving in a couple of days, before the Russkis get here."

"Where will you go?" I asked, astonished.

"Oh, I don't know, somewhere in the west where the Amis will be. I hear they're much nicer than the Russkis."

I was silent for a moment. "Rena, do you think it's true what they say about the Russians?" I asked.

"You mean about rape and all that?"

I nodded.

"It's true. My father has it from a good source. He says the Russkis are taking revenge on us for all the terrible things German soldiers did in Russia. They're raping and killing everybody without mercy."

"Girls our age too?" I asked incredulously. "We're only fourteen. We didn't do anything."

"My father says he heard that those pigs are raping eight- and nine-year-old girls. And Goebbels said that the Russians nail little children's tongues to tables."

I shivered. "Goebbels only says that because he's the propaganda minister," I replied. "That doesn't mean it's true."

"Well, if I were you, I'd try to make it out of the city too," Rena advised. "Things are going to be bad in Berlin, and I feel sorry for anyone who's staying." The air-raid siren interrupted our conversation. "Good luck! See you after the war maybe," she yelled over her shoulder as she hurried away.

For a moment I stood rooted. *The Russians,* I breathed, my fear like a vise around my heart. I watched Rena disappear around the next corner. Then the heavy drone of approaching aircraft broke through my daze and I ran home.

"Why can't we leave Berlin?" I begged Mother as we huddled in the cellar.

"Where would we go?" she replied, irritated. "Who would take in a family of six when millions of refugees are already flooding western Germany? And how do you propose we get there?"

"By train," I offered timidly, "like Renate."

"By train? I hear they're no longer running. And even if they are, they're perfect targets for bombers, and you have to have a special permit to get on one." She turned her dark eyes to me. "Do you suggest that we walk all the way to western Germany with two small children, exposing them to cold and disease and possible death? And all with nowhere to go once we get there?"

"I hadn't thought about all of that," I admitted, miserable.

More kindly, she added, "Look, we still have a roof over our heads. Maybe we'll be lucky and we won't get hit."

I nodded. *Yes, we have been lucky, and we're all safe at the moment,* I thought. *But what about when the Russians come?*

A few days later, in early April, Berliners were forbidden to leave the city under penalty of death. Now we had no choice but to stay and wait for the Russians to arrive. With the Russians only a few miles from Berlin, the city prepared for street fighting and house-to-house combat. Thankfully, Father's and Frank's status as Americans continued to keep them safe, but old men and Hitler Youth boys as young as twelve were called on to join the soldiers in defending the city in the name of the Führer. Barricades made of wrecked trucks, masonry, and wood logs were quickly erected. The old men and boys helped the soldiers dig trenches, bury land mines, and blow up the many bridges across the canals that encircled the city.

In the middle of these preparations, the oldest Basedow boy showed up at our place, an American wearing the gray-blue German Luftwaffe helper uniform. He was angry and agitated. When Mother asked after his remaining family, he replied in anguish, "I haven't been able to find out what happened to my sister and baby brother. When I start flying the fighter jets," he declared, "I'm going to shoot down as many Allied planes as I can to avenge my family!" I hugged Bassi as I listened to his angry words.

I couldn't block out the image of his parents passing the baby to strangers through the cellar window just before the ceiling collapsed. In my mind the Basedows' screams blended with the knocking from beneath the rubble of the building next door. The sounds haunted me.

A few days later, I bumped into a schoolmate on the street who told me with frustration, "My little brother is only thirteen. He's a severe diabetic. And can you believe it? They recruited him to accompany a tank battalion." Angrily she wiped away tears. "The worst part is that the stupid idiot is proud to be called to help, even though he doesn't know which end of a gun is up. Mother is beside herself with worry. She cries all the time. She says, 'I just know he won't make it!' It's all so senseless. I *hate* Hitler," she added.

I quickly glanced around to see if anyone had overheard her dangerous remark.

"He won't stop until we're all dead," she said.

I nodded and wondered for the thousandth time, *How can this one madman have power over so many people's lives?*

∽

Fear of Hitler's Gestapo reached its icy fingers into every corner of Berlin. Defeatist talk was punishable by death. On every advertisement pillar hung Gestapo directives: "Berliners fight with everything you have!" "Fight Bolshevism regardless of consequences!" "Berlin must remain free!" "The Capital is to be defended to the last man and the last bullet."

The rumor mill supplied plenty of stories of Berliners being dragged from their homes by the Gestapo and shot. Many were people who had been hiding Jews or openly resisting the regime by circulating leaflets urging surrender—they were trying to save lives. *It's so strange,* I thought. *Here we are caught between fear of the Gestapo and fear of the Allied bombers and the upcoming battle.*

Since regular newspapers ceased to exist, rumors became our main source of information. One day I heard that shoes were being given away at a store on the Schloss Strasse, the main shopping street in Steglitz. Mother and I, who now had the same size feet, had only one pair of leather shoes between us. We saved that single pair for special occasions, whenever those might occur again. My feet were always freezing and often in pain from the hard wooden shoes with the ersatz tops we usually wore.

As I hurried down the Schloss Strasse, I passed the Rathaus, our area's government building. There I saw something that made my blood run cold. A young soldier Frank's age dangled from a lamppost by a noose.

Attached to his trouser leg with a safety pin was a piece of paper that read, "I'm a cowardly deserter. I did not believe in victory."

Unable to move, I stared up at the open, unseeing eyes of the boy. *Who did this terrible thing? His only crime was that he didn't want to fight a war everybody knows is lost anyway.* I walked home without looking for shoes.

By April 16, we could hear the steady *vroom-boom, boom* of artillery fire. *Vroom-boom, boom,* day and night, like a distant thunderstorm hovering on the horizon. Rumors spread that over a million Red Army soldiers were poised along the Oder and Neisse Rivers in preparation for the great assault on Berlin. *What will become of us when they enter the city?* I worried.

Our family, like so many others, scurried around trying to find food and lay in provisions for the siege that was soon to come. Many stores began to give away their supplies rather than have them fall into Russian hands. We grabbed whatever we could. One time it was a bunch of packages of a red powdered pudding, another time a barrel of pickled beets. People frantically pushed, shoved, and grabbed, trying to get whatever they could.

I wanted to do my share to get food, but I often felt as if I were about to be crushed to death by the hysterical mobs. When I learned to use my elbows and kick at shins, I managed to get a head of cabbage. I was pleased and carried it home proudly, as if it were a trophy I had won.

Walking the streets became increasingly dangerous, as Russian fighter planes flew just above the rooftops and strafed citizens with machine-gun fire. The Russians seemed to particularly enjoy aiming at people standing in food lines, and many such civilians were injured or even killed, their bodies and blood strewn around the streets. *It's amazing how I'm becoming so used to the presence of death,* I often thought as I stepped out of a doorway or from behind a building where I had taken cover, walking around the bodies of the people who had been standing alongside me moments before. In the evenings when our family was back together again, I prayed to the Invisibles, *Thank you for keeping my family safe once more.*

One morning on my usual path to the stores, I walked through what was left of the little park across the street from us. I caught a glimpse of something bright yellow pushing through a fallen fence by the children's playground. When I went to investigate, I was astonished to find a forsythia bush in bloom. The tiny blossoms looked like unfolding angel wings, so delicate and perfect. I plucked some branches. For a moment I forgot the impending battle and thought with joy, *Spring is coming!* Instead of trying to find food, I happily ran home with my treasure.

Mother gave me one of her rare smiles as she arranged the forsythia in her best crystal vase. "Something for the soul," she said wistfully.

On April 21, there was no more water. Not even a drop fell from the faucets. Gas and electricity ceased for good. Berlin's lifeline had been cut off. Father built a little stove out of bricks in the hallway of our apartment and on top placed an iron grate he found in a bombed-out house. We gathered wood from the rubble outside and built a fire. We could now cook and sterilize water for drinking.

Clever foragers in the city had discovered water pumps left over from horse and buggy days. No one knew that they could still be activated until somebody thought of attaching a wooden handle, and with some vigorous pumping, water suddenly surfaced. Frank discovered such a pump just a block from our building. Soon the word was out and long lines formed, with everybody carrying buckets. We took turns running to the pump and filling up bucket after bucket with water. Bathtub, sinks, pots, and pans were filled to the brim.

Day by day the boom of artillery grew louder and closer. The Russians were advancing from the east, north, and south. Many civilians and soldiers tried to run away from the dying city. But signs everywhere warned, "Anyone deserting the city will be punished by immediate execution!" Berlin had become a city of gray terror.

Nobody talked anymore about the Americans reaching the city first, something we had all hoped and prayed for. People were saying that the Americans had stopped at the Elbe River, south of Magdeburg, and were coming no closer. It was now clear that Berlin would fall into the hands of the Russians. Every day I was busy searching for food and wood, and

I was glad I didn't have time to think about the upcoming battle for the city and what might happen to us.

"I wish we would get mail again soon," I said to Frank. "I can't bear not knowing how Omi and Grossvater and Grossmutter are. Are they still alive?"

"Don't worry. They're all in small villages, where there's no bombing. And in the country, there's always something to eat."

"I suppose they're more worried about us being alive," I said.

"I think you're right," he replied.

Father no longer went to pick up work at the AEG. It had become too dangerous. He helped Frank and me fix up our corner of the cellar with blankets, pillows, food, water, clothing, medical supplies, steel helmets, and towels to cover our faces in case of fire. We didn't know how long we might have to stay down there.

We knew by the increasingly loud bursts of artillery that the Russians were approaching fast. Rumors circulated wildly that the Russians were already in the suburbs of Berlin. The sky to the east of the city was black with smoke. The battle would be on us any day now.

As I returned from another store-raiding spree, I ran into Gabi, the daughter of a Nazi official in our neighborhood. "Thank God the war will be over soon," I bubbled, forgetting who her father was.

Vehemently she responded, "That's defeatist talk! It's treason!"

I gasped. *Now what have I done with my big mouth?* Mother's many years of warnings came back to me: "Always think before you speak. Never tell others what's discussed in our household. You'll endanger us all. Don't forget what has happened to your father!"

"Hitler promised us victory," Gabi said, interrupting my thoughts. "He's not going to let us down now."

"But, Gabi," I protested, "don't you hear the guns?"

Gabi shook her head and angrily replied, "I can hear them, but Hitler has some kind of secret weapon he'll use. Just wait and see. I could report you to the Gestapo, you know."

I was aghast. I imagined myself dangling from a lamppost like the boy at the Rathaus. Just then a loud detonation sent Gabi and me scurrying in different directions. For days afterward I froze each time somebody knocked at the door, petrified that the Gestapo was coming to take me away.

By April 25, we heard that the Russians had formed an iron ring around the city. Their final push to the inner city began in earnest. It came with sudden ear-splitting, earth-shattering noise. The roar of heavy artillery and the screaming and howling of missiles from multiple rocket launchers shaped like musical organs—Stalin organs or katyushas—tore into our neighborhood with a vengeance.

We grabbed the children and ran to the cellar, where we took up residence more or less permanently along with the members of the apartment house who had remained. We lived like a strange subculture, squeezed between suitcases, baby carriage, bunk bed, and lawn chairs. Day and night flowed together, one into the other. Candles and kerosene lamps suffused the cellar with eerie light, casting our own monstrous shadows on the walls, while above our heads the battle raged.

Even going to the bathroom became a risky business. Most of the time we relieved ourselves by squatting over a small grate in the concrete. But sometimes during a lull in the artillery fire, we ran upstairs to our own bathroom. The cardboard in the bathroom window and the window frame itself had been ripped to shreds. We had to be careful to keep our head below window level, as any movement could set off a flurry of machine-gun fire from the street. We had come so far, I didn't want to die on the toilet.

At one break in gunfire, somebody in the cellar reported that the Klugs, who owned the grocery store across the street, were giving away what was left of their inventory. Mother thought that since our food supply was dwindling fast, we should try to get whatever we could. Frank volunteered to go alone, but Mother insisted that she go with him. Father protested. "It's too dangerous. Stay here." For once I agreed with him. But to Mother the lure of food for the family was a stronger force than the threat of danger or our protests. During the next lull in firing, Mother and Frank crept on their bellies across the street to the store. Father and I listened anxiously for a sudden upstart of machine-gun fire and were greatly relieved when we heard the front door opening again. They had grabbed a twenty-five pound sack of flour and a box of fresh red beets, which they cautiously pulled and pushed back to our building.

I fell around Mother's neck, hugging her tightly and pressing my arms around Frank. *They're safe!* We laughed and celebrated having the flour and the beets, which we would share with other members of the cellar clan. Mother and Frank were heroes. I was secretly ashamed of my own cowardice. I hated myself for not volunteering, for being almost fifteen and still being afraid. Then I looked at Father and thought, *Why didn't he go?* Within minutes a new barrage of firing started.

Mother remained our source of stability. Tommy's and Bassi's needs for food, clean diapers, and attention had to be met. Mother insisted that we try to sleep and have regular mealtimes. She opened up the jars of preserves left from earlier seasons. We ate raw oatmeal and red beets, or Mother made a paste from flour and water and preserves. In the dim light I read or told the children stories and made up shadow plays on the wall.

Soon heavy street fighting began. We could hear the grinding, clanking chains of tanks and the staccato sounds of rifle and machine-gun fire slapping against our walls. There was no news, no radio. We couldn't tell what was happening outside. At one point during a pause in the shooting, Frank climbed up to the first floor and peeked through the window in the door. He caught sight of a Russian tank at the corner of our street. Suddenly he saw the turret swivel around and point its gun barrel directly at him. Then he saw a bright blast of yellow flame.

He called out. But the blast missed the window and hit the second floor, where we heard part of the wall crumble and fall. Visibly shaken, Frank stumbled back down the stairs to the cellar. He reported to us that German soldiers were firing from an office building on one end of Breitenbachplatz at the Russians on the other end of the square.

During another lull, when I was about to return to the cellar from a bathroom break, I heard a plaintive cry.

"Mutter!... Mutter!" Mother!... Mother!

Following the sound, I found a boy about my age in a German uniform much too large for his slight body, slumped in the doorway entrance, his chest ripped open by a bullet. He was bleeding heavily and was obviously near death. I couldn't leave him there, so I dragged him down the cellar stairs.

The air-raid warden immediately shouted, "He can't stay! If the Russians find a German soldier in our cellar, we'll all be killed."

"But what will we do with him?" I wailed. "We can't put him back out on the street."

The warden took a look at the moaning boy, whose eyes were already glazed. "He's not going to last long," said the warden softly. "I'll put him in the backyard in a protected area, where he'll be out of the line of fire." The warden carried him outside.

I worried about the boy. *What is happening to him?* I asked myself over and over. During the next break in the fighting, I crept upstairs to the backyard. The boy was still alive, but barely.

"Mutter!" he sobbed again, almost inaudibly.

I knelt next to him and cradled his head in my arms. Gently I stroked his clammy forehead, and out of somewhere deep inside me, I heard a voice saying, "Shhh! Mutter is here." He let out his breath for the last time. He was dead.

Down in the cellar, water was becoming a great concern to us. We had little left in our buckets and had to ration it carefully. After the worst of the fighting shifted from our area toward the inner city, Frank ventured outside to the pump with a couple of buckets. Shortly he returned, his face ghostly pale.

"You won't believe the mess outside," he gasped. "Tanks are rolling right over the dead bodies in the streets, as though they're nothing!"

We all crowded around Frank to hear his report.

"So many dead! They're all over the place—Russians, German soldiers, civilians, and horses. Katyushas are right outside our building, on the sidewalk." At that moment we heard the screaming missiles as they were fired into the inner city.

Then one day it was eerily quiet. All battle noises ceased. The silence was almost as nerve-wracking as the incessant noise had been. *What's going on?* Suddenly we heard sharp banging against the front door. My heart pounded. *Who is it? Germans or Russians?* Frank and the air-raid warden went to open the door.

We heard Russian soldiers declare, "Gitler kaput!" Hitler broken!

"The Russians are here!" somebody gasped.

I held my breath. *Goebbels spread so much propaganda about the horrible things to expect from the Soviets,* I thought. *What if his stories are true?*

CHAPTER TWELVE

LIFE UNDER THE RUSSIANS

APRIL 1945—MAY 1945

STRANGE GUTTURAL SPEECH and the thumping of heavy boots drifted down into the cellar from the apartment house entry.

"The Russians!" I whispered, terrified. I grasped Tommy tightly to me.

Moments later we could hear the soldiers tromping down the cellar stairs. The beam of a flashlight circled around our room, touching each one of us, wresting us from the shadows. When more beams circled the room I could make out several burly, battle-dirty soldiers in khaki uniforms with red stars on their shoulders. The Russians eyed us coldly. They each held a bayonet in one fist and a pistol in the other.

I glanced at Mother, who was clutching Bassi. For once, Bassi and Tommy seemed intimidated by strangers and didn't try to wriggle out of our arms.

One of the soldiers barked in broken German, "Deutsche Soldaten?" German soldiers?

I thought of my young soldier, glad he was dead and that they could not touch him.

Father answered, "No German soldiers here."

The Russians walked into the cellar room next to us, repeating, "Deutsche Soldaten?"

And then as suddenly as they came, they disappeared again. We waited for others to invade our cellar. But nothing further happened. I exhaled slowly. *Maybe my fears have been for no reason,* I hoped.

The explosions of mortar shells and artillery echoed from the inner city as street-to-street fighting continued. We stayed in the cellar for safety. Occasionally we could hear single shots followed by the *ack-ack* of machine-gun fire. We guessed that the Russians were trying to root out pockets of resistance in some of the buildings. Tanks and heavy trucks frequently rumbled by on the street outside our sandbagged cellar window. It was still too dangerous to be out in the streets or in our apartments.

As we huddled in the cellar, waiting for the Russians to complete their conquest of Berlin, Mother urged me to lie in the lower bunk bed to catch up on much-needed sleep. I was dreadfully tired, jumpy, and nervous.

"I'm not going to sleep in the bunk bed!" I retorted. "I can rest just as well on the lawn chair."

I could tell that she was annoyed and took my refusal as pure obstinacy. But I was afraid to tell her the real reason why I didn't want to sleep in the bunk. Since I had heard how the Basedows had died, I had been terrified that the ceiling would collapse and I would be crushed to death between the bunks. *If I stay in an upright position,* I reasoned, *I won't be suffocated.* A couple of times, sheer exhaustion drove me to stretch out on the bed, but then I had a hard time catching my breath. I felt like I just couldn't get enough air into my lungs, so I fled back to my chair.

At one point I dozed off into a deep, exhausted sleep in the chair. But then I felt someone pulling at me. I heard cloth ripping. A sickening stench permeated the air: rank body odor and tobacco mixed with perfume. I struggled to open my eyes. Then the realization of what was happening hit me. My eyes opened wide. I screamed and clawed and scratched at the Mongolian face above me, trying to wriggle out from under him. But he held me in an iron grip and continued to tear at my clothing.

Suddenly Mother jumped at him in a terrible rage, waving my American birth certificate and passport in his surprised face. "Amerikanski!

Amerikanski!" she yelled fiercely. The Russian loosened his grip, and I quickly fled behind Mother's back. Alarmed by the screaming and shouting, a whole gang of Russian soldiers with bayonets and cocked pistols crowded into the little room, their faces twisted with fury. Two soldiers shoved Father and Frank against the wall and leveled pistols at their heads. Others pointed their guns at Mother, the babies, and me.

This is it, I thought. *They're going to shoot us all.*

Undeterred, Mother kept waving the birth certificate, repeating, "Amerikanski! Amerikanski!"

We held our breath. *Will they believe it?*

After a few tense moments, grunting unintelligibly, the soldiers lowered their guns and passed my birth certificate and passport around. In the faint light I noticed that they were looking at the documents upside-down. Apparently none of them could read English. But the official red and gold seal of the United States seemed to impress them. They handed the documents to my mother and backed out of the room to find prey elsewhere. Only then did I begin to cry, shaking all over and pulling my torn clothes around me. Frank gave me a blanket and sat down beside me.

The soldiers kept coming in groups of ten, twenty, or more, wave after wave, searching the cellars for hiding German soldiers and weapons. Some of the men and women in our cellar were seized and, with rifles at their backs, ordered outside. We were all petrified. Those who eventually came back told us that the Russians had ordered them to bury the dead or to clear the rubble from streets. Others never returned.

After a few days, we felt that it was safe to emerge from the cellar and move back into our apartment. Father, encouraged by the Russians' positive reaction to our American connection, drew the Russian emblem of a hammer and sickle crossed by the Stars and Stripes and pasted it on the front door of the apartment.

It seemed to make an impression on the hordes of soldiers tramping through our apartment. They pointed to the drawing and clasped their hands together in a gesture of solidarity, saying, "Amerikanski, Russki, sooo!" But not long after that, new waves of Russians arrived. They sneered at the flags. With a mock karate chop they said, "Amerikanski, Russki, so!" We puzzled over this new, negative reaction and wondered if a split had developed between America and Russia.

We heard that Adolf Hitler had committed suicide in his Berlin bunker on April 30, 1945. And on May 1, the city surrendered to the occupying Soviet forces. On May 8, what was left of Germany was formally and unconditionally surrendered to the Allied forces.

When we realized that the war in Germany had officially ended, we laughed and cried. *The long war is over!* I couldn't believe it. But after the initial euphoria had faded, I caught a worried glance that passed between Mother and Father. *Oh no, is there still more to come?*

For years I had cherished the hope that once the war was over, everything would magically return to normal. We would get on the next ship and return to my beloved America. We would move back to Stratford, to the same old house on Union Avenue, where I would retrieve my childhood, and all things would be as they had been when I left there almost six years ago. This fantasy had kept me strong during very difficult times and had made life bearable.

But when I first wandered out onto the streets after the surrender, this fragile, childish hope shattered into a million fragments. The devastation was incredible. Wherever I looked were mountains of rubble, smoking ruins, and leaping flames. German and Russian tanks were overturned like upside-down beetles. Dead soldiers, felled by artillery shells or exploding rockets, and now bloating and turning gray-green, lay in pools of congealed, brown blood. Among the bodies of young Russian and German soldiers were dead women and children who had defied the shooting and emerged from the cellars to find water. The corpses' hands still clutched buckets. Neighboring apartment houses were burning like flaming torches, coloring the smoke-filled sky blood red.

Above everything hung a blanket of dust and dirt and acrid smoke like a black funeral cloth, blocking the sun. The weight and the intense heat from the katyushas that had been stationed in front of our building during the battle had demolished the sidewalk. *This is the end of the world as I have known it,* I realized. *How can life ever be normal again?*

A Russian field communication division confiscated our living room, the one room that was still intact, and set up their equipment there. In front of the sofa we had a large, square cocktail table with an opaque glass top which had somehow survived the bombings and the battle. One of the soldiers threw his heavy equipment on the fragile surface, and it shattered, crashing his equipment to the floor. The young soldier looked puzzled. Apparently, he had never seen a table made of glass before. He looked at us with an expression of genuine regret on his boyish face. Then his face brightened and he reached into his duffel bag, pulled out a loaf of bread, and gave it to Mother.

For the most part, these simple combat troops left us alone. We were actually glad of their presence because it prevented looting and raping in our apartment.

Our backyard became a bivouac site for many Soviet soldiers. They set up camp there, complete with mess tent, horses, chickens, and even a cow—the animals had been dragged along for thousands of miles. Almond-eyed Mongolians—short, squat men in ill-fitting, dirty uniforms—mingled with blond Ukranians, Cossack officers, and tall Belorussians with high cheekbones. Some arrived bareback on horses, carrying their muscular, tough-looking women behind them. Many of the women were barefoot, and looked used to roughing it. *How can they walk on the rubble in the streets and over burning embers without hurting their feet?* I puzzled. When they were seated and their legs were crossed, I got close enough to see that the soles of their feet were callused like thick shoe leather. I wondered if their feet had ever known the luxury of shoes.

One of these tough women walked into our apartment. She went from room to room. We didn't know what she was looking for and watched her nervously. In my parents' bedroom, she stopped and opened Mother's wardrobe. Her eyes lit on Mother's gold lamé dress. *Oh, no! Not that one!* I screamed silently as she tore it from the hanger with her grimy hands. I wanted to snatch it away from her but changed my mind when I spied the pistol in her belt. A grin spread over her coarse face as she roughly pulled the delicate dress over her big head and broad shoulders, where it promptly ripped to shreds.

Enraged, I wanted to hit her. "*You stupid, stupid woman!*" I felt like shouting at her. She had violated Mother, who always looked so beautiful and elegant in that dress.

Mother whispered sternly to me, "Get out before you do or say something dumb," and she pushed me out of the room.

Just as the Soviet woman had taken Mother's dress, the conquering Soviet soldiers felt it their right to seize whatever they wanted. In the days after the battle's end, they looted all over the city. The rough combat soldiers acted like children amusing themselves with toys. Some of the soldiers confiscated old treadle sewing machines from nearby apartments, and the rest stood in line for a chance to pedal them. Bathtubs were hauled out of homes, and soldiers gleefully splashed around in them.

Wristwatches were a special prize to them. One fellow displayed watches on his arm up to his shoulders. "Uri! Uri!" Watch! Watch! we could hear them demand when searching apartments for loot, until there was hardly a wristwatch left in Berlin.

Bicycles, the only means of transportation for Berliners, were coveted by the Soviets as well. The soldiers regularly stole them. We laughed behind our hands as we watched them struggling to stay on the two wheelers, like children learning to ride their first bikes.

One day Frank was on his old dilapidated bike, pedaling free-handed down the street. Suddenly a Russian soldier rounded the corner just behind him on a brand-new bike.

"Stuizi! Stuizi!" Stop! Stop! the soldier shouted.

Oh, no, thought Frank. *What does he want of me?* Nervous, he halted.

The soldier motioned, seemingly wanting to know how Frank could ride free-handed on that bike.

Frank shrugged and pointed to his bike. *It's the bike, not me,* he pantomimed. The man gestured that he wanted Frank's bike. So Frank offered the soldier his old bike in exchange for the new one. He then wasted no time swinging himself on the new bike and taking off down the street, briefly catching a glimpse over his shoulder of the soldier struggling to ride without hands.

～

The war was over, and an estimated 125,000 civilians had lost their lives in the Battle of Berlin. The once-beautiful city lay in ruins. For weeks we could not see the sun or a patch of blue sky through the dark, billowing clouds of smoke. We lived in fear of the Russians' looting, plunder, and rape.

We were without the simplest necessities. There was no drinkable water, no electricity, no gas, no transportation, no stores, no food. Our desperate hunger added a new torment to our lives. These conditions were worse than anything I had ever experienced before.

My family went about the chores of repairing and cleaning our apartment. We stood in long bucket lines for water or dragged water from a nearby reservoir, where dead bodies floated. Father's little makeshift stove burned continuously to boil the pots of water we set on the grate. Debris—crumbled mortar, broken glass, and splintered furniture—was everywhere in the rooms. Added to that was the terrible stench of urine and feces deposited in various corners of our apartment by the field communication unit. The Russians, unfamiliar with toilets, used the toilet bowls to wash themselves in and evacuated their bowels on the floor.

In the corner of the entrance hall we kept the small barrel of pickled beets from an earlier food-foraging expedition. We considered those beets lifesavers until we caught a soldier urinating into the barrel. *How many have done so before?* we wondered, horrified. We promptly dumped the barrel.

Mother, exasperated with having to clean up after the soldiers, took matters in hand one day. She led each man separately into the bathroom, indicating where he should urinate and defecate, and how to flush afterward with a bucket of water she kept beside the toilet. They delighted in watching everything disappear down the hole by magic and vigorously pumped Mother's hand in gratitude. They rewarded her for the lesson with a loaf of bread.

Bathing wasn't possible. There was no clean water to wash with. Lice and body odors began to add another kind of torture to our lives.

Among the many pots kept warm on Father's stove was the soup pot. Mother managed to make watery soups from the potato peels that our soldiers threw away. Sometimes we also scavenged for horse meat in the streets. We had to exercise stamina and courage to fight the crowds wielding knives, tearing at the dead animals like vultures. None of us had the stomach for it for very long.

Hunger—the painful, burning hole in our stomachs growing larger and larger—dominated our lives. It seemed that all I thought of and all I dreamed of was food. Frank and I talked mainly of food. We were obsessed.

One day one of our soldiers handed Mother a big, fatty sausage.

Mother thought it was for us and thanked him over and over again. "Spahseeba! Spahseeba!" she said.

Father quickly stirred up the fire, and the whole family gathered around. We inhaled the marvelous smoky fragrance and savored the rich flavor and texture of each piece as we ate it straight out of the frying pan.

The soldier suddenly reappeared, gesticulating and shouting something. We weren't sure what he wanted. Suddenly it dawned on us that he was looking for his sausage. He had instructed Mother to fry it for him. Fortunately, there was still a short piece of the sausage left. Panic stricken, Mother gave it to him and showed him all the grease in the pan, trying to convince him that the sausage had shrunk to that size. While we nervously watched, he frowned and looked from the small sausage in his hand to the fat in the frying pan. Finally he nodded, apparently satisfied with the explanation, and disappeared into the next room. We were thrilled to keep the treasured fat left in the pan.

Thankfully, one thing that Goebbels had so darkly predicted did not come true. The Russian soldiers did not abuse children. They seemed to love them. Frank and I quickly put this discovery to practical use. We coached our little Tommy, now a friendly, outgoing three and a half year

old and a born ham, how to hold his hands out and say, "Khleb?" Bread?
As the soldiers approached, we gently pushed him into their path while
we hid in the bushes.

Unafraid and seemingly aware of the importance of his mission, the
little fellow trotted up to the soldiers and, widening his blue eyes, he
clapped his hands together in a pleading gesture. "Khleb?" he repeated,
"Khleb? Bitte, bitte?" Bread? Please, please?

Frank and I watched from our hiding place, wondering if it was safe
to have sent Tommy into the street after all. But there was no need to
worry. The battle-hardened soldiers melted at the sight of the little
cherub. They knelt down and gave him bread. The next time we sent him
out, they gave him cookies, and another time candy, every time talking
to him in Russian. He always rewarded them with a sweet smile. After
they had gone, Tommy proudly carried his loot back to our hiding place
in the bushes, where we hugged and praised him. He never tired of this
game. But when Mother found out where we kept finding bread and
other treats, she promptly put a stop to it.

No milk or any other source of calcium was available, and Bassi, now
two, was beginning to show signs of serious malnutrition. She was frail
and thin, with dark circles under her eyes and foul breath. She seemed
listless and always begged to be carried.

Once when the communication group was out, two Russian soldiers
forced their way into our apartment. I was holding Bassi.

"You mother?" they demanded.

I nodded, knowing that they often showed mercy to women with
small children. Bassi was clutching her doll. The soldiers poked around
for something to loot. Suddenly the doll slipped from Bassi's grasp and
crashed to the floor, causing it to say "Mama!" Instantly, the Russians
whipped out their pistols and fired into the doll.

Bassi howled and almost fell out of my arms as she lunged for her
doll. The soldiers' expressions changed from alarm and anger to embarrassment. They dug into their pockets and handed candy to the crying
child. They must never have seen a doll that could talk, and suspected a
booby trap.

We were sorry when our field communication group left in the middle of May. Overall they had been decent to us and had given us a certain amount of protection from rape and looting. After they left, we were completely exposed. Soldiers wandered in and out of the apartment in endless succession, no matter the hour. Since we were on the first floor, the soldiers climbed through the glassless windows or broke down the front door to get in. Tired of constantly having to repair the door, Father finally left it unlocked.

When I heard soldiers coming I quickly hid under beds, behind clothing in wardrobes, and once in the attic, where I was investigated by big hungry rats who had taken up residence there.

Fearing that I would be raped, Father asked a German-speaking Russian officer for a protection note for me as an American citizen. The officer agreed, and for a while the Russian note he had written seemed to work. Whenever a soldier tried to get close to me or say the dreaded words all women feared, "Frau komm mit," Woman come along, Father whipped out the note. The soldier always looked at me with something close to loathing and backed away. We soon found out why. The note said I had venereal disease.

Once my disgust wore off, I tried to use this ruse to my advantage, pretending to be sick by emphasizing the dark shadows under my eyes and coughing loudly whenever a soldier's eyes lit on me. My behavior, combined with the note and my American passport, seemed to work.

Mother dealt with the threats of rape in her own way. Instead of making herself ugly by smearing charcoal on her face and dressing in old rags, as so many women and girls did, she emphasized her beauty and dressed in her best. Her manner with the soldiers was imperious and authoritative, traits that seemed to intimidate the ordinary, uneducated soldiers. This was a different kind of woman from those they knew back home. They weren't sure how to handle her. Mother shielded the other women in our apartment house who fled to her for protection and camped in our living room.

One day some soldiers were led into the apartment by a tall, handsome officer who looked and acted educated and fairly cultured. I was fascinated by his hands, which didn't look like those of a laborer or a soldier. They were soft and white, with long, tapered fingers. *Like a musician,* I thought. With measured looks the officer inspected the women in the room, including me, walking up and down in front of us, looking at each of us while occasionally commenting in Russian to the waiting soldiers. I could feel the other women's anxiety and fear as easily as I could my own. The officer stopped in front of Mother, and my heart skipped a beat. He looked at her with admiration and desire.

Mother pointed to Father. "My husband," she said, pointing to her wedding ring, and then picked up Tommy, who had just entered the room. I could see panic in Father's eyes and anger in Frank's as they watched helplessly. Mother then swept her hand around the room and informed the officer, "Americanski!"

"All family?" he questioned, gesturing to the women in the room.

"Yes," replied Mother, looking straight into his eyes. "All family! All Amerikanski."

He didn't say anything more. He seemed to accept Mother's explanation. Apparently he didn't think it was unusual for that many members of a family to share a small apartment.

"You make party tonight. Dance. Music," he ordered Mother. "All women come." And then he left with his men.

That evening Mother made me hide under the bed in my parents' room and shut the door. She wasn't taking any chances. I knew she didn't trust the officer.

The officer and his men arrived as scheduled, and I heard the clinks and thuds of the soldiers unloading something—food, I guessed, and probably liquor. Soon a gramophone played records of lively Russian dances and folk music. The officer, who seemed to be the only one who knew a few words of German, commanded, "Frau, tanz," Woman, dance. I assumed he was talking to Mother, and I knew Father must have been boiling mad. I only hoped he kept his mouth shut in front of the Russians.

The soldiers sang and shouted and danced their wild folk dances, pounding the floor with heavy boots so that the rough wood boards under my stomach vibrated.

At one point I heard Tommy open the door to the dining room and call, "Mutti!" Mother! The pounding boots stopped. I could just picture him shuffling out, his sweet face flushed from sleep. He probably wondered what so many strangers were doing in our home. The soldiers spoke in Russian to him, but then I heard Father say, "Off to bed with you, Tommy." I imagined Tommy was disappointed to be missing out on so much excitement, but I heard his little footsteps patter obediently down the hall to my bedroom, where he was spending the night.

They danced deep into the night. I knew Mother and all the other women must have been exhausted, but the soldiers didn't seem to be. I was totally stiff and cramped from lying for hours in one position under the bed. I prayed they would go and leave us alone.

Through the door I could feel the tension building. Then I heard the inevitable command, "Frau komm mit!" Woman come! Some women sobbed hysterically.

Mother, her voice loud and authoritative, called, *"Nyet!"* No! "You can't have me or any of these women. We're Americans!"

I imagined how she must have fixed the men with her dark, intimidating eyes. To my relief, I heard the officer give an order to his drunken men. After they left, I could hear them tramping down the sidewalk, probably seeking victims in other tenement buildings.

When the soldiers were gone, I was finally allowed to crawl out from under my narrow, cramped hiding place, my muscles stiff and achy. The dining room was a shambles. It smelled of liquor and the air was thick with cigarette smoke. Mother was noticeably pale. She sat on the sofa, rubbing her sore feet. The women were all going back to their apartments, safe, we hoped, for another night. Father, Frank, and I emptied ashtrays and carried glasses into the kitchen, wiping up food and vodka spills from the floor.

Mother pointed to holes in the carpet and white spots on the wooden floors. "That's from the vodka!" she said. "It must have been pure alcohol—150 proof." She picked up a bottle, still half full. "You know, I was so afraid the Amerikanski story wouldn't work once the officer and his men were drunk. I knew they would soon try to take what they wanted from us…. So when they were busy dancing, I poured out half the vodka from the bottles and refilled them with water."

"Were the soldiers angry?" I asked. Mother shook her head. With a tired smile she said, "They never noticed. They just went right on dancing their wild dances and drinking their vodka water."

I grinned back at Mother. She always knew what to do. And I was proud of Father too. For once, he had managed to keep his mouth shut.

Later, back in my bed with the sleeping Tommy beside me, I listened into the early morning hours to the screams of women in nearby apartment buildings, a terrible pain in my heart. I shuddered at what might have occurred if it hadn't been for Mother's courage.

A couple of days later, the officer reappeared and handed Mother flowers. He seemed to genuinely admire her.

But the Russians weren't finished with us yet. One afternoon Mother, Father, and Frank were out scavenging for food, and I was home alone for a few hours with the two little ones, who were napping. I was in my room, writing in my diary. Suddenly a Russian burst through the window, and I found myself looking down a gun barrel and feeling the sharp, cold point of a bayonet against my ribs. I was too terrified to scream. But he appeared intent on something other than rape.

"Uri! Uri!" Watch! Watch! he demanded. "Uri! Uri!"

He jabbed my ribs. I knew that to save myself I had to find a watch somewhere. *But where?* The Russians who had been invading our apartment for weeks had already depleted our household supply of watches. But he was very angry and bent on a mission.

Holy Mary! I silently prayed, quickly glancing at the picture on the wall. *Help me! Send the Invisibles.* And suddenly I remembered the gold watch with the red ruby stem that Grossmutter Rump had given me for communion. I had hidden it in my raincoat pocket some time ago when I learned that the Russians were after watches.

The demand of "Uri! Uri!" got more insistent and the soldier's stance more threatening. His eyes were cold and brutal. I was paralyzed with fear. From another room I heard Tommy call my name, and suddenly I was spurred into action.

With one hand I motioned to the wardrobe and with the other I pushed aside the bayonet. He nodded and tucked the pistol into his belt. Frantically, I groped through the pockets of the raincoat, hoping and praying I had remembered correctly. *I never realized that this raincoat had so many damn pockets,* I thought desperately. But finally I fingered the watch and gratefully pulled it out of its hiding place. I laid the delicate little thing with the red ruby stem into the dirty, grubby hands of the Russian soldier. Satisfied, he disappeared out the same window where he had entered. When Grossmutter gave me the watch at my first Holy Communion, I never suspected that one day it would save my life.

CHAPTER THIRTEEN

FIFTEEN AND I'M GOING TO LIVE

MAY 1945–SUMMER 1945

BERLIN CONTINUED TO SMOLDER. Choking, poisonous yellow smoke and gray dust hung motionless over the dead city, shutting out the sun. And as the weather began to grow warmer, the sickening stench of decaying bodies, burst sewers, and broken gas pipes permeated the air. It seemed as though the ghosts of the dead were rising from the rubble to protest their violent deaths.

I sensed a hopelessness everywhere. It lurked behind tightly closed doors where broken families lived. It seeped out of the ruins where bodies were buried. It hung heavily off emaciated people digging through debris for something to salvage. It stared from the hungry eyes of the orphaned children searching for food and shelter. It showed in the gaunt faces of the endless masses of refugees from Pomerania, East Prussia, Silesa, and other eastern provinces, who sought food and a place to stay in a city that had nothing to offer. It emanated from the ashen faces of returning soldiers in tattered uniforms and dirty bandages, limping through the streets trying to find their families.

No food could be found. Hunger was a constant, relentless ache we couldn't forget for a moment. It gnawed at our insides and our minds. Mercifully, in sleep we could escape it, but it was there again to torture us when we woke up.

For the first time since I could remember, I didn't look forward to the future. Life was dull gray. Nowhere could I see a single bright spot. I didn't even enjoy Tommy and Bassi, who had so often brought cheer to my life.

I no longer had access to fantasy, to the magic of imagination. I was cut off from the inner world of images that had always sustained me. Dreams of returning to Stratford lay buried in the ashes of the city. No matter how hard I tried to remember them, they wouldn't form in my head. The Botticelli Madonna was only a painting now. I no longer spoke to her. Worst of all, I could no longer feel the presence of the Invisibles. They were gone too.

In the middle of May the Russian Kommandantura, or command post, issued ration cards. They were rated in five levels. Those people who contributed to cultural events—like musicians, singers, actors—as well as city cleanup crews were given the highest rating and the most food: weekly rations of 600 grams of bread, 30 grams of fat, and 100 grams of meat. Housewives, jobless people, and former Nazi party members were assigned the lowest rating: daily rations of 300 grams of bread, 7 grams of fat, and 20 grams of meat. "Hunger cards," the Berliners called these meager rations. Our family got the hunger cards.

We went back to the daily routine of standing in line in front of stores for distribution of supplies, this time provided by the Russians. Our ration cards didn't automatically guarantee a loaf of bread. Sometimes the shelves were bare long before I reached the counter, and I had to wait until the next day to try again.

In the morning Mother usually gave Frank and me our daily ration of three slices of bread with a little salt. This was to last us the whole day. At first I wolfed down all of them at once, but I learned very quickly to save some for later, when hunger returned with a vengeance, gnawing a hole through my belly. The Russian bread was like nothing I had seen before. It was a blend of rye and sourdough, heavy, grainy, and chewy. It lay so heavy in my stomach that I felt like I had eaten one of the huge chunks of concrete piled in the streets. Often we found roaches baked right into the bread. We were too hungry to care, though. Mother just plucked them out.

Mother used the fat ration to make concoctions that managed to fill our bottomless stomachs, but only for a while. Tommy and Bassi cried and begged for more after every meal. I overheard Mother complaining to a neighbor, "It hurts me so much to have to deny my children food—especially the little ones, who don't understand why they can't have any more." Now that it was safe to do so, Mother sent me back to picking dandelions in the park, which she steamed and pureed for baby Elizabeth and Tommy.

One day Frank and I were walking down the street when Russian soldiers shoved a huge wooden barrel off a passing truck. We immediately investigated and found to our great joy remnants of honey still clinging to the inside of the barrel. We reached way inside to scrape and lick the sticky sweetness with our fingers. But we had no time to find something to put the honey in and take it back to Mother. In just moments, other children spotted us working the barrel, and soon it was as smooth and clean inside as if it had been scrubbed and washed.

Shortly after Bassi's and my birthday, I woke up to the roar of trucks and chatter of voices coming from the little park across the street. I shook Frank.

"Wake up! Something's going on out there."

He jumped out of bed. "C'mon, let's find out."

We quickly dressed and crept outside. A grisly scene presented itself in the moonlight. Russian soldiers were guarding a group of men, like ghoulish shadows, who were digging up corpses in various stages of decay from trenches where they had been dumped right after the battle. Among the workers, we recognized several neighbors who had been active Nazi party members. They loaded the bodies onto trucks and hand-pulled carts and trudged off to bury them somewhere else. This scene repeated itself for weeks in other parks, fields, and gardens—anywhere the ground had been soft enough to dig shallow trenches during the battle.

In all the burying and reburying, there were no caskets, no undertakers, no ceremonies, no flowers, no tears, and no prayers. With the coming of summer and heat, both the Russians and the Berliners feared typhoid, dysentery, and other diseases, and they rushed to bury the dead. So many dead were in the city that individual grave sites were a luxury no longer available. Mass graves had to be dug deep enough and long enough to accommodate all the corpses. Many of those who had died didn't get a resting place at all—thousands remained buried beneath tons of concrete and bricks.

I could not imagine that these bloated, disfigured bodies I saw everywhere were once alive, were real people like me. *Why am I still alive and they are not?* I asked myself over and over again. *Why?*

$\sim$

We heard that a local store was distributing milk to families with small children. Anxious to get out of the house, I volunteered to go. A long line had already gathered at the store. Ahead of me I recognized a schoolmate. "Anneliese!" I cried, thrilled to see a familiar face. A big smile spread across her face as she spotted me, and we hugged. We had had little contact in school beyond a quick greeting in the hallway, but she too appeared happy to see an acquaintance in all this misery. We exchanged stories of suffering—who hadn't made it, who had lost their homes, who had been raped.

"My father and brother were killed at the Russian front," she told me flatly. Then she added, "My mother, baby sister, and I all survived the bombings, but our apartment was destroyed by artillery fire when the Russians came. We're now living in the basement of a bombed-out building."

After we received our shares of the precious milk, I knew I should go directly back home. "The streets still aren't safe," Mother had warned me. But I didn't see any harm in going with Anneliese just a little way to talk. I couldn't bear to part with her yet. After we had strolled several blocks, though, my conscience began to nag me. "I have to go home, Anneliese," I said. "Mother is waiting for the milk."

She nodded. "See you in school soon." I watched her as she waved and rounded the next corner. I turned to go home.

Just then I heard trucks roaring down the street behind me. Tires screeched, doors slammed, and loud, angry voices spoke in guttural Russian. I dashed through some bushes and pressed against a building. I heard running footsteps—wooden shoes clattering and scraping against the gritty pavement—then screams of terror, followed by the *ack-ack* of machine-gun fire. *What's going on?* my mind shrieked as I pressed my hands against my ears, my eyes shut tight. The screaming seemed to go on forever. *Please stop, please stop,* I prayed.

The screams did stop. Then I heard the slamming of truck doors and the roar of engines that faded down the street. After a few minutes, I cautiously crept to the corner where Anneliese had disappeared from sight. People were running from all directions to see what had happened. I gasped in horror as I saw Anneliese. Her small, thin body lay sprawled in a pool of milk that was stained red with blood. She was still clutching her blue tin can. Many other bodies lay scattered in the street around her.

"What happened?" one woman asked.

A man pointed to the attic window of the building next to us. "Two Russian officers were shot from up there a couple days ago, and they haven't found out who did it."

"It was probably some fanatic Hitler Youths who can't believe the war is lost," replied another angrily. "The Russians retaliated by simply massacring people who happened to be walking down this street."

Poor, poor Anneliese. I couldn't look at her body. I turned to walk away, but then I stopped. *Oh no! I have to tell Anneliese's mother. But where can I find her? Where is she living now?* I realized that I couldn't help Anneliese or her family.

My sense of hopelessness was now complete. I was barely fifteen, but I couldn't imagine living a normal life, wearing a pretty dress, going to a dance, knowing what it was like to fall in love. *Most of the boys my age are dead,* I reminded myself. I thought about Hans Joachim in Stolp, Hans and Ernst in Waldenburg, and Frank's friends. *What happened to them? So many have suffered and died. So much is destroyed. How can I ever be happy again?*

With no electricity, we didn't even have the small pleasure of listening to the radio. There were no newspapers, no magazines, no libraries, no books. The few stores still around were empty.

∾

The routine Mother insisted on kept our lives going, although in an automatic, mechanical way. We spent our days caring for Tommy and Bassi, scavenging for food, hauling buckets of water, digging through ruins for wood for our hallway stove. At night nightmares haunted me.

I moved dully through days and nights. I couldn't laugh. I couldn't cry. Now that the war was over, I felt more dead inside than I had during the worst bombings.

I thought often of Annemarie and wondered if she had survived. She and I hadn't seen each other since long before the battle, and it was now the end of May. Some law and order had returned to the city under the Russian Kommandantura. The free-for-all rape and plunder seemed to have stopped for the most part, and the streets had become a little safer.

I finally couldn't stand it any longer. I had to see if Annemarie was still alive. Deeply absorbed in dark thoughts, I walked along the debris-littered street toward Annemarie's house, but a sound broke through my daze. *What was that?* I heard it again. I stood still and listened. It was an almost forgotten sound, strangely sweet, like the trill of a flute. *What is it?* I searched my memory. *Is it a bird? No. There* are *no more birds in Berlin. The firestorms from the bombings and the battle—the intense heat, noise, smoke, and destruction of trees—killed or drove the birds away.* I hadn't seen a bird for months. *There it is again!* My eyes wandered up to the branches of the badly scarred tree next to me.

There, perched on a blackened limb, was a robin redbreast. We measured one another in mute recognition. He tilted his tiny head in my direction and again broke out into ecstatic song. And then something happened in the deepest part of me, like the gushing forth of a long-dammed-up spring, picking up volume and speed, then turning into a rushing, thundering river. It beat against my temples, roared in my ears, and pounded my flesh with a wild, primitive, ecstatic surge of life.

In that moment, all of the death and destruction became not reasons to surrender to hopelessness but inspirations to fight, to live.

As though blinders had been torn from my eyes, I suddenly discovered signs of spring all around me. There in the moist spot between the fallen beams were brilliant purple violets. And there beside the charred garden gate were my favorite flowers, lilies-of-the-valley, dancing in the breeze, claiming their right to life. Purple lilac offered a touch of color to a blackened wall nearby. And the tree on the corner was covered with green buds. *Why haven't I seen this before?* I sucked in deep breaths of air. Sooty or not, it was, after all, air. I ran from wonder to wonder, reveling in as many vibrant strokes of color as I could find, admiring nature's palette. And there in the sky, like the eye of God peering down at me, was a patch of brilliant blue and a ray of light as though the sun were trying hard to break through the gray curtain.

Suddenly I knew in my heart that Annemarie was alive.

"I'm fifteen, and I'm going to live!" I cried, stretching my arms up to the almost visible sun in the sky. Before me lay a future filled with unimaginable possibilities.

As I walked quickly toward Annemarie's, I became aware of renewing life in other areas. A banner across a theater proclaimed that a play would soon be performed there. A crude sign over the basement of a bombed-out house read "Hair salon opening soon. Bring your own soap." Oh, just the thought of having my hair washed made me skip and leap.

I neared the Teschs' and saw that at the Botanical Gardens, the glass enclosures had long been shattered, and steel girders lay about in grotesque sculptures. But here, too, the urge to live was visible in the rare plants, trees, and bushes thick with buds, ready to burst into bloom, defying war and devastation.

I saw that Annemarie's beautiful villa on the Arnoholzstrasse had survived the bombings and the battle. In fact, somehow the entire street of villas had escaped severe destruction, although many of the lovely trees had been cut down—for firewood, I assumed.

I rounded the corner and saw that the garden in front of the Tesch house also showed signs of spring. Its bushes and flowers were budding, and blades of green grass sprouted thick. But then I spotted, at the far end of the lawn, a lone Russian soldier and his grazing cow. I stopped and quickly looked for a place to hide. The man sat on a tree stump, smoking a cigarette, lazily watching the cow, looking more like a farmer than a soldier. When he showed no signs of being a threat, I nodded to him and ran up the front steps.

I knocked at the door, still a little afraid of what I might find. But when the door opened, there she was, Annemarie, my beloved friend, pale and thin but otherwise in one piece. We fell into each other's arms, laughing and crying at the same time. She pulled me into the house. We had so much to talk about, so much to share.

"Oh, it was dreadful," Annemarie said. "Christoph is still with the Paulsen school, which evacuated to Posen. He couldn't make it back to Berlin," she reported, her eyes and voice dropping. She hesitated for a moment. "And," she added softly, "the Russians were terrible. Whenever we had enough warning, we hid in the secret attic room."

It feels like a lifetime has passed since we played in that little room, I thought.

"Imagine!" she continued, shuddering. "They even tried to rape Ömi, such an old woman."

"Oh no!" I gasped.

"But somehow," Annemarie continued, "Ömi found the strength to escape from the soldier. She ran screaming into the street. And he let her go!"

"Poor Ömi," I said, barely able to hide a smile about the image conjured up in my mind of the cantankerous, dignified old lady fending off the soldier. We were silent for a while.

Then, on a brighter note, I recalled one of the signs I had seen. "Did you know the Ahornschlösschen is opening soon with Shakespeare's *As You Like It?*"

"And guess what? I heard the Philharmonic is practicing at the Titania Palast."

"Erika left before the battle. She should be back soon."

"I heard Inge and her family fled to the countryside before the battle. They aren't back yet."

"Where is Rena?" Annemarie asked.

"Last time I saw her, her family was trying to leave Berlin." Then I paused, sad again. "Anneliese didn't make it." I told her the dreadful story and broke into sobs. Annemarie cried with me. We gradually quieted. We knew we would hear many more tragic stories in the months to come.

～

Early in June the lights went on. Electricity was back! Frank quickly turned on our radio. "This is England here," started the first broadcast we heard. *England!* We were reconnected to the world. We listened to the entire BBC report of the postwar situation without fear of reprisal. Best of all, the radio brought music. It cheered our dreary lives and shabby surroundings. Electricity was on only sporadically, but at least the promise was there.

But the radio and newspapers also brought devastating news. Millions of people—Jews, Gypsies, Resistance fighters, Poles, and many, many others—had been exterminated in death camps. Those persons who had survived were barely recognizable as human beings, emaciated and abused. "That can't be true," I gasped. *What kind of people could have done such terrible things? And why?* I agonized.

I had known about the Nazi concentration camps and prisoner-of-war camps, prisons where people served sentences and then were released. *Where were the death camps? Is this what happened to the man behind the barbed wire in Waldenburg?* I looked anxiously to my parents to see if they had known about these horrifying places. But the stricken looks on their faces told me they had not. When I spoke to my friends about it, they were just as shocked as I was. *What other evils will come to light?* I wondered.

Rumors spread that Berlin was to be divided into four sectors, each to be controlled by one of the four main Allies: the British, French, Americans, and Russians. For weeks we heard much speculation about the Americans. Would they come? And if so, to what section of the city? Of course, everybody hoped that their part of Berlin would be put under

American jurisdiction. Every day I prayed, *Please let the Americans come to Steglitz.*

And then late one afternoon Renate knocked on our door. "Rena!" I shouted, hugging her tightly, so happy to see her again. "Where have you been? I thought you had left Berlin."

"We tried," she explained, "but couldn't get the travel papers. We were told that no more civilians could leave the city. So we stayed in our cellar, and we all made it!" She beamed.

"Guess what?" Rena bubbled. "Today I saw an Ami on the Schloss Strasse!"

"An American soldier? Hooray!"

I couldn't wait to tell the family. "The Americans are here!" I burst out importantly as everyone gathered at the supper table for our usual ration of thin soup.

"Really?" Frank said, his face brightening.

"How do you know that?" Father demanded.

"Rena was here today, and she said she saw an Ami on the Schloss Strasse."

"What's an Ami?" asked Tommy.

"Ami," echoed Bassi.

"That's short for an American," Mother explained.

"Yes, and you're Americans too," I told the two little ones. "Because Father is an American."

Frank turned to Father. "Maybe we'll be lucky and Steglitz will be put under American jurisdiction."

"I sure hope so," Father replied, looking at Mother.

In my heart I already knew it would be true.

I've been waiting for this moment, I realized, *for so many years.* I had always felt American. I had been born in America, had spent the happiest years of my life there. It was my homeland. My loyalty to the United States had never wavered. Neither the rituals of the Hitler Youth and the Nazi propaganda nor the terrible Allied bombings had changed my heart. Suddenly the Stratford dream leaped to life again. I dared to hope we could return at long last.

A few days later I saw them with my own eyes: tall, proud American soldiers from the 82nd Airborne Division. They looked like the conquerors they were, well nourished, clean, dressed in neat uniforms—unlike their sloppy Russian counterparts. Excitedly I listened to the familiar language and wished I had the courage to go up and speak to them.

As I had hoped, Steglitz came under American jurisdiction. But some of the American occupation troops were not, after all, the gods I had made of them. I was walking home from Annemarie's house one day when two American soldiers approached me.

"Do you want an orange?" one soldier asked, holding it out to me.

Did I ever! I could barely remember what an orange tasted like. I hadn't seen one since we had left Stratford almost six years before. Besides, I was starving, and all I thought of was food.

I thought, *Here's a chance to practice my English.* I replied, in the best English I could muster, "Yes, thank you. I would like an orange very much." Then I proudly added, "I'm an American too."

"Sure you are," sneered the soldier with the orange. "Isn't everybody in this cussed country?" And with that, he threw the orange down the street. "You want it? Go fetch it."

I felt as if he had slapped me in the face. Tears flooded my eyes. The soldiers laughed and turned away. Mesmerized, I watched the orange roll down the street and stop in the gutter. I was torn between running after the precious fruit and walking away with my pride intact. Hunger, and the thought of taking home a treasure to share, won out.

At home, after Mother had cleaned the orange, I handed it to Tommy. We all watched his reaction.

With great curiosity he turned it over and over, squeezed it, sniffed it, shifted it from hand to hand. "Ball?" he asked.

"No, you eat it," I urged. "We have to peel it first, though."

But before I had a chance to take the orange from him, he bit into the rind. His face screwed up into a shocked grimace; then he shook himself at the strange taste, and we all laughed.

～

Annemarie stopped by one day, bursting with good news. "Guess what? I heard this afternoon there's going to be a concert by the Philharmonic at the Titania Palast!"

"A concert! A real live concert!" I cried. "Let's see if we can get in."

I was amazed to see how many people showed up, in spite of having no transportation and seeing no posters. The only news of the concert had been spread by word of mouth. People came on foot and on mangled old bicycles.

Russian and American soldiers sat side by side with Germans. Men and women, young and old—everybody was eager to forget hunger and worries for just a little while and escape into the magic of music. The emaciated musicians put their hearts and souls into playing the music of Mendelssohn, Mozart, and Tchaikovsky. *I am alive to hear this music,* I thought as the wondrous notes took me away. My throat tightened, and tears began to run down my cheeks. All around me I heard people sniffling and their clothing rustling as they wiped their eyes and noses.

In the coming days, signs of human life sprang out of the ashes all around me. Movie houses—showing mostly Russian and American films—and theaters in various stages of repair were opening again in various sectors of Berlin. Annemarie, Renate, Erika, who had recently returned to Berlin, and I went to the opening of Shakespeare's play *As You Like It.* The cost of admission was a carpentry item, like a tool, nails, screws, or paint. Who cared if there were bullet holes in the roof and walls and not enough chairs to go around? We were thrilled just to watch a play again, to have the chance to be transported to a world very different from our own.

❧

The American Occupation force arrived—countless clean-cut Navy boys, battle-weary 78th Infantry soldiers, and fresh-faced 82nd Airbornes—all clearly pleased that the war in Europe was over and they were at last in the capital of the infamous Third Reich.

With the coming of the Americans, our food situation began to improve a little, but we still struggled to find enough to eat. And the black market shifted into full swing. Because German marks were practically worthless, cigarettes became the real currency. Even though bartering and dealing in the black market were forbidden, everybody participated. It made the difference between life and starvation. We were desperate.

Frank, who was sixteen, became a skilled trader on the black market, and the family's main food provider. Although Mother did not approve of it, necessity forced her to close her eyes to the danger and seamy activities. Father didn't like Frank's involvement with it either, but Father had been out of work for months and had no hope of finding a job in the ruined, chaotic city anytime soon.

Father was more irritable than usual and lashed out at us at every minor provocation. Most of the time Frank and I tiptoed around him and tried to be away as much as possible, Frank on his deals and me with the two little ones in a stroller to Annemarie's. But one day Father became especially angry with Frank and tried to hit him. Frank pushed Father back on his bed and pinned him down with his now six-foot frame. He calmly looked down at Father and said quietly, "Don't ever do that again." Father never did.

I knew that some of the dealings Frank had become involved in were very dangerous. He was able to bring home food that the whole family desperately needed, but he had told me about some deals that had gone bad, when he had had to escape down the street with bullets whistling over his head. He said everything was available if you were offering the right kind of goods in trade. Expensive Bavarian china, crystal glasses, diamond necklaces, beautiful artwork—all were expendable in the face of starvation. Canned ham, coffee, butter, powdered milk, and powdered eggs were far more valuable than a solid gold bracelet.

The U. S. Navy confiscated some of the less damaged buildings on the other side of our little park to accommodate a contingent of American sailors. Frank worked with one of these sailors in the black market, and said that the fellow's room was stacked to the ceiling with goods worth thousands of dollars, all of which he collected by trading G. I. food supplies and cigarettes on the black market. The sailor was shipping his new treasures back to his family.

Most of the time when I passed the Naval office, I was greeted by friendly sailors. But one day two sailors were standing out front, smoking cigarettes, and as I passed the building, I overheard one talking to the other about me.

"Look at that skinny Kraut. I wonder if she's any good in the sack?"

Blood rushed to my face. *They're talking as though I'm a whore!* I spun and faced the startled sailors and yelled at the top of my lungs, in English, "Who the hell do you think you're talking to?"

Shocked, the men just looked at me.

"I'm an American, just like you." I pointed at each of them. "And I demand to see your commanding officer!"

"Sorry, ma'am," one of the soldiers replied, red faced. "We didn't know you were American."

"Well, you never know. Do you?" I snapped. I walked away, immensely pleased with myself.

Sometimes Frank brought American soldiers or sailors to our apartment. When this happened, I became aware of how I looked in the clunky, klutzy wooden shoes and the dingy, ill-fitting, patched clothes I was wearing. I desperately wished I were pretty. Mother still had several nice dresses from Stratford that had survived the war. One in particular, royal blue with a border of white lilies, was my favorite.

"Please may I borrow it?" I pleaded. "It's the only dress that can make me pretty."

Usually Mother scolded me. "For heaven's sake, Eleanor, stop being so vain." But on rare occasions she gave in.

I had noticed one American soldier in particular. Frank told me his name was Richard. He came from Philadelphia, where I had been born, which made him even more attractive to me. I wanted to impress him. So one day when I knew he was coming, I invited Annemarie, Erika, and Renate over and all three helped me get ready for his visit. Each one of us girls had something to add to this glamorous wonder I wished to create. We dug up a lipstick from an old purse, a bit of rouge and powder to cover my freckles, and hair curlers to put a wave into my straight hair. We had to do all of this while Father was out of the house, of course, because he absolutely did not approve of lipstick and rouge. "Only prostitutes wear makeup!" he often declared.

The mirror and the admiring smiles of my friends told me that the finished version of me wasn't too shabby. With confidence I waited for Richard, ready to hand over my heart to him.

The reward for all my effort was Richard's remark to Frank as he walked into the house, "So this is your little sister?" And he patted me on the head.

～

The scope of our world expanded more and more, thanks in large part to the Americans. Now that we had electricity some of the time, we began to enjoy immensely the jazz and swing music often broadcast on the Armed Forces Network. What joy it was to listen to the sounds of Duke Ellington, Glenn Miller, Benny Goodman, and Harry James on the radio after years of nothing but boring speeches, Hitler's and Goebbels' tirades, news of disasters at the front, and the inevitable warnings of approaching bombers.

My friends and I were quick to capitalize on these new developments. We began to meet one afternoon a week at Annemarie's house for what we called Tanzstunde, dance hour. Her big library room was ideal for dancing. There, for a while, we forgot the ever-present hunger and the misery all around us. We turned on the Armed Forces Network and jitterbugged and fox-trotted with each other, dreaming of our true loves who were sure to come. We made plans for the future.

"I think I'll be a baby nurse," said Annemarie.

"And I'm going back to Guatemala. Maybe I'll manage a coffee plantation," piped up Renate.

"Well, I'm going to marry a rich man," said Erika, rolling her beautiful blue eyes, "and I'll travel all over the world."

"And we know what you'll do," said the girls, turning to me.

"Yes, I'm definitely going back to the States." I beamed. "Maybe I'll come back sometime as a diplomat in the foreign service, and then I can visit you."

It was exciting to think about all these things, to have a future again. We never tired of talking about what we wanted for our lives.

But we knew sadness was never far away. The Teschs received news that Annemarie's Tante Alice had vanished from her apartment in Charlottenburg. Devastated, Frau Tesch and her niece, Lili, went from one Kommandantura to another trying to find information about the missing aunt. But no one was able to help her. Then, a few weeks later, a woman appeared at the Teschs' house and told them that she, Tante Alice, and other women had been picked up by the Russians and deported to a work camp in Poland. The Russians had released her because she was ill, she said, but she was at the camp long enough to find out that Alice and many other women at the camp had been forced to stand all day in an icy river and that they had all died of exposure. The news devastated Frau Tesch, Annemarie, and especially Lili, who had been so close to her mother.

But the Teschs also had reason to rejoice. Christoph, Annemarie's brother, suddenly appeared at the house. Starving and with sores all over his feet, he had walked all the way from where his school had been evacuated in Posen. Annemarie and Frau Tesch were overjoyed. They had despaired of ever seeing him again.

～

One morning early in July, I found that I couldn't open my eyes, no matter how hard I tried. They were solidly glued shut with pus.

"Mother!" I screamed, "I can't see!"

She ran into my room and gently dabbed my eyes with a damp cloth. Gradually I was able to open them, but was immediately thrown into a panic when I couldn't see anything but a white blur.

"Oh God! I'm blind!" I cried hysterically, stumbling around, bumping into furniture. "What's happening?"

After several days of flushing my eyes with water without improvement, Mother went in search of a doctor. Doctors were hard to find. Many had lost their lives on the battlefield. Those who had returned were overburdened with the tens of thousands of wounded and dying in the city.

Somehow Mother managed to persuade a young American medic to take a look at me. He interrogated me intensely, and I quickly became embarrassed by the questions he was asking.

"Were you recently with a man?" he asked. "Did he touch you, and if so where? Were you raped? Did you use a public toilet and not wash your hands afterward?"

I didn't understand why he was asking me these questions. But for some reason I felt ashamed. Later Mother explained that the medic had suspected I had syphilis. But he eventually came to the conclusion that it was some other kind of infection, and he gave me medicine that eventually cleared up the problem.

Many strange diseases emerged from the dirty, unsanitary conditions in the city. Summer had come, and the weather was hotter than usual. We had no escape from the dreadful odor of decay. Rats overran the city, and typhoid and epidemics were rampant. And the flies—big black flies that I had never seen before—added their own torment. The Americans told us that the fly larvae probably had been brought into Berlin on the clothes of Russian soldiers. Those larvae were now hatching by the millions and feeding on us. A painful infection always followed a bite from one of those nasty creatures. We were constantly on the lookout for them.

Sometimes it seemed as though life was going forward only to slip backward again the next day. I felt a growing, desperate impatience to get on with my life.

CHAPTER
FOURTEEN

OCCUPIED BERLIN
SUMMER 1945–SPRING 1946

ON AUGUST 6 we heard on the radio that the Americans had dropped an atom bomb on the Japanese city of Hiroshima. "The bomb," the announcer read, "had a detonation power twenty thousand times greater than the English ten-thousand-kilo bombs that were dropped on Germany." I couldn't imagine bombs worse than those that had fallen on Berlin. The announcer read an eye-witness report: "On the ground in Hiroshima, an unimaginable incandescence swallowed the sky and out-shone the sun. With a horrendous blast the bomb pulverized the entire city and reduced it to ashes."

I shuddered and imagined the thousands of people who must have died terrible deaths in that fiery furnace. It conjured up nightmare images which I tried to push away as fast as they appeared. *Don't think about it*, I told myself. *I have all I can handle right here and now.*

Three days later, we heard that the United States dropped a second atom bomb, this time on Nagasaki.

I turned to Mother. "After all the death and pain we've seen and lived through, I don't understand why countries fight wars."

"I don't either," Mother replied softly. "It's always the innocent who suffer."

Then on August 14, the radio reporter announced, "Japan has surrendered to the United States. The war in the Pacific is over." After six years the guns were finally silent all over the world.

The Allies had now established a provisional four-power government. They were trying to find ways of feeding the Berliners, including the many tens of thousands of refugees that were daily pouring in from the east. Each sector had set up its own military command post to establish the rule of law.

By fall 1945, a certain amount of order was emerging from the chaos, although we still heard occasional gunshots. We had to show identification papers to go from one sector of the city to another. Cleaning operations were in full swing. Streets were being cleared, brick by brick, mostly by women who were called the Trümmerfrauen, rubble women. Among them were housewives, mothers, and many professional women of all ages and backgrounds. Two generations of men had been killed, imprisoned, or maimed by this terrible war, and now it was left to the women to clean up Berlin. They labored from dawn till dusk at this backbreaking work. Heavy labor was rewarded with the top ration cards, so the women were able to help save their children from starvation.

Father finally had some luck. He got a job as an interpreter and secretary for a Colonel Stahl in the American Command Post, a ten-minute walk from our house. Frank and I breathed easier now that he was out of the house.

My family was constantly worried about Bassi's health. I yearned for fresh vegetables to feed her, but our garden had long ago been destroyed by the Russians. Thankfully, because we were American citizens, our family was now eligible to receive Red Cross care packages. The powdered milk and eggs and the canned meat came just in time to save Bassi from severe complications of malnutrition. When we began to see some improvement in Bassi's health, we were all relieved.

Just as electricity and the music of the Armed Forces Network had helped bring color back into our lives, so did the re-establishing of postal services. We were actually getting letters now and were reconnected with family living in other cities. The first card that had reached me since 1942 came from Tante Lina and Onkel Carl in Philadelphia. It was a belated card for my fifteenth birthday. I displayed it proudly on my dresser. We received notes from the Münster grandparents and Tante Elsbeth and from Omi Ramrath, confirming that they were alive. They were worried about whether we had survived the battle. We learned that Onkel Werner, Mother's brother who had brought us the treasured goose fat years earlier, had been taken prisoner at the eastern front and sent to a Russian prison camp. Our immigrant friends in the United States wrote, anxious for news from us—mainly trying to find out if we were still alive.

It must have been difficult for the postal carriers to deliver the mail because so many addresses no longer existed. Luckily, we still had our home. But the only remaining traces of thousands of families were scraps of paper tacked to heaps of rubble. These read "Schmidt family alive, now living in Bavaria," or "Giesingers living in the Schwarzwald." Often the posted notes were desperate attempts to find missing loved ones. They read "If anyone has news of the Reintal family, please contact Hannelore in Zehlendorf," or "Looking for Friedrich Herman formerly at this address, please contact...." Sometimes a photograph of a child was pinned to the remnants of a house wall with the plea, "Have you seen my child? Please contact me at...."

A letter came from my friend Helga in Waldenburg.

Dear Eleanor,

I'm giving this letter to Herr Richter who is going to Berlin. Here is what happened to us since you left Waldenburg. On May 8, we were thrown out of our place. We trekked across the mountains in the direction of Czechoslovakia. We got as far as Gablonz but had to turn around on account of the Russians. For seven weeks we stayed in Polaun in the Iser Mountains. Finally, with nowhere else to go, we returned to Waldenburg. On the way the Czechs took all our belongings. Also in Waldenburg at the Police Presidium where we used to live, everything we had left behind was gone. We now live with Herr Richter along with Russians and Poles in the same apartment.

There is still no school. Remember our teacher, Hofi? He returned home with thirteen grenade splinters in his body.

Your relatives too were ordered out of your apartment on the Pflugstrasse. Frau Mettner's husband is a prisoner of war somewhere in Russia. But they have no news from you.

We are still trying to get back to Germany. There's no news about my father. Eleanor, please try to find my relatives in Zehlendorf and let them know we are alive.

No news yet from Hans and Ernst Novack. They were drafted at the last minute and forced to fight the Russians. Write to me, but I don't know if mail will reach us yet.

Helga

I was overjoyed to hear from her and immediately went to Zehlendorf to try to find her relatives. I found, however, that their house had been destroyed, and neighbors there had heard no news of them. I wrote Helga a lengthy letter but doubted she would ever receive it. The whole area of upper and lower Silesia had been turned over to Poland, and there was little communication between Germany and Poland.

A while later, I was glad to get a note from Hans Joachim from Stolp.

Dear Eleanor,

I hope this letter reaches you. I'm alive and so is my family. I was drafted along with many other Hitler Youths. We were thrown as last ditch defenders into the ferocious resistance against the invading Red Army, where many of us were shot or froze to death or died of hunger. I was one of the fortunate ones. I lived!

Hans Joachim

One day that fall, Tante Mieze and Onkel Adolf showed up on our doorstep. Stolp, like Waldenburg, had become part of Poland, and they had been evicted from their apartment. After we hugged them, we sat down to catch up on news.

"Oh, the most awful thing happened!" Tante Mieze told us. "I had packed a big bundle of money inside my corset. Since I'm…er…somewhat stout, I didn't think the additional padding would be noticed. Onkel Adolf and I managed to find seats on a train heading for Berlin."

She took a breath. "But the train was stopped and raided by Russian soldiers searching the passengers for valuables. A soldier looked closely at my waist. Then he poked me with his rifle and demanded that I pull up my dress! Oh, I was mortified!"

She looked away, her lips pursed but her chin twitching. Then she took another deep breath. "He ripped off my corset, and all the money fluttered to the floor." Tante Mieze looked away again, dabbing her eyes.

"There, there, Miezchen," Onkel Adolf said, patting her shoulder. He continued the story for her. "Your Tante Mieze informed that soldier how rude and coarse he was, but he just growled at her and shoved her back onto the seat with his rifle butt."

I could see that it must have been a frightening, humiliating experience for my proper aunt. Just the same, when I thought of Tante Mieze lifting up her dress, I couldn't help but be a little amused.

Then I reminded her, "Tante Mieze, the money wouldn't have done you any good, anyway. There are no stores and no goods to buy, not even the barest necessities. You risked your life for something worthless."

I was happy to see my relatives alive. I had mostly good memories of my visits to Stolp in 1941 and 1943, and I loved my aunt and uncle. They remained with us to recuperate and to wait until trains to the west were running more reliably. Then they planned to go to Wellingholzhausen, where Grossmutter and Grossvater Rump had moved.

But living with these two spoiled old people in our already cramped quarters wasn't easy, particularly for Mother—it was as stressful as it had been when we had stayed with them in 1943. Some of the old tension between the two strong-willed women quickly resurfaced. Mother, Frank, and I had to scrounge around even more to find enough food for the additional mouths, and Mother had to be even more imaginative with the way she created meals.

The previous spring we had found some red powder, which when mixed with hot water made a thick pudding. We loved it because it was sweet and invitingly red, and it could fill that constantly empty hole in our stomachs like nothing else. Tommy and Bassi jumped up and down when they saw Mother preparing it.

Mother now had just enough powder left to make two small dishes of pudding to feed the little ones. She set them on the windowsill to cool, then went next door to visit a neighbor. I took the children for a walk to Annemarie's house. When we returned, Mother confronted me, enraged. "Did you eat the pudding?"

"No, I didn't," I replied, hurt. "I wouldn't take it away from the children."

"Well, somebody did!" she said, waving at the dishes in the sink. "The bowls are clearly empty!"

Tante Mieze stepped into the kitchen. "Onkel Adolf and I did," she said, giving Mother a withering look. "I didn't think you would mind. We were hungry."

"That pudding was for Tommy and Bassi," I spat out before Mother could say anything. "They need it more than you do." I recalled the old blueberry episode, and my anger rose up hotly.

Tante Mieze turned on her heels and strode out of the kitchen, mumbling about children with no manners.

Later I overheard Mother complain to Father, "Tante Mieze took the food right out of the mouths of our children. I was so mad!"

We were relieved when, some weeks later, the two old people left.

～

Later in the fall we heard over the radio that schools were reopening. Schools that were still standing doubled up to accommodate students from bombed-out school buildings. School was held in double sessions, morning for some grades and afternoon for others. My old school was being used as a temporary clinic now, so we were ordered to attend the Königen-Luisen Stiftung in Steglitz. I never thought I would welcome going to school, but after a year's absence, I was actually excited and happy about attending again.

That first day we were sent to a room to be deloused with a dreadful-smelling chemical before entering class. Some girls who had severe lice infestations had to have their hair shaved off and were given bandannas to cover their new baldness. Many cried with shame. *I'd cry too,* I thought. I felt so sorry for them, and relieved that I got to keep my hair, as straight and stringy as it was. *These poor girls will have to wait a long time before their hair is longer than boys' hair.* The overpowering odor of delousing chemicals seeped into my pores, and I wondered if I would ever be able to wash it off. But I was grateful for the relief from the constant itching.

The class reunion of those of us who had survived the war was bittersweet. We felt awkward, almost embarrassed, to see each other alive when we could easily look around and see that so many classmates hadn't made it. No one seemed to know if we should laugh with relief or cry. So much had happened in the past years. It felt like practically a lifetime since the last normal school attendance in 1943, before the city was evacuated of women and children. So many tragedies had befallen us and those we cared about. I heard endless sad stories.

"Did you know Susanne died? There was a direct hit to her house. Her whole family was wiped out."

"Rita is the only one left in her immediate family. She lives with her aunt in Bavaria now."

"Heidi was raped thirteen times. They say she isn't right in the head anymore."

"My favorite aunt was raped thirty-six times. She took her own life."

"My father came home from the eastern front. We were so happy to see him alive. But two days later the Russians deported him to God knows where in Russia, probably Siberia. I don't think he'll ever be back."

"We lost everything in a bombing raid. We now live with my aunt, and she doesn't like it. She complains all the time."

"My mother never gets out of bed anymore since my two brothers were killed. They were in the Volkssturm. One was thirteen and the other sixteen."

"They raped my poor old grandmother. She was eighty-five and died of a heart attack."

"My little ten-year-old sister was raped. Now she cries all the time."

One girl sobbed, "Oh God! I think I'm pregnant with a Russian baby. What am I going to do?"

We shared story after tragic story. I was relieved when our geography teacher entered the room and the stories stopped.

Annemarie, my beloved friend, sat next to me again. As so often in the past, her presence comforted me. I looked around the room and thought, *Will we ever be normal, happy teenage girls?* Sadly, I doubted it.

In English class our teacher struggled with the difficult English "th" sound. She asked those of us who had a small mirror to bring it to class and practice pressing the tip of our tongue to the back of our front teeth.

"Now! Al-to-ge-zer! Za man in za moon," she instructed.

I couldn't help laughing. "No! No! That's wrong!" I said. I showed her how to pronounce it correctly. But my effort to help didn't go over very well. It earned me a 3 in English—a C—in what should have been my best subject. I had a hard time explaining the poor mark to Father.

Russian was added to our already heavy curriculum. Science and math—physics, trigonometry, and algebra, especially—continued to be difficult subjects for me, and my familiar anxiety about failing returned. I studied hard and tried my best, but it wasn't enough. Frau Dr. Clausius, our new math instructor, was used to teaching university students, not high school students. She was able to reach the few brilliant math students in our class, but left the majority of us far behind.

I struggled hard in her classes and finally resorted to cheating during tests. I found that if I wrote a formula on the back of my hand, I could actually solve some test problems. I sensed that Dr. Clausius was onto me, but for some reason she never stopped me from using these aids. Anyway, my cheating didn't make much of a difference. I was failing math anyway.

As winter approached, classes became irregular again due to lack of coal. Before and during the war, Berlin had been supplied with coal from Silesia, but since that region was now part of Poland, only trickles of shipments came through. So, as we had during the war, we occasionally had coal vacations. And as before, these days were hardly vacations. We were given loads of homework to do and were almost as busy at home as we had been in school.

By early December, the weather forecasters told us that this winter was already breaking all records for cold. Temperatures hovered well below zero for days on end. What trees were left in the inner city parks were chopped down for fuel. Berliners picked over the city's ruins for anything that could be burned.

Houses still standing had so many holes in them and were so weakened by bomb explosions that they provided little protection from the wind. Windows still had no glass and were boarded up with wood or cardboard. Roofs leaked. Snow drifted in between cracks and through shell holes in outer walls.

When classes were in session, we sat at our desks wearing mittens, coats, wool hats, and shawls against the piercing cold. Our teachers regularly had us jump around to keep our feet from freezing. The wooden shoes most of us wore made a considerable racket, clumping on the brittle classroom floors. We were so cold and uncomfortable; it was even harder than usual to memorize the capital cities of all the states in America and the square roots of numbers.

After school, Frank and I scavenged among the ruins for anything we could burn in Father's little stove in the entrance hall, which was the only warm spot in the house. Sometimes Frank was able to barter for coal briquettes, which provided extra warmth.

Father had gone from a strapping 160 pounds to a thin 133, and little Elizabeth still looked like a tiny waif. Frank had grown tall in the last couple of years, but he was just skin and bones. Mother, Tommy, and I somehow had fared better. We managed to hang onto the little fat we still had left.

Despite all our hardships, I knew my family was luckier than many— if not most—others. We had a solid roof over our heads and some heat and food. But more important than anything else, my family was miraculously still intact.

In the middle of the many dreadful days below zero, it snowed. Gentle snowflakes covered everything with a mantle of pure white. I put on warm clothes and walked alone through the deserted neighborhood, breathing in crystal-clean air in deep gulps. Snow mercifully covered the ugly ruins, the charred tree branches, the heaps of rubble. It transformed everything into an immaculate dreamscape. I walked to the bombed-out building next to ours, where I knew many bodies still lay buried beneath the tons of concrete.

Even though the actual tapping had stopped long ago, I still had nightmares that I could hear those doomed people knocking. I had tried to tell Mother about my recurring dreams that the people were still alive. "Don't be silly," she replied. "That was over two years ago. Stop that nonsense." After that I didn't talk about it anymore, but the tapping in my head hadn't gone away.

The sharp edges of the ruins were now made softer by the snow. I listened into the swirling silence of the falling snow. Now all was quiet, outside and inside my head.

~

Day-to-day life seemed to take more and more effort. Nothing was simple anymore. Just washing clothes was a major undertaking. We started the process at night, when Mother and I carried our dirty laundry three flights up to the Waschküche, washing kitchen, in the attic of our apartment house. There we soaked the clothes in a giant tub. The next morning, we used what little coal and wood we could spare to light a fire under the tub and bring the wash water to a boil. Then we soaped the clothes, scrubbed them on the washboard, drained the tub, rinsed the clothes, and wrung them out by hand.

In the warm months we had carried the heavy wet clothes downstairs and hung them out on a clothesline in the backyard. In the winter, however, we had to hang them in the attic, where they promptly froze on the line. Once the clothes were frozen solid, we could shake the ice off them, whereupon they were completely dry. But we had to be careful not to tear the worn clothes while we were shaking off the sharp ice crystals. In the subfreezing temperatures, at least the drying process was quick. The clothes, however, were always ice-cold, stiff, and very uncomfortable to put on again.

Because this process was so involved and exhausting, we left the sheets on the beds for a month or longer and changed our clothing only once a week. I dreaded the monthly wash-day ordeal. Before we went to Stolp, when we still had Lucie, I had been excused from it, but now Mother had no help. So it was up to me to pitch in.

Sometimes after a snowstorm, Father and Frank rolled up the rugs in our apartment and carried them out back. They spread out the carpets on the new snow and pounded the dirt out of them with a bamboo rug beater. I loved to watch the swirled patterns of gray dust settling on the fresh snow. We moved the carpets from one place on the snow to the next until they came out clean. Afterward, the whole apartment smelled fresh.

～

During the winter, when I was fifteen, I finally got my first period. I had been fretting over it for some time, since all my friends had already had theirs, and mine came one morning very unexpectedly. *Now I am a real woman,* I told myself proudly. I hoped in some magical way that everybody would see the difference in me and stop treating me like a child.

That afternoon when no one else was around I told Mother. "It happened! I finally got my period!"

"That's normal," she replied without a hint of emotion. "Welcome to womanhood."

Unfortunately, sanitary napkins, like toilet paper, hadn't been in stores for years. Now that the toilets were working again, instead of toilet paper, we used newsprint. And since we didn't have sanitary napkins, Mother and I tore up old bedsheets and towels and made our own. The messy things had to be soaked, washed, and hung up to dry after each use. I soon wondered why on earth I had wished for my period to come. It was nothing but an annoyance.

Before I knew it, Christmas was just around the corner, and I began to feel the stirrings of the old magic of the holiday. While I spent hours making a cloth doll to replace Elizabeth's old one, left in Waldenburg when we fled in such a hurry, Frank scavenged through ruins and found an old Easter basket. Then he found a bamboo rod and four small wheels. He made axles, put on the wheels, and then attached them to the bottom of the basket. He fastened the flexible rod to the basket with rope, to serve as a handle. He had created a fine doll carriage. I sewed pillows and blankets for it by hand, and the doll I made rested happily in blue and white comfort.

Frank used his coping saw to cut out wooden zoo animals for Tommy, which I then painted. We made lions, tigers, and zebras, even an elephant. Frank also built a small dollhouse with furniture while I created little people out of cardboard. Working on these Christmas projects brought Frank and me together again. I felt close to him as I had in the Stratford days.

Somehow, through Frank's black market efforts or Father's connection to the American Command Post, we managed to have a scrawny little tree, which we decorated with stubs of candles left over from years before.

The best part of Christmas 1945 was the reassuring knowledge that the war was over. My beloved family was safe.

At midnight on Christmas Eve the bells that still existed rang out all over the city in one glorious chorus. I stood in the doorway of our apartment house listening into the night until they died away. And in the silence that followed, I thought I could hear the flutter of wings.

The children loved their gifts. Elizabeth gleefully pushed her doll carriage from room to room like a little whirlwind. Impatiently she rammed against the furniture—or us—screaming at the top of her lungs with frustration until the obstacle in front of her was removed.

Tommy spent all day arranging and rearranging his zoo animals. He liked playing with the dollhouse so much that it became more his than

Elizabeth's. Soon his animals took up residence in the house with the dolls.

My family was making it through the postwar months all right. We had little to eat, but we weren't starving anymore. We were cold, but we weren't in danger. We were together. We were alive.

All around us in that harsh winter of 1945 to 1946, thousands of people in the city were freezing or starving to death.

~

I longed desperately for spring, and it came at last. I spotted the first signs of crocus and snow bells pushing through the melting snow in Annemarie's garden. The sun returned after months of cold and darkness. I felt pure joy when I heard the first robin sing.

One sunny afternoon I sat on the front step of the apartment building and lifted my face to the warm rays of the sun. Mother Nature had again brought her gifts of spring and new life to the destroyed city. *I only have to look,* I thought. I smiled as I spotted the thick green buds on one of the few remaining chestnut trees in the little park across the street.

I drifted back to memories from my early childhood, when I had stayed with Omi in Eslohe. She taught me to care for and respect the natural world of that small village and its surrounding forests and mountains. *Well, Omi,* I thought, *I can see now that, despite her terrible winters, and despite the destruction that humans have wrought, Mother Nature always brings new life. Thank you, Omi, for showing me how to find hope in nature's gifts.*

~

In that spring of 1946 the city truly began to return to some semblance of normal life. Brief bursts of machine-gun fire still sounded sometimes, but other aspects of life were getting back to normal. Stores opened up everywhere, albeit with sparsely stocked shelves. Streets were being cleared of rubble. The subway system was working again in most areas. And the open-air market in Steglitz reassembled, filled with entrepreneurs selling potatoes, rutabagas, and an odd assortment of goods obtained on the black market. People seemed friendlier. They greeted each other with "Guten Tag," Good day, and stopped to chat for a while or to exchange the latest Berliner jokes. I sensed a general feeling of optimism and hope that life would go forward again.

Also, thankfully, Else came into our lives. Like Lucie, she helped our family during the day, but she went home at night. With her assistance, things became easier for Mother and me. Often I had so much homework that I had little time left to be a real help to Mother.

Something else was emerging that spring. I suddenly found myself becoming more interested in boys. Whereas before I had thought of them only on occasion, they were now taking up a lot of my thoughts. When a handsome young soldier looked at me, my heart beat a little faster and I could feel blood rushing to my cheeks. I became aware of my appearance, my hair, my clothes, and how I walked. Annemarie was going through a similar change. Boys became *the* topic of conversation at our dance afternoons at Annemarie's house. I became even more envious of Erika because of her beauty, her blond curly hair, and her well-developed breasts—all attributes I lacked. None of us were surprised that Erika was the first to have a real boyfriend.

Our curiosity about boys led us next door from Annemarie's house to a villa that the Russians had confiscated from a doctor, driving him and his family out. When the Americans had occupied Steglitz, the Russians left the villa in shambles. They had tossed all of the doctor's medical books into the garden, where they were gradually being destroyed by the snow and rain. We girls began to sneak next door and pore through the books that were still in good shape, repulsed but also fascinated by the graphic details of both healthy and diseased sexual parts of the human anatomy. We tried to stifle our embarrassed giggling and ignore our queasy stomachs. But when Papa Petke found out what we were doing, he promptly burned the books, thereby ending our impromptu anatomy lessons.

After dinner one night in April, Father called us together. "I have applied to the American Embassy for our return to America," he announced.

Both Frank and I were ecstatic. *We're going home! After so many years, we're finally going back to America!* I couldn't wait to share the news in class.

"I'm going back to America," I happily announced to my schoolmates the next day.

But the news fell oddly flat. Instead of an enthusiastic response, I received only polite mumblings of "That's nice." In a flash, I understood why. I would be leaving for a new, exciting, safe life in a country untouched by bombs and battles, whereas their lives would continue in the ruined and struggling city. I regretted having blurted out my good news and became aware of the deep bond I had developed with my German friends, a bond forged in large part by shared horrible experiences and tragedies. I would never be able to forget these friendships.

The most painful thought, however, was that I would be leaving my best friend, the only true friend I had ever had. Of course, as soon as I told her my news, Annemarie and I made endless plans.

"I'll move to America," Annemarie immediately vowed.

"Oh, yes, and we'll get jobs and live together," I added.

But deep down we both knew that these were only pipe dreams. Where would we get the money for travel when our families often had to go without the barest necessities of food and clothing? The ocean was so broad that it took nine days to cross by ship. We realized all this, but couldn't admit that we would probably never see each other again.

Sometimes at night I cried about leaving Germany and my friends, but I didn't want Mother to see my tears. I knew she wouldn't understand. I knew she would say, "I thought this is what you've wanted for years, Eleanor, to go back to the States! Why are you crying?"

Arranging our return to the United States proved to be a lot more difficult than we had expected. Exit visas were hard to get. Father had to visit the American Consulate often and write countless letters to Washington. He had to undergo harsh CIA interrogations and interviews.

The interrogations were meant to establish if Father had ever been a member of the Nazi party or if he had been a Nazi sympathizer. As part of their investigation of Father, CIA agents talked to neighbors in our apartment house about our family. The interviewer told us that one of the neighbors remembered Father back in 1940 flying the Stars and Stripes on Hitler's birthday among all the swastika flags. We never knew if this incident finally convinced the American investigators that we weren't Nazi sympathizers, but I liked to think so.

∾

After weeks of anxious waiting, we finally heard the CIA officials' decision: Father, Frank, and I were granted permission to return to the States as American citizens. But Mother had to stay behind. The U. S. government would not loan her the money to return. It was a terrible, painful shock to all of us.

We hadn't expected Mother to be denied the passage. How could we leave her? She was the one who always said we must stay together as a family. *We can't split up the family,* I thought, *not after all we've struggled through. Perhaps we shouldn't go.* Mother and Father discussed the situation deep into the night. Anxiously I tried to listen, but eventually I fell into a troubled sleep.

The next morning, Father turned to Frank and me at the breakfast table. "Mother and I think it's best that I go ahead to the United States and that you two come with me." He looked at Mother, and she nodded. He continued. "We think it's important for you two to go to school over there as soon as possible. The Americans didn't say she cannot go to America. They just said that they won't pay for her passage. So I'll try to get a job as quickly as I can and earn the money to bring Mother and the little ones over. Hopefully it won't take too long."

"And Mother?" I whispered, close to panic. I turned to her. "You'll be all alone!"

"No," she said, "I'll be okay. I have Tommy and Elizabeth to keep me company. Anyway, before you know it, we'll all be back together again."

She's trying to sound brave and reassuring, I thought. But she kept her eyes cast downward, so I couldn't tell what she was really feeling.

Moving across the ocean without Mother and the babies.... How will we manage? How can we abandon them in this ruined city and leave for the safety of America?

Christmas 1943 in Stolp, with Tante Mieze and Onkel Adolf, both at right. Father and I are standing, to the left, and Mother and Frank, seated, are holding Bassi and Tommy. After months of separation, all of us are together again as a family.

Bassi (age 14 months) with the dirty, ragged doggie that she refused to allow to be washed.

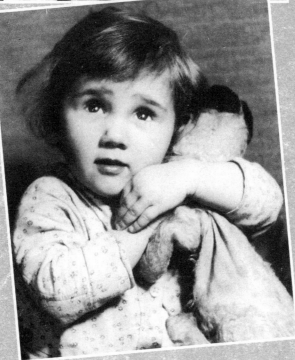

*Bombing raids
decimated the city.*

*The apartment
building next
door to ours after
it received in 1943
the direct block-
buster hit which
buried many
in the rubble.*

Our building at the end of the war in 1945. Note the cellophane in the windows and the scars on the exterior from bullets and phosphorous.

The Botticelli Madonna, which hung over my bed during all the awful, frightening times. Note the thumbtack hole that I used after I had to remove her from the frame to fit in my suitcase. Her gown and cape were scratched by flying shrapnel.

Christmas 1945. Tommy (almost age 4) and Bassi (age 2 ¹/₂) opening their presents. This was our best Christmas ever because we had survived the bombings, the Battle of Berlin, and hunger.

Late spring 1946, just before Father, Frank, and I departed for the United States. I am at left (in one of my mother's dresses and the patent leather shoes from the Red Cross) with Annemarie and Renate.

Helga (top right), my Waldenburg friend, and Erika (bottom right).

July 1946, sailing back to the United States aboard the U.S.S. Marine Perch. Frank (age 17), Father, and me (age 16).

Fall 1947. Mother (recently returned to the United States with Tommy and Elizabeth) with Father, Frank, and me.

CHAPTER
FIFTEEN

RETURN TO AMERICA
SPRING 1946–JULY 1946

DURING THE SPRING of 1946, we still heard occasional sniper shots and bursts from machine guns, but Berlin generally felt much safer for civilians.

It was obvious that any good feelings that may have existed between the Russians and the Americans had deteriorated to outright animosity. Radio reports and newspapers told us that Stalin in Russia was angering the Americans by imposing repressive Communist regimes on conquered countries. The occasional rifle shots we heard around the city were generally fired by testy Russians and Americans when one crossed into the other's territory.

Over the radio we heard that the Nazi leaders continued to be on trial in Nuremburg for their unspeakable crimes during the war. I only wished Hitler could have been there, too, to face the aftermath of the evil he had begun. Instead, Hitler, SS chief Heinrich Himmler, and propaganda minister Joseph Goebbels had all committed suicide before the Russians could capture them.

Now that the Americans and British were flying large cargoes of food into Berlin, we were eating more and better quality food. But the average ration was a bare fifteen hundred calories or so a day, and I was still always hungry.

Housing continued to be virtually nonexistent for many refugees. Those who had survived the harsh winter in drafty ruins—and many did not—were relocated into requisitioned rooms in houses that were still standing. People had to double up wherever possible. Many rooms in Annemarie's home were converted into temporary housing for bombed-out families.

But even though the citizens' most basic housing and food needs were being taken care of, few jobs existed in Berlin for fathers or mothers to earn money to pay for additional needs. No factory work was available—those factories still standing had been stripped bare by the Russians, who had dismantled all of the machinery and shipped it back to the Soviet Union. Using the black market and bartering continued to be a way of life.

My family was still anxiously awaiting news from the U. S. State Department about Father's, Frank's, and my departure date for America. Officials at the department frequently made promises to us of specific dates, then informed us of unexpected delays. Sometimes I despaired that we would ever go.

As we waited, my family settled into a routine. Father set off every morning for his job as translator and secretary at the American Command Post, and Frank and I went to school. Mother took over the chore of standing in line for food while Else cared for the children and the household.

We rejoiced in the small improvements in our daily lives. Electricity was becoming more and more reliable, we had running water, and many branches of the subway were working again.

Across the street from us, in the little park, someone had cleaned up the children's playground and cleared the sandboxes of artillery and bomb debris. Once again children's laughter and gleeful screeches echoed across the street, pulling other children from the neighborhood to join in the fun.

"We want to play in the sandbox too," demanded Tommy, now four, standing with his fists dug into his hips.

"Me too," echoed little Elizabeth, almost three, giving Mother a determined look.

It was a sunny spring afternoon, and Mother and I escorted the two happy children across the street to the sandbox, where other kids had gathered. Several children were barefoot, which didn't go unnoticed by Tommy. He sat down and took off his shoes. Elizabeth promptly copied her brother.

"The sand is warm and soft," he said to Mother.

"Don't you dare lose your shoes," Mother warned, shaking a finger at her two youngest children. "You know we can't replace them. These are the only ones you have, so guard them well."

The children nodded and carefully placed their shoes on a low wall alongside the playground.

Mother and I had chores to do, so we waved good-bye. "One of us will come and get you in a while," I said. They were already deeply absorbed in play.

Sometime later the two trotted home alone, barefoot.

"Where are your shoes?" Mother demanded, an icy edge to her voice.

"They're gone," said Tommy softly, looking regretfully down at his sandy feet.

"Both pairs?" she asked, near panic.

Elizabeth nodded, her eyes big.

I felt so sorry for them and wanted to hug them, but I knew the seriousness of the situation. Shoes weren't available anywhere.

Mother and I frantically searched the playground. We looked in every corner, under every bench, on the far side of every wall, but the shoes were gone.

When we returned home, Mother lost her temper for the first time in years. She seized the trembling children and spanked them mercilessly, then sent them into separate rooms, where they cried bitterly. They had never been disciplined like that before.

Mother turned to me, reading my mind. "Don't you dare go in there and comfort them! I forbid you!" She clenched her hands, wailing, "Where will I get shoes for them?"

Fortunately, when Father learned of the lost shoes, he went to Colonel Stahl, his employer, about our plight. The Red Cross supplied the children with new shoes.

During the war, everyone in our family had been expected to help keep up the household. This did not change after the war. Father did his part by working, Frank continued his involvement in the black market, Mother and I took care of the children, and little Tommy took the trash out to the cement garbage hut behind our apartment. Every day he dutifully trotted off to empty the trash baskets. But one day he refused to go. Father threatened him, but Tommy stood his ground.

"I'm not going!" he finally blurted out. "There are too many rats!"

Frank ran out back and returned with the news that the place was indeed overrun by huge, black, hungry rats. After that, either Frank or I went with Tommy, banging pots and making as much noise as we could to scare the rats away.

That spring, Tommy was enrolled in a kindergarten that had opened up in my school. The kindergarten started and ended at different times than my classes, and it was too far for Tommy to walk there, so every morning Father pedaled him to school on the way to work on his bicycle and picked him up again at noon. On rainy days, I took him with me on the subway. I liked that he was in my school, and whenever possible, I'd sneak a peek into his classroom to watch him playing with blocks or singing in a circle of children.

Frank, Father, and I began spending more and more time with Tommy and Elizabeth. Once we left for America, we didn't know how long it would be before we saw them again. On Sunday mornings, Tommy crawled into bed with Father and sang him all the songs he had learned in school. Father ordered me to write down the lyrics in my diary so they wouldn't be forgotten. I was flattered that Father asked me to do this and happily recorded the words. I liked one song in particular, about how many stars are in the heavens, and asked Tommy to sing it to Elizabeth when I put her to bed at night. Tommy never tired of singing his school songs, and it wasn't long before we were all singing them.

On a beautiful spring day in May 1946, Annemarie was confirmed in the Protestant Church. Since clothes were still impossible to get,

Annemarie's mother had been pulling dresses out of Ömi's trunk and tailoring them into clothing for the family. She also used her sewing machine to transform brocade drapes into clothing.

Mother allowed me to wear her royal blue lily dress, but not before she warned me repeatedly not to get spots on it when Renate, Erika, and I celebrated with Annemarie that afternoon in her family's garden. Annemarie was chic in a black dress with a white lace collar and a brand-new perm in her hair.

Mother had baked a cake for the occasion. She made it from potatoes. I gave Annemarie a book titled *Demian* by Hermann Hesse, which I had found on our shelves at home. Mother knew we couldn't take many books back with us to America—we just didn't have the room, and they were heavy—so she encouraged me to give some away. Books and magazines were still hard to get, and Annemarie was thrilled with the gift, since she too was an avid reader.

The afternoon was filled with laughter. As we talked and celebrated Annemarie's special day, I felt young and alive. I wondered what all of our futures would bring.

We ate Mother's potato cake under Annemarie's old walnut tree, which was budding with tender green leaves.

"It's the best cake ever," everybody agreed.

～

In June, at the end of the school year, I said painful good-byes to my classmates. I realized I would probably never see these girls again, and they realized it as well.

"Don't forget us," they said. "Write when you can. We want to know what's happening to you. We'll miss you." I had grown up with these girls. We had been through horrifying times and joyous ones. I knew I would miss them too.

As I said my good-byes, my math teacher, Frau Dr. Clausius, called me into her office. With a warm smile on her face and a mischievous twinkle in her eyes, she said, "Eleanor, I can't let you go to America with a poor grade in math. What will they think of our German schools?"

I squirmed, remembering how I had repeatedly written the formulas on my hand for the tests.

Still smiling, she continued. "You know what? I'm going to give you a 3 in math for effort."

My mouth fell open as I stood in front of her. I had never expected such a thing. I quickly mumbled my thanks and left. I was grateful for the grade, but it brought little pleasure because deep down I knew I didn't deserve her kindness. I had cheated.

The State Department finally gave us a mid-July departure date. As the day drew ever closer, I was torn between excitement and anxiety. I worried about all kinds of things, not the least of which was leaving Annemarie.

"We'll write every day," Annemarie and I promised each other.

"We won't keep any secrets from each other, especially about boys and love."

"Let's share everything that happens, the good and the bad."

But I couldn't help worrying that when I was gone I would lose my special place in Annemarie's heart.

～

Thoughts of leaving behind Mother, Tommy, and Elizabeth were upsetting in a different way from those of leaving my friends. The sixteen-year-old, grown-up me was excited and ready to strike out into the world alone, without Mother. But the little-girl me still wanted to cling to her. I now knew how quickly a safe world could turn against me.

I spent many moments looking hard at Elizabeth and Tommy, trying to memorize their faces. I felt their soft hair and held their tiny hands. *How long will it be before we're together again?* I fretted. *What if they forget me? What if I become just a stranger to Elizabeth, a stranger in a new, strange land, as Father was to me when I first returned from Germany?*

At night I cried, already feeling lonely. *I can't make it without Mother,* I sobbed. But with the arrival of daylight the situation always looked brighter and more encouraging. That was when my adventurous Stratford spirit reawakened.

In the middle of June, Mother and I sorted through my clothes, trying to decide which items I should take with me.

"They're not very nice," she sighed over the pile of clothes that still fit me.

"I know. I haven't had anything new in years," I wailed. "I wish I could take your blue lily dress."

"No!" she said emphatically. And seeing my disappointed face, she added, "You'll still have plenty of years left to wear pretty dresses, while I don't. Anyway, you're too sloppy to have nice things." To prove it, she pulled one of my dresses out of the wardrobe and showed me a torn hem I had fixed with a safety pin.

"If I had something really nice, like your lily dress, instead of that old rag," I said defensively, "I'd take care of it."

But she didn't put much faith in that argument. She gave me another one of her dresses that wasn't, to my way of thinking, nearly as pretty as the lily dress. Then she discovered a linen bedsheet tucked away in the depths of a drawer. "This will make a beautiful suit," she said, holding the sheet up to me.

"An old bedsheet made into a suit?" Ignoring my protests, she gave the material to a local seamstress. And to my surprise, I was delighted with the results: a smart-looking outfit, a pleated skirt and a jacket decorated with large wooden buttons that Mother had taken off an old jacket of hers.

When I tried it on, it fit perfectly. Along with the new black patent leather lace-up shoes I received from the American Red Cross, I thought I looked quite fashionable. I leaned in closer to the mirror and examined myself. *Now, if only my hair were naturally curly, my nose didn't have so many freckles, and I had bigger, rounder breasts, I could actually be pretty.*

Mother caught sight of me looking at my reflection. "For heaven's sake, Eleanor, stop being so vain!" she snapped.

❧

Then it was time to pack. We were allowed only one suitcase each. When it was time for Mother to leave for America, she would give the furniture, and all the other things we couldn't take, to her cousin in the Russian zone, Maria Koppe, who had lost everything.

I made sure I packed my diaries, notebooks from school, and drawings. Just as I was closing my suitcase my eyes fell on the Botticelli Madonna. I took her off the wall, blew the dust off the top of her frame, and placed her on top of my folded clothes. But the suitcase wouldn't close. The frame was too big. The Madonna had been such an important part of my life during the Berlin years that I couldn't leave her behind. I removed her from the frame and lovingly placed her between my clothes, where she would be safe.

Finally, our big day dawned, July 12, 1946. Just before leaving Berlin that morning, I went outside and looked up at our apartment house at Breitenbachplatz 15. Miraculously, it had withstood all the bombings, the Russian tanks, the katyushas, and the artillery barrages. It was a little worse for wear and tear, but it had kept us safe when we needed it. I said a silent prayer of thanks to the building. The day of departure reminded me of 1939, when I had said good-bye to the Stratford house and dived into the unknown future.

Frank had stored under his bed several jars of gasoline that he had obtained on the black market. Now it came to good use. A friend of his had just rebuilt an old truck, and with the offer of the gasoline Frank persuaded him to take our family and our luggage to the United Nations Rehabilitation and Reconstruction Administration Camp at the former SS barracks in Zehlendorf.

When we arrived at the camp, Tommy raced from the truck, darting in and out of the crowds preparing to travel to the United States. Elizabeth was content to stay in my arms. Her little body felt more solid than a few months earlier, and the dark circles under her eyes had faded to faint smudges. I hugged her close, trying not to think of how it would feel to be separated from her.

Jews, Americans, GIs, and people from all over Europe were going to the United States. I listened to the many languages bubbling from different groups, knowing we all had one thing in common: we were all survivors of a terribly cruel war. The UN workers weighed our luggage and gave us ration cards for meals.

Trucks soon arrived to take us to the train depot at Wannsee. Just before we boarded, Annemarie, Erika, and Renate showed up to see me off. A lump grew in my throat that I just couldn't swallow. We all hugged and kissed and made more promises. *We've shared so much. Will I ever see them again?*

Out of the corner of my eye I saw Father hugging Mother. I could imagine how sad they must be feeling at the thought of being separated again. Frank stood alone, looking forlorn and miserable. I knew that he probably hated leaving Mother without his protection.

Finally we gave our last hugs and kisses to Mother and Tommy and Elizabeth. As Father, Frank, and I climbed into the back of the truck, I fought back tears. *Another good-bye; I have had to say so many over the years.* After a last blown kiss and shouted promises to write, we rattled off for the train depot.

In Wannsee we were transferred to a waiting train to Bremen. UN workers gave each of us a little cheese, some crackers, and liver paste, which were to last us until the next day. Late that afternoon we crossed the Elbe River near Magdeburg, where the Americans and Russians had met as victors a year earlier. As far as I could see, charred fields and villages, abandoned farms, and ruins of houses and barns haunted the barren landscape. Few people were about. An occasional bent-over old woman or man on a muddy road struggled to pull a wooden cart holding few possessions. No one ever stopped to look at or wave to the passing train. I closed my eyes to the joyless scenery outside the window. I let the gentle swaying and rhythmic clatter of the train lull me to sleep.

The sounds of loud, angry voices jarred me awake. I looked out the window to see that we had stopped in the middle of yet another burned field. "What's happening?" I asked, rubbing my eyes. "Are we in Bremen already?"

"No," Frank replied. "We're in Russian territory. They're coming on board to check our papers. Quick, get your passport out."

I could hear heavy boot steps in the passageway outside our compartment. The door jerked open, and Russian soldiers with pistols in their belts glared at us. "Pass!" Passport! they demanded, their narrowed eyes moving from one person to the next in our crowded compartment. My heart pounded. *What are they looking for?* Rumors flashed through my mind of Russian soldiers dragging people off trains for no apparent reason. Those poor people vanished somewhere in Russia, never to be heard from again. Fear showed clearly on all the passengers' faces.

After the Russians examined our papers, they left. I could hear some cars being unhooked from the train. After what felt like forever, the train slowly lurched forward. We were on our way again. The train stopped often that night, and each time I felt the icy grip of fear. *What now?* But it was too dark to see what was going on outside.

In the morning we heard that the Russians had stolen the mail and luggage cars. Luckily Father, Frank, and I had put our suitcases in the rack above our seats. When we arrived in Bremen, we were again loaded onto trucks and driven to the Schaumburgschule, a former school, where we received visas, were given medical examinations, and were deloused. While we were there I shared a dormitory room with fifteen other women. Father and Frank stayed in the men's dorm.

We spent days just waiting, and time dragged. *Will we get to go at all? Or will we be rejected at the last minute for some reason?* Names of the lucky ones were posted daily on bulletin boards along with departure dates. First thing every morning, Frank and I scanned the board for our names, only to be disappointed again and again. We had thought we were so close to finally getting to America. I was bitterly disappointed.

The only things that broke the monotony of our days were mealtimes. I eagerly waited for each meal because I was obsessed with food. But although the meals were regular, the portions were small, and I was usually hungry soon after I finished.

Later in the week, after a quick check of the board confirmed that my father, brother, and I were not yet scheduled to leave, I took the bus into Bremen and met with Ruth, my school friend from Waldenburg who had moved to Bremen with her family after the war. We caught each other up on what had happened to us and our families, talking away the sunny afternoon in a café. Then we said good-bye and I made more promises to write.

A little less than a week after we had arrived at the Schaum-burgschule, Frank and I read RAMRATH on the list. "That's us!" I shouted, waving my arms and jumping up and down. "C'mon, let's tell Father!" Now it was absolutely certain that we were going to America. All three of us went to the office and were given boarding passes for the *U.S.S. Marine Perch.* Departure date: Thursday, July 19, 1946.

On the morning of the nineteenth, we were delivered by truck to a wait-ing freight train along with many other waiting passengers. We crowded into one of the hot, stuffy boxcars. The locomotive broke down halfway to Bremerhaven pier, and we waited for what seemed like forever until the machine was finally repaired and we were once more on the move. Every-body was irritable and anxious. But finally we arrived at the pier and had our first glimpse of the iron-gray *U.S.S. Marine Perch,* a 7500-ton troop transport ship—a far cry from the huge luxury ocean liners I had traveled on before. But most important, the modest ship would take us home.

I was assigned to a cabin with five other girls in what had once been officers' quarters. Poor Frank and Father found themselves down on the *D* deck, deep in the bowels of the ship with fifty other men in a poorly ventilated room with only one porthole.

At five o'clock that afternoon the ship quietly, without fanfare, pulled out of the harbor. Father, Frank, and I stood silently with many other passengers at the railing and watched Bremerhaven recede into the mist. Each of us was silent, following our own thoughts and memories. I was about to begin my fourth Atlantic crossing in sixteen years. Oddly, what I had expected to be the happiest moment of my life was tinged with a terrible sadness. Tears rolled down my cheeks. I felt a deep loneliness that I couldn't explain.

Back in my cabin, though, things were lively. My roommates were busy claiming berths for themselves and arranging their belongings. We introduced ourselves and discovered that we were all Americans. We became fast friends. At sixteen, I was the youngest in the room. The old-est was twenty.

We sat on the edges of our berths and shared our stories of survival. Each of us had sad stories to tell. One girl, Ruth Meyer, said, "My father was an American industrialist in Berlin. He was killed when our apartment house received a direct hit. Mother and I crawled out of the rubble." She paused. "You know, it was strange. After Father died, Mother's hair turned completely white overnight, and I got diabetes." Again she paused, this time swallowing hard. "Because Mother is German she wasn't given an exit visa."

I nodded. I knew how that felt.

"I'm going to friends of ours in the Bronx," Ruth continued. "I'm going to get a job and sponsor Mother as soon as possible and bring her to the States."

Their stories were all similar; they were children of American fathers and German mothers and for various reasons had found themselves in Hitler's Berlin. Each of these girls had suffered a terrible tragedy. One girl had lost both her parents and was being sponsored by a relative in New York. Once again I couldn't believe how lucky my family had been. But I also felt that strange tug of guilt. I asked myself again, *Why did we survive when so many others perished?*

My roommates and I played card games and explored the ship. I spent much of my time with Ruth. All of us shared a favorite pastime, though: eating. We were in the dining room at every opportunity. We couldn't believe that we could ask for a second helping and even a third. One morning I ordered six eggs for breakfast and ate them all, then promptly threw up. Still, I always ate whenever food was offered, no matter how stuffed I felt. Hunger was still too fresh in my mind.

One night loud crashes and the heavy swaying of the boat woke us up.

"Is the ship sinking?" someone whispered.

"What's going on?" asked another girl.

Shivering, I sat up in bed and reached for the light switch. We all laughed with relief when we saw the cause of the racket. Our suitcases, toothbrush glasses, shoes, and odds and ends were on the floor tumbling from one end of the cabin to the other.

"It's a storm," I said, squinting out the porthole.

With blankets pulled up to our chins, we listened to the waves crashing across the *A* deck above us. *It sounds just like the* boom, boom *of artillery shells,* I thought. Waves lifted and dropped the *Marine Perch* in an unending cycle of ups and downs, like a seesaw. The frightening crashes and roar of the storm made sleep impossible. *Have we survived the war only to be drowned at sea in a storm?*

The next morning I opened the porthole to huge, frothy white waves stretching as far as I could see. The sea raged and tossed our ship around as though it were a child's toy. Again and again the *Marine Perch* slid down into a deep trough and then climbed back up to the next crest. Icy cold saltwater splashed into the cabin and I quickly shut the porthole.

Because of the storm, even the simple task of balancing on the toilet became a major undertaking that morning, as each wave tried to unseat me. Showering involved a feat of remaining upright while the soap bounced and slid from corner to corner, always just out of reach. As each girl took her turn in the bathroom, the rest of us could hear, between the booms of the waves and creaks of the ship, the thumps and crashes and giggles.

After my dancing act in the shower that morning, I began to feel slightly queasy, but there was no way I was going to miss breakfast. Somehow I lurched to the dining room while hanging on to guardrails in the corridors. I was surprised to find the dining room practically empty, except for my roommates, who staggered in one by one.

"Everybody's seasick," explained our steward.

Because my roommates and I were the only ones present, we were treated like royalty. The stewards were all young and seemed to enjoy waiting on us.

"You're real sailors," they praised. We ate heartily as usual, very proud of ourselves.

I didn't let on that I was feeling increasingly woozy, as that would have spoiled my reputation as a good sailor. To save face, I had to make it back to the cabin as unobtrusively as possible.

"I think I'm going to read this morning," I declared airily, pushing my chair under the table. "I'll see you later!"

In the cabin I promptly crept into bed, pulling the blanket over my head and trying to calm my rebellious stomach. Much to my regret I had to forfeit lunch. It was the first time I had skipped a precious meal, but I just didn't dare eat.

But by afternoon I was feeling myself again. Ruth and Betsy-Lou, my pretty eighteen-year-old cabin mate, ventured with me up on *A* deck to watch the spectacle of the storm. Giant waves battered the ship. We clutched the railing tightly to keep from being tossed into the angry, gray sea.

We didn't stay on deck for very long. Seasick people were lying everywhere, looking pale and miserable. Vomit made the decks slippery and smelly. We quickly fled back to the safety of our cabin.

The storm continued for days, and we could do very little without becoming queasy. Every day I went down to the *D* deck to check on Frank, who was terribly seasick. He was pale and thin. I worried about him, but I couldn't remain down there for long. The ship rocked even more at that level, and the roar of the ship's engines, the smell of vomit and soiled clothes, and the lack of fresh air all gave me a bad headache. I had to climb back on deck for fresh air.

Father fared better. He wasn't sick and was usually in surprisingly good spirits. He spent a lot of time in the smoking lounge, where I sometimes joined him.

There were times, though when I could tell he was worried. "I'm not sure how quickly I can find a job that'll pay enough," he told me. "I need to earn enough to pay for our keep, and still save enough money to bring your mother and the little ones over as quickly as possible." He sighed. "When we left the States, we were only four people," he said wistfully. "Now we're six people, living on two continents."

I knew that nothing I could say would make him feel better. Besides, I was worried too. But I was proud that Father was speaking to me like I was an adult. He had never done that before.

~

I noticed that the sailors and GIs on board were paying a lot of attention to Betsy-Lou, whereas they paid no attention to me at all. I figured it was because she looked so sophisticated and self-confident smoking cigarettes.

"Teach me how to smoke," I asked her one day.

She was happy to oblige and showed me how to light a cigarette, how to hold it between two fingers, and how to inhale. I practiced in a quiet corner of the smoking lounge where no one could see my coughing, bumbling efforts. I hated the taste and couldn't imagine why anyone really enjoyed smoking. *But if it gets me noticed,* I figured, *it's worth the effort.*

Finally I felt ready for my debut. I borrowed a dab of lipstick from Betsy-Lou, donned my new white bedsheet suit, laced up my black patent leather shoes, and ambled on deck. I found a good spot in the direct line of sight of several working sailors. With my hair falling over one side of my face in what I hoped was a sultry fashion, I leaned against the railing. After several failed attempts, the cigarette finally glowed in my hand, and I held it as instructed between my second and third finger. *So far, so good,* I thought.

I took a few puffs of the awful-tasting stuff. Suddenly I was overcome by a dreadful urge to cough. I tried to suppress it, but my cheeks bulged out and then I was seized by a sudden uncontrollable fit of coughing that drew everybody's attention to me. Out of the corner of my eye, I could see the sailors laughing. Mortified, I threw the cigarette into the ocean and fled. I wanted to die with embarrassment. *Oh, I hope no one I know saw me,* I agonized. I vowed never to smoke those nasty things again.

The stewards continued to be very attentive to us girls. They were always asking if we needed something. An Italian steward kept us supplied with apples, oranges, aspirins, magazines—anything we wanted. A black American steward wanted us to teach him German. He had a terrible time pronouncing the words correctly, but luckily he had a good sense of humor because we couldn't help laughing and joking with him.

After six days of storms, the weather finally calmed. As we approached the Gulf Stream we saw little pieces of moss floating on the water, and the air became soft and mild.

One day our friendly Italian came to tell us a piece of interesting news. "We're meeting a ship headed for Europe this afternoon," he said. "They have a sick man on board with appendicitis. And we're going to pick him up."

We looked forward to something exciting after days of boring routine. Everybody who wasn't recovering from seasickness crowded on deck to look for the approaching ship.

"There it is!" someone shouted. "I can see it!"

At first only the smokestacks were visible, and then gradually the gray hulk of the ship, like a floating elephant, heaved into sight. The two ships signaled back and forth. As the other ship came closer we could make out passengers waving to us, and we waved back to them. Our engines stopped. Sailors on the other ship lowered a motor launch, which ferried the sick man alongside our ship. With ropes and pulleys our sailors hauled the man in his stretcher on board. After the two gray ships exchanged all-clear signals, they parted ways, one to Europe and the other to America.

The next morning we woke up and realized it was our next to last day on board ship. We welcomed the warm and sunny weather after days and days of storms. The ocean was smooth and dark blue. Father and I stood by the railing, watching seagulls swoop and screech around our ship.

"The gulls mean we're not far from land," he noted.

I thought of the next day with increasing excitement. *We'll be back in America!*

At lunch that day we feasted on canned ham. But by late afternoon I became violently ill with vomiting, abdominal cramps, and diarrhea. *Why am I so sick when the sea is as smooth as glass?* I wondered. Then all my cabin mates became ill too. No sooner had one girl left the toilet when the next was hanging over it.

We soon found out that many passengers on board had the same malady as we did. Those of us who had eaten the canned ham for lunch were sick. Apparently the meat had become contaminated, and we all had food poisoning. *Never again,* I vowed, *will I eat canned ham.* Poor Frank, who was just beginning to recover from seasickness, suffered terribly from the food poisoning. He was so thin, he looked like a walking skeleton. Father was ill as well.

The next day, July 27, 1946, I woke up early feeling mostly recovered from my illness. The voyage had seemed unending, but we had been at sea for just nine days. My cabin mates had also recovered and were busy packing suitcases. Excited, I climbed down from my berth and joined them. Then I put on my new white suit and black patent leather shoes and went on deck. Father and Frank were already there. Together we watched for the first signs of land. In the distance Coney Island rose out of the pink mist of the morning.

"I can see the Statue of Liberty!" a soldier shouted, pointing to the famous lady holding the flaming torch of freedom aloft. She was bathed in the golden glow of the early morning sun. "I never thought I'd see her again," the soldier murmured softly.

"Neither did I!" I whispered.

As we slowly passed her I spotted the poem inscribed on Liberty's base written by Emma Lazarus in 1883.

> *The New Colossus*
> *Give me your tired, your poor,*
> *Your huddled masses yearning to breathe free,*
> *The wretched refuse of your teeming shore,*
> *Send these, the homeless, tempest-tost, to me,*
> *I lift my lamp beside the golden door!*

The enormous statue and the freedom she symbolized brought tears to most of our eyes.

As tugboats maneuvered the *Marine Perch* to her pier in the harbor, the first rays of sun slashed across the skyscrapers of New York, reflecting in the windows like millions of sparkling diamonds. Small yachts and fishing boats cruised across the smooth surface of the water. The landscape looked untouched by war, so peaceful. *I'm home at last,* I sighed.

An odd memory struck me then: I remembered the day my family visited the World's Fair, just before we boarded the ship to Germany in 1939. I recalled standing on a slow-moving platform and looking down at the World of Tomorrow, thinking of how peaceful it looked. I had told myself that day that was where I wanted to live.

Now here I am, I thought. *I'm finally where I've wanted to be for so long. Will life in the States be all I've dreamed it would be?*

CHAPTER SIXTEEN

HOME IS THE STRANGER

JULY 1946–DECEMBER 1946

AFTER MANY DELAYS—checking passports, going through customs, hugging my shipmates good-bye with more promises to write—we finally arrived in the huge waiting area at the wharf in late afternoon. Tante Lina and Onkel Carl were there, looking just as I had remembered them from Stratford.

"We didn't think we'd ever see you again," Tante Lina laughed, hugging us. "And here you are at last, alive and well!"

I stepped out into the streets of New York in the early evening. It had been nearly seven years since I left the city. All around me were towering skyscrapers, bright blinking billboards, endless streams of honking cars, stores brimming with merchandise and the latest fashions, and well-fed and smartly dressed people rushing along the sidewalks with somewhere to go. *What a contrast to the gray, ruined city I just left,* I thought.

I gaped at the stylish passersby and the dazzling displays in the store windows, and then looked at my suit. *Oh my God!* I realized in a flash. *All these people are going to know that I'm wearing a bedsheet!* I had been so proud of the suit in Berlin, but in America it looked shabby and completely out of place. I was humiliated. I wanted to melt into the sidewalk. The black patent leather shoes, given to me by the Red Cross, were not the stylish shoes I had thought them to be—a fact Tante Lina quickly pointed out. "Those old-lady shoes just *have* to go," she promptly announced. "They're *not* for girls like you."

I glanced down at the shiny, laced shoes. How could I explain to Tante Lina that these were the first real shoes I had had in years?

As we walked along, Frank didn't say much. He mainly seemed to be looking at all the different cars, at the pretty, well-dressed girls, and at all the goods in the store windows.

We stopped at a delicatessen. "What would you like?" Tante Lina asked. "You can have anything you want."

I was overwhelmed by the many choices and the tantalizing aroma that surrounded the place. Somebody nearby ordered an ice cream soda. *That's it!* I thought. "An ice cream soda, please!" I replied.

It came in a tall glass. The dark soda at the bottom was piled high with ice cream, whipped cream, and topped with a bright red cherry. Every spoonful was like heaven. I savored every sweet, creamy bite, trying not to eat it too fast. I couldn't remember eating anything so delicious.

~

During the years we were gone, Tante Lina and Uncle Carl had moved from Routledge to Newtown Square in Pennsylvania. They had generously offered to take us in until Father found work. Their dark brown house, tucked away as it was between big trees on the edge of the woods, reminded me of Hansel and Gretel.

Father soon realized that finding a job wouldn't be easy, because he had lived and worked for years in an enemy country. He was forty-three years old and he had to begin again from scratch. Even the furniture we had put in storage before we left in 1939 was gone. Our payments to the storage company had lapsed, and we had been presumed dead.

Father didn't talk much about his problems to us now that we were back in America. But several times I heard him say wistfully, "I wish your Mother were here!"

As I arranged my things at Tante Lina's, I pulled an envelope out of my suitcase pocket and opened it. In it was a five-dollar bill that the father of a schoolmate in Berlin had given me to buy his daughter some chocolates. Although I planned to earn some pocket money and send the girl her chocolates, as promised, for now the money came in handy for my family. Those five dollars enabled Father to ride the many streetcars and buses he had to take for interviews.

I missed Mother so much. I needed her no-nonsense practicality to help me with these painful times of readjustment. But Tante Lina was helpful. She had organized a used-clothing drive among her friends and neighbors for us. I delighted in trying on all of the dresses, and those that didn't fit I carefully put aside to send to my friends in Berlin. At last I could retire the now-revolting bedsheet suit. I turned in the old-lady shoes for stylish brown-and-white saddle oxfords.

Eating remained my favorite pastime. Tante Lina always kept a bowl filled with fresh fruit on the dining room table. "You may take some any-time," she urged. "You don't even have to ask me."

But I found I could take a banana or an orange only when I thought nobody was looking. Then I quickly rearranged the fruit to cover up what was missing. I just couldn't let myself accept that all this food was available anytime I wanted it. It was difficult to let go of survival habits.

～

Seven years had passed since my childhood sweetheart Bobbsy Kurash had given me a ring and his solemn pledge, and I heard that Bob, as he was now called, was eighteen and a sailor in the U. S. Navy. His sis-ter, Eleanore, was engaged and planned to wed that fall. And their brother Hans had gone into business with his father.

On one of Bob's furloughs, Eleanore invited me to her family's home in Routledge as a surprise for him. Although he and I were glad to see each other, we stumbled awkwardly through a conversation, trying to find a connection to our childhood. We were strangers to each other. He was a man instead of the boy I had last seen. I became acutely conscious of how I had changed as well. *How different I must look to him,* I thought, glad I had decided to wear my soft lavender dress. I knew it comple-mented my blond hair and brown eyes. We sat across the table from each other, and every time Bob looked at me—which was often—I felt my cheeks burn. It was the first time I had felt a man look at me as though I were a desirable woman and not just as a child or an object to be violated. *Is this what falling in love feels like?* I wondered.

After that weekend, Bob and I met whenever he was in town on furlough. Since Father didn't allow me to date yet, we were always supervised, usually by my brother. Once, though, Bob and I managed to be alone. It was a beautiful, sunny, fall afternoon, and the leaves on the trees behind Tante Lina's house were just beginning to turn red and gold. Under the pretext of getting wood for the fireplace, we met outside and slipped into the woods. It was wonderful crunching through the fallen leaves, holding hands, and being alone at last.

Bob stopped and leaned against a tree. He pulled me close. "I think you know how I feel about you, Eleanor," he said softly.

I nodded, feeling a delicious sense of what was to come. He kissed me, and a shiver ran through my body like a current of electricity. Unsure of myself, I pulled away from the embrace and ran to the house.

I didn't know what to make of this new, bewildering sensation. The kiss was unlike the innocent kisses of my girlhood. I was sixteen now, and I didn't know how to respond to it. *If only Annemarie were here to talk to,* I despaired.

Images and sounds popped into my head like unwelcome intruders— of the Russian soldier ripping my clothes off; of the screaming women in our apartment block; of the empty, gaunt faces of rape victims; of a priest shaking his finger at us, declaring "Sex outside of marriage is a sin!"; of Edit in Stolp, warning "Kissing a boy must be confessed."

Soon after the kiss, Bob went to sea for a lengthy tour of duty. We wrote love letters to each other, which I cherished. But I came to realize that I was more in love with the idea of love than with Bob.

Images of rape and other horrors continued to haunt me. Dark scenes rose up uninvited in the middle of fun and laughter. Like black-and-white photos that flashed before my eyes, I saw images of people suffocating beneath tons of debris, of a wooden cart loaded with children's frozen corpses, of a man without a head, of a boy hanging from a lamppost. During the day I could chase the mental pictures away, but at night I couldn't escape from these nightmares. I was always so glad when morning came, relieved that the terrible memories were just spooks of the night. *I am back in America,* I reminded myself. *I'm safe here.* But even ordinary, minor things in America prompted my fears. I jumped when a fire engine screamed down the street, thinking for a moment it was an air-raid siren. I ducked when I heard a car backfiring, thinking it was a sniper.

I had no one to talk to about these troubling things. Tante Lina hadn't been in the war, so she couldn't possibly understand. Frank and I had both changed and were growing in different directions. He didn't appear to be troubled by nightmares or to react the way I did to these sudden noises. At one time I could have talked to the Invisibles or prayed to the Botticelli Madonna for her magic, but now I was practically grown up. Mother was far away. I had no one to rely on but myself.

～

In mid-September the first day of school in America arrived. I was plagued with all kinds of anxieties. *Will I feel like a foreigner? Will I be looked at as an enemy alien? Will I fit in? Will my English be good enough?* It had been seven years since I'd spoken the language. My English language comprehension had stopped at age nine.

That first morning a school bus picked up Frank and me, and I was glad to have my big brother with me. When we arrived at school, the principal wasn't sure which grade to place me in because of the irregular schooling I had received in Germany. For a trial period I was entered as a sophomore, a year behind where I should have been. "In a couple of months I'll move you up to the junior year," he said, "if your work is suitable."

When I entered the classroom I was assigned to, I saw a jolly-looking, middle-aged man perched comfortably on top of a desk. As boys and girls entered the room, they happily slapped his back and called, "Hey, Harvey. How are ya? Good to see ya!" I was puzzled. *Is this a student or the teacher?* In Germany students had to keep a respectful distance from teachers. We always had to address teachers formally and bow our heads in polite acknowledgment.

But Harvey, or Mr. Harvey as I called him, was indeed the homeroom teacher. He must have seen me standing at the back of the room because he strode right up to me and shook my hand. "You must be the new girl we're expecting," he said warmly, putting his arm around my shoulder. He turned to the class. "This is your new classmate. Her name is Eleanor, and she just returned from war-torn Germany. I want you to make her feel at home with us."

Those kind words quickly put me at ease and lessened my fear of the unknown. The students were friendly and made me feel welcome. *This day is so unlike my terrifying first day of school in Berlin back in 1939!* One girl introduced herself as Dot. I had never heard of such a name. With astonishment I said, "You mean your name is Dot, like a dot on an *i* or a dot at the end of a sentence?"

"Yes," she laughed, "it's really short for Dorothy."

I carefully noted what Dot and the girls were wearing, the bulky, over-sized sweaters and long full skirts with white bobby socks and saddle oxfords. I felt out of place in a dress and stockings and quickly made a mental note to ask Frank if I could borrow one of his big sweaters the next day.

That first morning I followed the crowd to the assembly hall. As we rushed down the stairs, everybody pushed and shoved to get into the hall. A tall, pretty girl just ahead of me created quite a stir when every-one noticed that her pink panties had fallen down around her ankles. Apparently the elastic in her underwear had snapped. All of the girls gasped, but the boys howled with laughter.

Then the girl did an extraordinary thing. She nonchalantly stepped out of her panties, picked them up, and twirled them around on a finger, facing her tormentors. "Now don't tell me that you silly little boys haven't seen girls' underwear before," she said sarcastically. "Because if you haven't, take a good look!" All laughter ceased, followed by an embar-rassed silence. She then turned on her heels and strode, head held high, into the restroom.

Wow, I thought, *what an incredible girl! If only I could have that kind of self-confidence, then nothing would ever bother me again.*

After everybody was seated in the assembly hall, a group of pretty girls ran up on stage and jumped up and down, clapping their hands, and shouting something that sounded like, "This is a bo-bo yell, bo-bo ski whatin' dotin', whata had a shoe, how d'ya like your boyfriend, sweet, sweet, sweet. Yay team!"

I was bewildered and looked around for my classmates' reactions, but they watched the girls calmly. *What is going on?* As the girls continued their chant, I thought, *Surely a teacher will put an end to this nonsense.*

The girl next to me must have noticed my astonishment because she smiled and asked, "Did you have cheerleaders in Germany?" I shook my head. "These are our cheerleaders. It's a custom in the States for schools to cheer their football teams to victory. I guess it would seem kind of strange if you've never seen it before." We laughed together. "By the way, I'm Jeanne," she said. "We're in the same classroom."

Jeanne became my first girlfriend in America. She took me under her wing and explained the workings of an American high school. She made school life a little less confusing.

Academics challenged me in America as they had in Germany. Just reading English was difficult. I found that many words completely eluded me, and I couldn't read most of the library books I checked out without constantly having to refer to a dictionary. When we were assigned a book report, I finally chose *Little Lord Fauntleroy,* which I could read without having to look up words. My classmates snickered at the childish book I'd chosen, and I wanted to die with embarrassment.

Math soon proved to be a problem as well. That first week, our math teacher dictated figures to us and told us to come up with the solution. He was puzzled when my figures were way off. Soon the problem became clear. In German the last numbers are said first, so that twenty-four becomes four and twenty. I had to mentally reverse every number to complete the dictated problems. After that, instead of dictating the numbers, my teacher kindly wrote them down for me.

Of the many shocks and adjustments I experienced upon my return to American school, the worst by far occurred in history class, where we discussed current events. There I learned that the rumors I had heard after the war about the Nazi death camps really were true. Pictures in newspapers and magazines showed evidence of the horrendous atrocities committed against the Jews, the Poles, the Gypsies, and others.

When I saw these photos, I sat at my desk and cried in disbelief and shame. *How did such terrible things happen without our knowing about it?* I felt responsible somehow because of my German heritage.

Then, as we studied the tragedy of the American Indians and the horrors of black slavery, and discussed the legacy of the atom bombs on Hiroshima and Nagasaki, I suffered this guilt all over again, as an American.

I tried to express my thoughts in my Poesie album:

> *Who lives in me*
> *And knows me well?*
> *Who is she who*
> *Awakens my spirit*
> *Who looks out*
> *Through my eyes?*
> *A stranger*
> *And yet familiar.*
> *Who is this someone*
> *Who quickens my inner space,*
> *Who loyally stands by me*
> *In good times and bad?*
> *Who is she who is immortal,*
> *Who was before and always is?*
> *Oh, if only I could know her*
> *I would know who I am!*

After the first glow of excitement of being back in America wore off, I was left with a sense of rootlessness, of not really belonging anywhere— not in America or in Germany. I wanted so much to be like everyone else, to be popular and pretty, and I worked hard at fitting in. But even after I began to understand the workings of an American high school, I was lonely and isolated. My classmates treated me kindly, but I always felt like an outsider looking in, as I had felt so many times before.

While Frank and I went to school, Father spent the days following every lead he could in trying to get a job. But he couldn't find work. No one wanted to hire a man who had worked in Germany during the war.

Father, Frank, and I couldn't forget that half our family was still facing the difficulties of postwar life in a crumbled city. We sent frequent parcels to Mother and the children. We thought of them and wondered about their situation all the time. But mail to Europe was a gamble, and it could take many weeks and often months to get there, if it reached its destination at all. Often the packages were stolen or lost.

I missed my Berlin friends painfully, so I threw myself into a frenzy of writing letters and sending packages to them, especially to Annemarie. My life began to center on the mail delivery. I earned pocket money baby-sitting for Tante Lina's neighbor across the street, and with the money I bought canned food and other items to send overseas. I begged discarded clothing from the kids in school and from neighbors and mailed endless packages.

But the needs of my friends in Germany were so great, I despaired at ever being able to meet them. Often I felt that my puny efforts would never make a difference.

Annemarie and my other friends in Germany wrote regularly, keeping me up to date on their lives and their bleak situations. They asked for sugar, flour, darning thread, shoes, and old clothing. Their families were cold, poor, and hungry. Annemarie wrote regularly and kept me informed of the conditions in Berlin.

September 1946
Berlin
Dear Eleanor,
Here things look economically very bad. Nobody has money or paying jobs. We literally don't even have one penny in our pockets. We

are trying to sell our island in Spandau, but no one has the money to buy it. We haven't been able to pay the taxes on it for at least half a year.

My grandmother had two strokes and had to be moved downstairs with us, and as you remember, she was always a difficult person to be with. Papa Petke, who has done so much for us, also has to be fed. I often feel so sorry for my poor mother. Father is missed in every area. I'm looking forward to a time when I no longer have to be a burden to Mother and I can be of help to her.

I can't tell you how much I miss you. I haven't seen Erika for a while. We have become somewhat estranged. We never got along as well as you and I did. I'm sending you a turquoise as a remembrance of me. It belonged to my great-grandmother.

Annemarie

October 1946
Dear Eleanor,
I wish you were here, but unfortunately we can't change anything. Tomorrow our entire school is invited to our old Gertraudenschule by the American students who are now occupying it. Their fathers are part of the occupation force. I'm anxious to find out how it will go. Just think twice a week the 14–18 year olds receive Swiss food donations, cocoa, two zwiebacks, a piece of cheese, and sometimes even soup. It helps to fill our bottomless stomachs for a while. Our school is supposed to enter into a letter exchange with the Quaker school in Pennsylvania, called the Georges School.
Annemarie

November 1946
Dear Eleanor,
Not much happiness to report from Germany. We have no more potatoes. Bread is hard to get, and the weather is icy cold. We can heat only one room now. Everybody longs for spring.
Annemarie

November 1946

Dear Eleanor,

Your package arrived and brought much joy. It's touching how you always try to make us happy. I know you don't have much money either, and still you share. Some day I will make it up to you. You will get the best room in our house.

Everything is available in stores again, but nobody has the money to buy anything. Good thing we have our garden and nut trees. My horoscope promises lots of luck in life. I haven't noticed much of that, though. But one thing I have noticed is that, in spite of hard times, I feel again and again how wonderful it is to be alive and young. Do you feel the same?

Annemarie

December 1946

Dear Eleanor,

You can't imagine how much happiness you gave me with the arrival of your latest package. The blouse is adorable. I wore it right away and was admired by everybody. The lipstick is exactly my color. The sweets tasted heavenly. There is so much hunger and craving for sweets so long deprived that one goes crazy. I just don't know how to thank you enough. We get only two hours of electricity a day. We can't even go to the movies except in the Russian sector to see Russian movies. I'd rather do without.

Annemarie

December 1946

Dear Eleanor,

I know this will make you sad. We are going to sell the house in the spring. We can't afford it any longer. We had to spend a lot of money we don't have on roof repairs, and still it leaks everywhere. I miss you so much.

Annemarie

I couldn't wait to get home from school to open my mail from Germany and hear every detail of my friends' lives. Sometimes I got as many as five letters in a day. But not all of the letters were filled with bad news. Some offered encouraging news that my friends' lives were moving forward too. I delighted in the news of Annemarie's first boyfriend, and of Erika's meeting a cute American soldier she was crazy about. I commisserated with Renate when I read that her boyfriend had dumped her for another girl. My friends' news about American occupation forces was wonderful: the Amis had opened a teen club in the neighborhood where kids could meet, play Ping-Pong, and have dances.

One day I received a sad letter from my schoolmate Gabi, whose father had been a Nazi official. I remembered seeing her for the last time on the street toward the end of the war, when she had refused to accept that Germany had lost, and had told me she could report my defeatist attitude to the Gestapo. I had written her a number of times, but had never before received a response.

> *December 1946*
>
> *Dear Eleanor,*
>
> *Thank you for your letter. It made me so happy. I have a big request. Could you possibly send us some darning thread? Mother doesn't have a single thread left. We don't know if we can keep our clothes mended. Life in Berlin is terribly hard. The cold weather again is claiming many lives, and the rest of us just want to give up. You know, Eleanor, I would give up too if I didn't know that we Germans did many terrible things that are all coming out now. Somehow we must pay for that and pray that God will forgive us. Hopefully he will hear us, but first we must become a better people.*
>
> *I don't know where Father is.*
>
> *Gabi*

The letters and requests for help streamed in endlessly, and while I was glad to hear from so many friends, I also felt overwhelmed. The little money I earned all ended up in postage and stationery and food. Mother had taught me that letters had to be honored by a response, and my letter writing left little time for anything else.

I knew my friends in Germany were going on with their lives as best they knew how. I tried to send them all the goods and words of support I could, but I also tried to go on with the new part of my life in America. And gradually, Jeanne helped involve me in school activities.

Taking part in high school events and trying to have fun helped me forget my worries for a little while. I was fascinated by all the ceremony surrounding football games, like cheerleading and marching bands. I even joined the bugle drum corps, mainly for the cute white, blue, and gold uniforms and because I had a crush on the handsome young band-leader, Johnny. Unfortunately, I was unable to master the bugle despite my strenuous efforts. All I got out of it was cracked lips, a few squeaky, off-key sounds, and an embarrassing plea from Johnny.

"Eleanor, please do me a favor," he begged. "When we march out on the football field Thanksgiving day, just pretend you're blowing the bugle. For God's sake, *don't blow!*"

Jeanne urged me to go to the Friday night dances in the school gymnasium, where the students danced to jukebox music or sometimes to live student bands. I knew she wanted me to go, but I also knew that she hoped that if I went, then Frank would too. Jeanne and Frank were starting to date; she was becoming Frank's first real girlfriend.

A sock hop was announced for one Friday night, and I turned to Jeanne for an explanation. I had no idea what a sock hop was. Jeanne said, "It's a dance, but before we enter the gymnasium, we all take off our shoes in the cloakroom."

"Why?"

She laughed at my puzzled expression. "We jitterbug in our socks. It's fun!"

That night we slipped and slid across the highly polished wooden floors in socks. Wearing socks definitely added to the fun of jitterbug-ging—as long as no one stepped on my toes. I watched Frank and Jeanne dancing and laughing together, and was reminded of sliding through the Sanssouci Palace in felt slippers when Frank and I were little.

After the dance, we all crowded into the cloakroom to find our shoes. It proved to be no easy task because some wise guys had mixed up all the shoes and put them into a big pile. Since all our shoes were saddle oxfords, it took a long time to untangle them. We all crowded around to sort out the shoes, which involved cussing, shoving, grabbing, and loud shrieks of laughter. I laughed and laughed as I hadn't for years. In the end we all just tried to find a pair of shoes that fit—not necessarily our own.

Won't Annemarie love to hear about this silly night? I thought.

～

One Sunday in early winter, Frank and I took a bus to Stratford. I had dreamed for so long of returning to where I had spent the happiest time of my childhood. For years I had reviewed every bit of the town in my head, despairing of ever seeing it again.

As we walked down Union Avenue past the fields, the red brick school, and the fire station where we had our Halloween parties, memories swirled around me like silent ghosts. Children's laughter and cries echoed from familiar places and then vanished into silence.

When we finally stood before the beloved old house, Frank broke into my thoughts.

"It looks smaller than I remembered," he said.

"Yes. And a little worn, but otherwise the same," I replied. "Look, Frank, the old apple tree is still there."

"Yeah, but they tore down my tree house," he said.

"I buried a treasure box under the tree just before we left for Germany," I said. "Did I ever tell you that?"

"No," he said. "At least, I don't remember if you did."

We didn't knock on the door to see who was living there or look inside. As we paused in front of our old home, I realized how much this house had meant to me during those traumatic war years. But I also understood now that I could never go back again. *I have changed and the town has changed.* And in that moment, the Stratford dream that had been so alive for me, dissolved into the mist of time. Home had become the stranger.

I took one more look at our old house, then walked with Frank toward the bus depot. It was time to go.

EPILOGUE

IN DECEMBER 1946, Father was offered a job as an engineer at Allis Chalmers in Boston, Massachusetts. While Frank and I stayed with Tante Lina and Onkel Carl, Father moved to Boston. Our family was split between two continents and three cities, but Father would finally be able to earn the money to bring Mother and the little ones over. We all looked forward to the day we would be together again.

In June 1947, almost a year after we left Germany, Father finally had earned enough money to bring Mother, Tommy, and Elizabeth from Berlin to the United States. Initially, they too stayed with Tante Lina until Father could find a place for us all to live in Boston.

By late fall of 1947, our family was finally reunited. We moved to the Hyde Park area of Boston, where Father had found a small one-bedroom apartment down the street from Hyde Park High School, my new school. These were cramped quarters. All four of us children shared a room, but at least we were together.

In 1948, after all my academic struggles through the years, I graduated from high school with honors. I found a job at an insurance company that summer and, come fall, I attended Boston University at night. In 1950 our parents bought an old house in Hyde Park on Blake Street. Owning a home of our own finally gave us a sense of permanency, of belonging somewhere. The slow process of rebuilding our lives began in earnest.

Over the years, the roots of my transplanted self reached down again into the soil of the country of my birth. I never forgot the words Annemarie had written to me: "In spite of hard times, I feel again and again how wonderful it is to be young and alive!"

AUTHOR'S NOTE

AFTER ATTENDING BOSTON UNIVERSITY, I worked for Donnelley Advertising Company, where I met Louis Garner, who during the war had fought as a member of the 78th Infantry Division in the Battle of the Bulge in the Ardennes, the crossing of the Remagen bridge, the Ruhr pocket campaign, and who was among the first American troops into Berlin.

We married in 1951 and had two sons, James Louis in 1952 and Thomas Joseph in 1954. In 1957 Louis's job moved us to San Diego, where we raised our sons. I worked for a number of years with a social service agency and in 1980 joined the College Textbook division of Harcourt Brace Jovanovich, where I worked as permissions editor until I retired in 1993.

Our son Jim and his wife Christina have two daughters and live in Fullerton, California. Our son Tom, a graphic artist for high fashion houses and a fine artist in his own right, lives in Italy with his wife and their two sons.

Over the years, Father and I made our peace. After his retirement he visited me often in California, where the healing between us began. We had long talks about our expectations and regrets. We expressed our common interests and experiences and bridged our differences, so that shortly before his death, at age ninety, we could unreservedly say the words "I love you."

After difficult years of rebuilding and raising my little brother and sister, Mother was physically and emotionally exhausted. That, and the trauma of those war years, left an indelible imprint. She suffered from frequent depressions and was unable to regain her former joy. Our much-loved mother died on December 12, 1999, after a long heroic life. She found her peace at last.

Frank, a retired engineer, has three children and seven grandchildren. He lives with his second wife Astrida, a refugee from Latvia, in the Boston area.

Younger brother Tom enlisted at an early age in the 8th Air Force, the same unit that had bombed Germany during World War II. He retired from the Air Force as a major and is now an executive in technology. He lives in Albuquerque with his wife Jeri, two dogs, and four cats.

Little sister Elizabeth, an accountant, has one son and lives in San Diego.

None of the immigrants who used to gather on Sunday afternoons in our Stratford home are alive anymore.

I never saw my Grossmutter and Grossvater again after 1942. Grossvater died in 1959, and Grossmutter died a year later. Omi visited us for a year in the United States in 1952. She died in 1967. When I visited Germany in 1971, I managed to see Onkel Adolf. He died shortly after. Tante Mieze is also deceased. Tante Elsbeth, Mother's sister, lives in Wellingholzhausen. Onkel Franz and Tante Trudel are both deceased. Their daughter, Ursula Wohlers—the little four-year-old cousin who visited us in Berlin in 1941—now lives in Hamburg, Germany with her three children and seven grandchildren. She recently completed a professional translation of my book into the German language.

Onkel Werner, Mother's younger brother, died in 1994. He had been taken prisoner during the war by the Russians and sent to a prison camp. Ten years later he was released. He walked across Russia only to be captured by Polish authorities just before he could climb the mountains to Waldenburg, where his wife was waiting for him. He had to work another five years in the Silesian coal mines and helped to rebuild Warsaw before he was allowed to return to his wife. He is survived by his wife, a daughter, and a granddaughter in Stuttgart.

Through publication of this book, I rediscovered cousins Reiner, Margaret, and Giesela Koppe after fifty-seven years. They lived with us briefly during difficult times in the tiny apartment in Waldenburg, Silesia.

At the time I left Germany in 1946, Annemarie and I did not believe that dreams come true. However, seven years later, my husband and I sponsored Annemarie to the United States. She and I were reunited in New York in 1953. She became a ground hostess for Swissair and lived in New York, where she met Kurt Groh. They married, settled in Switzerland, and adopted two sons. Annemarie and I have remained the closest of friends. We continue to share our lives through frequent correspondence and occasional visits. Our friendship deepens and becomes more precious every year. She is an angel made visible.

Beautiful Erika died in 1997 of cancer, but not before we were able to reaffirm our long-ago friendship by writing frequent letters up to the time of her death. Unfortunately I lost touch with Renate and Gabi. I have had no news of their whereabouts since 1948. My friend Inge lives somewhere in what had been East Germany. She is married and I believe has two children. She and her family fell on hard times under the Russians because her father had been a Nazi judge. He had been executed for war crimes in Holland. She wrote to me a few times in the early fifties, but later asked me not to write anymore as she was having difficulties with the authorities because of our correspondence.

Helga and Ruth from Waldenburg are also lost to me. I never saw Ruth after our visit in Bremen just before my departure from Germany. My correspondence with Helga stopped after 1950.

I kept in touch with only one of my shipmates from the *U.S.S. Marine Perch.* Ruth Meyer was able to sponsor her mother to the United States several years after our arrival in the States. They lived in Washington, D.C., where Ruth worked as a secretary. Unfortunately, Ruth died young due to complications from severe diabetes.

Our Berlin neighbor, the SS Officer Schmidt whose children I babysat on Saturday nights, moved his wife and three children to safety in 1943. We did not hear of them again until the 1960s, when we read an article in *Stern* magazine which told of Schmidt being indicted for war crimes. As I recall, the article said that as an anthropologist, Schmidt had been responsible for measuring prisoners' skulls to judge whether they met Hitler's idea of an Aryan or not. His decision often determined whether the individuals would live or die. It was hard to believe that the same man who had been a devoted father and husband, and a good neighbor, could have been involved in such gruesome work. After a trial, he was imprisoned for a number of years. (In this book, a pseudonym has been used to maintain his family's privacy.)

I saw the Gadows again briefly when I visited Berlin in 1971. Both were still elegant and charming. They have since died.

Many of the boys who dug tank trenches with Frank near the Polish border were later handed rifles and grenades and ordered to defend the ditches against the oncoming Red Army. Most of the kids, including our Waldenburg landlady's son, lost their lives. They were only fourteen or fifteen years old.

Frank recently tracked down Georg Geutler and other buddies from the Berlin days. Georg and his family were twice evacuated from Berlin between 1943 and 1945. In March 1945, he was drafted into the Air Force as a fifteen year old. He was sent to an air base near Torgau, which was heavily attacked by American fighter planes. After the Russians overtook the air base, Georg managed to find his way back to his mother and brothers.

The little porcelain elephant I gave to Mother in Stolp survived the trip to and flight from Waldenburg, the Allied bombings of Berlin, artillery fire in the battle of Berlin, Russian occupation, and a stormy trip across the ocean. It is still intact today and remains a valued part of our family history. One of my most important diaries, the one that described in detail the day-to-day events during the battle of Berlin, survived the war, only to be lost in a fire that destroyed Marple High School in Newton Square Pennsylvania.

In the year 2000 the city of Berlin was once again dedicated as the capital city of the reunified Germany. After its total destruction in 1945 and the dismantling of the Communist wall that had cut the city in half until late 1989, Berlin is now completely rebuilt and restored to its former vital beauty.

Since publication of the book, remarkable things have happened. After sixty-three years, on September 24, 2002, my brother Frank and I were reunited with the town of Stratford, New Jersey and with our former schoolmates from the third- and fourth-grade class of 1939. People came from all corners of the United States to share this special day with us. I spoke to the local middle school and to the community. The mayor, Stratford City Council, and the community honored me with the key to the town.

Upon visiting the old house at 8 Union Avenue, Frank and I shared memories of those early years. A next-door neighbor told me a fascinating story. Several years ago, lightning had struck the old apple tree that bordered the two properties. The tree had to be removed. As the tree was pulled from the ground, the woman noticed finger-like roots clutching a small rusty tin box. Curious, she extracted the box and pried open the lid. She found, among other things, an arrowhead, a small blue toy Indian chief with white head feathers, a pink ribbon, a piece of netting with sparkles, and an illegible note. Not knowing what to make of it, the woman tossed the rusty box out and gave away the arrowhead and the toy Indian chief. She kept the ribbon until about a year before our visit and then threw that out too. Shortly before my arrival in Stratford, the local librarian recommended she read *Eleanor's Story*. Upon reading the book, she was thrilled to realize that she had found the treasure the nine-year-old Eleanor had buried just before she left on her incredible odyssey. The illegible note found in the box was my promise that some day I would return.

With the return to Stratford, the meeting with my former playmates, and the coming to light of the buried treasure, my life has come full round.